Seven Days

Bobbie McMorrow

ISBN: 1451583311
ISBN-13: 9781451583311

For Lyndsey and Justin—refusing lies and digging deep for courage, insight and wisdom, you continue to open my heart and illuminate my mind.

And for the wolf counselor, who gives roots to my wings.

Author's Note

The story you are about to read is as true as I can make it. I have attempted to stay as close to the facts as possible, and I have referred to my journals and many notes from the period covered to keep me honest. Wherever my recollection departs from that of someone else's or their story, I ask indulgence; the foibles of memory and the subjectivity of impressions are sometimes inescapable.

To respect the anonymity and well-being of those I write about, many names have been changed. However, the names of the "public figures," specifically Howard Weitzman, Michael Zavis, Alan Muchin, and Martha Morrison are real. I also used the real names of my own family who have stood beside me and approved of this book and its possible impact on them. They are a courageous lot! In addition, the last family session is an amalgamation of events that occurred in quick succession over the course of that day.

Lastly, you will see that I used these words, "The Teacher," by way of a shortcut to give full credit for years and volumes of brilliant teachings from many voices. As you will read in the acknowledgements section at the back of this book, it would be almost impossible to give every teacher the praise and exact quote they deserve. Therefore, I took "poetic license." I hope I do their words justice, for their contribution to my life, my work, and teaching has been profound.

I didn't grasp this in the way I came to understand. All that I was sure of was the untethering of all things known.

October 1990

Los Angeles, the City of Dreams, creates illusion to be consumed whole. But it is the light, sun rising over the San Gabriel Mountains, kliegs illuminating the Hollywood sign, the sun setting on Santa Monica's beaches and evaporating golden into the Pacific, that draws and seduces us into the open arms of possibility.

The light is nothing without the dark. Light gathers into itself in dark, hidden, but beating in expectation of exposure. At the sun's bidding, heat grows out of the earth, and infiltrates steel-framed brick and mortar; buildings sigh that even they are alive.

Few conjunctures display this communion of light and dark as does Century City on the western boundary of Beverly Hills, southeast of UCLA and the mansions of Bel Air. Bordered by Twentieth Century Fox Studios, it houses LA's leading law firms, image makers, and businesses, including mine.

Over-sized, open-air shopping and innocuous high rises are boxed in next to buildings of style and note. My office at 1925 Century Park East and its twin tower, 1875, sit in the center of this development, one block east of Avenue of the Stars and north of Constellation Boulevard. The towers rise to thirty stories, slicing the sky at forty-five-degree angles to create an envelope of shadow facing light.

Throughout the day, angles change in relationship to each other and fold in on themselves. Fused corners give way, melt seamlessly. At other times demarcations, sun to shadow, face off. Stern and independent, they become razor-edged.

Protected by man-made shade, I squint into the morning sun, approximate depth and speed of change without, I think, the risk of being blinded by the reflection of window, sky, or steel.

I wait in that triangle where building meets glass, and entry opens to outdoors for a car that will take me to LAX to catch a plane for Chicago, where the assignment is to accelerate the biggest deal of my career.

Another day and into the night of negotiations, pressure, performance, set to the romance of adrenalin is all that is promised.

In the conflict that is untethering me, I am aware of the desire to step out and be swallowed whole by light. Or to escape into undefined darkness. Disappear.

I watch the envelope folding the opposites. Light and dark die and rise—create and define each other. Exist for the other. I wonder at the consequence that is both.

∾ 1 ∾

"9:45? Christ! He's late! I told him, hell, I begged him, 'please Howard pick me up no later than 9:30 or we won't make that 11 a.m. plane!' He's probably still at the gym, oblivious to schedules! Whaddya think? Try his cell?"

"I'll try his cell…he's always late. Relax, Bobbie…he'll be here."

1990 was the year when the barriers came down between my personal battles and my professional success. Definitions of who I was, of why my life no longer made sense bombarded me, brewed within me, rode turbulent seas in my head and gut. Lies escaped amidst my life's unraveling. At the same time, the first threads of a new weaving, vague and uncompromising, peeked out around the edges of confusion. Bidden or unbidden, the tearing apart, coming together, darkness of despair, explosions of grace, of light, moved as one through me. All at once. Separate and together.

"I know he's always late, Katy, that's the point. I begged him. 'Not this time… this meeting is different, this meeting…'"

"Well, hell, Bobbie—he is the meeting!"

We laugh, rueful, wise, and relax again.

"Yeah, you're right. Of course you're right…but, God this is crazy making… he knows he's the meeting and plays it for all it's worth. Then he gets bored or distracted and forgets for awhile—only to remember and play it again… ANYWAY, I knew I should have gotten the car to pick me up first."

Kate and I are standing in the shadow of a forty-five-degree angle that cuts the sun-wrapped plaza to our left. We crane our necks, shade our eyes, and pray to see Howard's car.

Introductions, interviews, and months of preparation have led to this day. Completed, it will be the largest merger of its kind for a California law firm and one of the largest mergers in the country. And my company is in the middle of it.

"And then what? I can see it now, you dragging him out of his office… face it, Bobbie you have NO control here, you are now in the game of the master control freaks. You'd better just hold on for the ride."

Five years earlier I left thirteen years of teaching to start my business. I can't remember exactly what expectations I had; I knew just this: there was excitement and promise in the revolution we called the women's movement. There was the energy of new and bold, of tightropes to walk without the net of tradition. The time had come for women to step out from shadows of generations of should and have to. New limits tested the time. New definitions pushed the limits.

There was, for me, the practical too, supporting my family beyond the restrictions of a teacher's salary. I worked for six years to get to the point that leaders and executive teams, 99 percent male driven and determined, value my contribution and see me as a vital part of the team. Hired for my judgment, insight, and information, I found my views and experience deemed worthy, even essential, to the nation's most accomplished lawyers. I had proven myself and taken my company, McMorrow Associates, an executive-search service specializing in law firms, along with me.

But, for all that, I also know that Kate is right: settle for influence and remember control is an illusion. I fake disgust. Shrug, look at my watch. Shift anxiously on too-high, high heels. There is comfort for me in moving left to right to left, to the rhythm of expectation, pleasure in leaning into the excitement of the day. And in playing with someone like Howard.

To LA the entertainment industry is "the industry." The conceit infers there is no other industry as special—nothing as important. Howard is an industry insider. He is Hollywood in its flash and shine—who you know, and what they owe you; where you were seen and with whom; what you own and who owns you; and what they have on you and you have on them. But he never forgets the street where he came from. He grew up far from the Hollywood lights and was an up-by-his-cleats baseball star who went all the way to the minors. He is whip smart, combines scholarship and raw brains. He gives *kinetic*, *brash*, and *king-of-the-courtroom* a whole new meaning. He is made of himself and by himself.

"Did he answer his cell? We've got to make drinks with Allan and Michael before the fireworks begin!"

Kate knows this. I know she knows, but I say it again. We squint into the sun. We wait.

The past six years had been audacious. McMorrow Associates broke all the barriers of entry into the pristine and prestigious world of international law firms and the global business they control. Our company plunged out of the ranks of the unknown to dominate a substantial part of the game by moving top legal talent to the best places and in the process we helped construct global law firms. And, with each step and every deal, nothing stopped the onslaught of deconstruction inside me that demanded a reckoning.

In this time of things falling apart and first beginnings, grace dissolved to anxiety, rebirthed joy, and fell away to sorrow. Sadness clung to me as sure as achievement exalted me, bubbled up inside of me until my skin crawled and my mouth ran dry. Rewards of the marketplace, humor, passion for the hunt, enthusiasm, intelligence, and teamwork lived side by side within the personal vortex of struggle, redemption, confusion. Dominance and victory without collapsed to a silent siren pulling me inside myself. Two things, one thing, fragmented then whole, then split again.

"Maybe we should try him at his office...maybe he had to stop there on his way... try it will ya?"

I am crazed; Kate tries to be the reasonable one and dials Howard's number. I hear her relief at getting a live voice on the phone. She laughs with an assistant, shrugs her shoulders at me; *"He's not there."*

Howard has become the lightning rod of the top entertainment law firm Wyman Bautzer, where stars of the screen and the courtroom were made, destroyed, and remade for two generations. Former partners, such as the legendary Frank Rothman, who became CEO of MGM, went on to run the major studios, and be confidantes and agents to the biggest names in movie land. Howard, now the leading trial attorney in the firm, has become the plum in this proposed merger.

Celebrities love Howard because he's one of them and respect him because he isn't. Before *Court TV* made household names of lesser talents, if you were anyone who knew anyone, Howard Weitzman was the guy you called. Headline clients included celebrity car designer John de Lorean, who created a sports vehicle with winged doors and set Detroit's auto industry on its head. De Lorean hogged magazine covers with his sleek designs and beautiful women, until the law decided maybe he was raising capital for his new company by trading in cocaine. The sexiest star of her era, Kim Basinger, beautiful, maybe wronged, but on trial nonetheless, turned to Howard to defend her.

Howard's magnetism shone in the battle between the Jordache brothers, who popularized blue jeans in the 1980s, and their rivals Guess Jeans' Marciano brothers, who all filed multiple lawsuits against each other in a bloody, protracted, and expensive battle. They agreed on only two things: they hated each other and loved Howard.

Maybe more important are those devotees we don't know, kept anonymous by their power and Howard's skill at keeping them out of jail and headlines. They are the ones who owe him big time, and on that debt he cuts a wide swath through LA's inside group.

"Do you have the proposed agenda with you?"

Kate checks with me but knows I have it. She prepared it twice. Put it in my briefcase twice. Shift left, right, right, left. Laugh but stay focused on the high-stakes game—all energy, all performance, real and not real at once.

"Maybe you can work on it on the plane... in case you miss..."

"Katy! Don't even say that! It's not about the agenda. It's about a sit down with the three of them and making sure there's some male bonding."

The full merger committee meets tomorrow morning at 9 *a.m.* Before that the principals, Allan Muchin, Michael Zavis from the Chicago firm, and Howard from Wyman Bautzer, must look each other in the eye to assure themselves of the basic trust necessary for a merger to be possible.

The room tomorrow will be filled with male partners from each firm. These three men are the most powerful among them, and their opinions the most important; they wield that authority and leadership because they are aware of the delicacies of internal politics. They know tomorrow's meeting is part performance and that their developing relationship needs to be tested tonight to see how it will play before a crowd. They have to ask themselves who among all tomorrow's participants must be pleased and who impressed.

"And who to trust or not trust?"

Kate asks it as a question but knows the answer. I only have to raise my eyebrows in her direction for us to agree.

"Hard for these guys, partners on both sides, and all business owners of their firms, not to have their own agendas. Trust can be an elastic word in the heat of a deal."

Deals are about nuance, ego, and style as sure as they are about assets and market position. Each step is gauged, reassessed, and measured. Trust. Teamwork. Loyalties. All shift, mean different things to different people; manifest in different forms.

The consolidation of the law firm industry is in its infancy. In 1990, the acquisition of one large firm by another is big news. Deals are devised out of a dynamic strategy, the promise of global reach, better brand and marketing value, or the platform that a larger organization can provide. Politically and politely we call them *mergers*, but a lot of the time, they are really an acquisition by a stronger firm with a strategic objective. Even when one firm is hurting, stressed in serious ways by market forces, it may provide the stronger firm with additional talent, clients, geographic advantage, or practice areas that extend its power and reach instantaneously.

In firms with financial, management, or strategic challenges that the partners are unable to solve independently, a merger with a stronger organization brings partners stability, hope, and shelter. Firms with something of value left to sell and protect, namely, clients, community status, professional experience, and partner loyalty, choose merger as the best business opportunity. Still others are trying to avoid the disaster that the dissolution of a partnership means.

"He'll be here... I'll try his cell again. They all like each other anyway—don't they... didn't you say?"

Kate asks as she punches in the numbers, holds the phone up so I hear the busy signal with her.

"Yeah, yeah, but it's a dance... you know... one with no missteps allowed. Stepped-on toes can happen in a second and can have disastrous ramifications. Remember that deal a few years ago when the litigators from the New York firm almost came to blows with the L.A guys over a ten-year-old case they had been opposing counsel on? Blew the deal to hell over drinks."

My role in a deal is to identify the possibilities, search the marketplace, and evaluate the choices. I analyze which firms or groups of partners will be most valuable to my client. I bring the potential acquisition into focus; align it with the articulated vision. I help make the hopes and dreams of clients tangible.

Because the process of merger and acquisition is human and dynamic, I also lend point and counterpoint to its evolution. These contributions give me chits to play, as bystander or on center stage, depending on what the deal demands.

The deal that includes Howard is my first significant national merger, combining Katten Muchin Zavis from Chicago, with Wyman Bautzer from Los Angeles. But I know enough to worry that the deal is too fragile yet, too new. No one has bonded in a way that could smooth over egos, insecurities, or screw-ups. And tomorrow, additional players enter the game, and anyone could change the odds of success, throw a curveball, or hit a homer. All want to be noticed, make a contribution, or just raise hell to make sure someone recognizes that they are there.

A merger may be each firm's preferred option, but it is never perfect and never without cost. Never does everyone involved feel complete. Egos, male and territorial, are rarely satisfied. Tomorrow, added players will change the focus and rearrange the issues.

"Craig and another 'Alan,' Howard's partners from the Wyman side of this deal, are joining us. Then there's a cast of supporting characters, maybe as many as ten partners from KMZ will drop in during the day. Plus there'll be accountants and managers, marketing and PR personnel, and who knows who the hell else!"

The list of attendee names clicks through my mind—whom I know; whom I don't. What I should expect, what to prepare for and when to just pray.

My company's first clients are New York and Wall Street's most formidable players. Their expansion and rise to dominance in the 1980's fueled the growth of my company. In order to represent them, I educated myself about their politics, pecking orders, and internal organization. I immersed myself in understanding the businesses that made up their client bases. I came to understand what created New York's dominant economic position.

The rest of the world toils and is distracted, plays hard, tries to love and be loved, is determined by personal things, while New York, the financial markets, and an appallingly small number of people run the world. In the 1980s a group of such people from both coasts created an extraordinary bull market.

Michael Milken, the arbitrageurs, Drexel Burnham, KKR, junk bonds, and hostile takeovers drove the market with unprecedented economic extravagance. Mergers and acquisitions ruled and created vast new wealth. They left in their wake a river of dead companies, smaller dreamers, and dreams. By late 1987, however, a pall settles over Wall Street. The bottom has gone out of an overheated, unsustainable market. The feds move in, and some top dogs go to jail for the greed of many. New York is all but dead. But not California…yet.

The illusion Gateway to the Pacific Rim propels the entire region, especially LA and us, its inhabitants, forward. Belief in destiny dominates the landscape. Screw New York—we are the new aristocracy of business and power.

The warp speed of the twenty-first century's interdependent markets is not at full acceleration. In the late 80s it takes three years for markets to follow each other, to tumble. California has hope, resilience. This is LA before the Tokyo stock exchange falls and before the savings and loan industry collapses. California real estate is robust, and the defense industry is riding high.

By 1991 California succumbs to the same problems that swallowed New York. Before we run out of the fuel for growth, however, the Chicago law firms target Los Angeles in the national race for dominance. Midwest stability helps Chicago firms also remain unscathed. The City of Broad Shoulders wants part of the West Coast dream. And my company picks up an entire new client base.

Led by the name partners Michael Zavis and Allan Muchin, Katten Muchin Zavis created, in less than ten years, a business law firm that rivaled the Chicago brands established over hundreds of years. The strategy of their aggressive partnership now called for a substantial acquisition in LA to establish position while New York firms licked their wounds. Was a once famous Hollywood law firm, Wyman Bautzer, the best resolution for their plans? Was the situation too volatile or was it a unique opportunity—a clever move that others couldn't see? This was the week to find out.

"9:55! Is he kidding...? He's got to be kidding—never again!"

"There's the limo. Better move out to the curb. Save a minute or two."

"Hey, Kate, where did I put my sunglasses?"

"A black stretch, of course. God is this ostentatious enough?"

Kate drawls this out in her best Sugarland, Texas, disgust. It's the, "honey-can-you-believe-it?" half-admiration, half-disbelief, shake-your-heads-in-unison voice I love.

"He's a Hollywood boy, Kate. You wouldn't expect anything else, would ya? After all, only the best..."

My answer is lost in our shared laughter of recognition. A stretch? It is funny, and it is so Howard. Appropriate too because the adventure of timing, focus, and merger has begun. Action gives way to reaction to action. Mind, body, and heart are engaged. Drama and dramatic effect are now common. Every moment the promise of challenges to solve expands, convulses, closes, opens decidedly, or reluctantly. Ideas, personalities, and viewpoints introduce themselves; strategies are created, deconstructed, recreated, found faulty or brilliant or both, and are reframed until they gather momentum or die.

Adrenalin is the one consistent factor in the deal world; it's the rush that can motivate, thrill, and bring focus and precision. It can also blind and be addictive; it can take you to the brink or take you to the bottom of the pit. Like all highs, it has its own idea of where it is going and who to take along. That is a part of the game too. The part few people see. In this storm's eye, I ride the wave of adrenalin adventure for all it is worth—to be alive and purposeful and move forward. Always forward.

Kate smirks, it is her signature, kept between friends,

"It's not him I'm wowing on girl. Remember, I know where you're from… it's a hoot… wasn't so long ago I watched you climb trees after cats and kids. I don't think you owned a pair of high heels, and now this?… got to admit…"

Clients recognize Kate as my assistant: trusted, professional, has my ear, and my back. She is that and more. Neighbors when my kids were toddlers, she had just adopted Jimmy, who was serendipitously nine months older than my son, Justin, and six months younger than my daughter, Lyndsey. We became instant friends. Kate and her husband, Bob, purchased the house across the street from us in Pacific Palisades, Los Angeles, suburbia by the sea, hoping to impress the adoption authorities with white-picket-fence stability.

We both loved/hated exurban living. She and Bob had a dozen years of marriage, and the company of LA social, entertainment, and career upwardly mobiles. They'd lived the sailboat and cocktails at sunset life. Kids and two car garages moved them into the slow lane.

I was a '60s activist who pushed against the restrictions of mundanity by starting things: schools, community projects, and co-ops of all kinds. I escaped the tightness of agreed-upon mores with hikes up the California canyons or runs on the beach, usually with all three kids in tow.

Together Kate and I laughed. Her humor, so quick and close to the bone, missed no opportunity to comment on the foibles of self-important, middle-class values with her incisive screening. But her kindness and humanity wouldn't allow her quicksilver mind to take too acid a turn of the tongue.

By the time I started my business, Kate had lost Bob, her one-and-true love, to cancer of the esophagus. The two-year ending of his life was excruciating. Night visits to emergency rooms when the body's systems failed, rallied, then failed again laced with the terrible tedium of cancer's details: the exact measuring of medications, the collection of blood and urine samples, and the constant explanations to a child who was soon to lose a second father. Kate was vigilant throughout. She kept her humor, which was ballast and nurture for Bob's soul, as a shield against the devastation of her man's body.

When I started my company, Kate was the first person I thought of. Her career had been notable for its right-hand-to-the-executive status. I wanted her advice and loyalty; I knew I could count on her telling me the truth and rely on her business experience and dependable teasing. She would have none of it, balking and complaining, *"Happy in early retirement,"* *"Too done in,"* by Bob's death, by the raising of a preteen boy alone. I was relentless, figuring the arrangement would be good for us both. Once engaged, *"Just to get you up and running,"* leasing furniture and space, and meeting the gathering team, she became more interested.

Unleashing her wit and wisdom on a growing and attentive audience, becoming, once more, the center of things, she decided to stay on board. We know each other in small and large ways, and like all girlfriends are surprisingly similar and wildly different. But on that day in 1990, we shared the incredulousness, the thrill of finding ourselves in the middle of mergers and acquisitions—doing business with familiar faces from the evening news,

"So she buys the theory that no one steals shabby luggage?"

It's Howard, ignoring my staged impatience, talking over my head to Kate. All ebullience and energy, he bolts from the limo, phone to his ear, and looks down at what passes for my luggage, inelegantly plopped on the curb. He hauls the offensive pieces into the trunk faster than the driver can come to a full stop.

"You should see the shit she's dragging around."

He barks into the phone.

"I have to get into the car before anyone sees me with it."

Fluid drama, car to curb, swinging door, voice exuberant, all laughter and purpose, he gathers us into his game.

"Who's on the phone?"

He ignores my question, as I quicken into motion, with him, the moment, the space of fun and possibility. I loosen up but don't relax, just exchange the energy—tense to perform, to play.

"Must be one of your partners. Someone we both know—who the hell else would care?"

I say aloud to myself. Laugh. Keep moving. In one gesture Howard trades barbs with the cell phone, tells the driver we have ten minutes to make the twenty-five it takes to LAX, blows me a kiss, and winks hello to Kate.

"It's 10:00 AM!!"

I remind Howard who is not listening, exaggerate the roll of my eyes, match his energy, shout last-minute instructions to Kate, and slide into the backseat.

"I'll be at the store buying you new luggage."

She calls after me for Howard's approval.

"Try upgrading to Kmart."

Howard yells back as he slides in next to me leaning out the window, waving good-bye to her.

The driver avoids the 405 south, taking National to a maze of streets I've never seen before. Blur of asphalt and street signs—forget laws and limits. Howard leans over the partition of the backseat, and in one breath, speaking bravado and bullshit, directs the driver and teases me. His words are laced to shock and caress, everything done for effect but true in its way. *"I told you we'd make it… any earlier we'd be sitting around looking for something to do."*

Howard says as we pull up at UAL curbside in twelve minutes with no time to spare. Harold, travel agent to the stars, was a gift to Howard from celebrity friends. He whisks us through security. It's his job to grease VIP's through the airport. Anyone who is anyone cannot be bothered with the details of mortals.

"Sitting around? We are running… do you notice me? I am running in high heels… hello… running here…"

I try to show sympathy for Harold, but he knows this drill. Laughing, he drags all of our bags and gets us to first class, seats 1A and 1B, on time—barely. The flight attendant meets us at the door with a full tooth, cat-bird smile. She says she knows Howard from an earlier trip. Does he remember? He laughs, of course, says something to prove it. She's impressed. "Little ole me?" she smiles.

"Knew you'd make it when I saw your name on the roster; knew you'd be late too."

She laughs with him, exchanges comments on the talent agent he was traveling with the last time they flew together.

"Saw him on the news…"

Says she saw Howard too, admits that she bragged to all her friends. Howard answers laughing.

"We had a great time; for a guy who never flies commercial, he turned out to be a good sport."

At no time in this push from Century City, to limo, to airport, to seats has Howard stopped entertaining. His energy is contagious, and big-hearted, he exploits the average day into something bigger. I catch the attendant's wink. Hollywood, private jets, of course. She is wondering, too, if I get it, get him, and if by chance, I am also someone she should know. After all, she thinks, Mr. Weitzman, I mean Howard, he insists on being called Howard, is always with *"someone."*

I say to her questioning look,

"Click your heels, Dorothy, we are nowhere near friggin' Kansas."

She gets it, laughs and nods; yes, working girls, we get it, and we know. Coiffed, sprayed, and beautifully suited but never quite manicured perfectly, I'm grateful to take my seat, check my watch, and exhale for the first time in hours.

"Made it," I say to no one.

* * *

Journal Entry, Winter Meditation Retreat, January 1990: First day of retreat, it's suddenly upon me how far away I am from the safety of noise and performance. Can I sit for five days? I don't know, but with merger possibilities bubbling around me, and the confusion of family, work, the company, if I don't do this now, then when? So I come, and I sit, walk, eat in silence. So slowly, it agonizes my jaw, clenched too tight, too long. Then this: The Teacher asks at the end of a long day "What is your true name? Tell me who you are." Beginners almost all, we do not answer. We do not get it… know it is a trick question. This is Zen. Nothing is as it appears. We know that much. So he picks someone, she answers timidly, questioning him back. Is this right? Is this what you want? He never really answers. He bows slightly to each person, smiles faintly, goes on to the next expectant face. It goes on this way. Then me, I know it is the wrong answer, but I cannot be clever or quick, so I say the names I have named myself, the names I've been named in the world chronologically: daughter, sister, friend, student, teacher, wife, community organizer, mentor, what else? I laugh and ask, now? Now. Then I add, head hunter, merger queen, entrepreneur, CEO. I try to say it sing-songy so they know I know these are not important…But tears well up suddenly from somewhere unprotected. Long day. Tired. No energy to push away the unexpected, I swallow, try again to say the word I care about most… no longer laughing I finally say Mother… Mother…Mother. I choke up. I pause… grab hold of myself. He asks, then who? Then what? True or not, I think but don't say, these are the names I am known by—no, more importantly, know myself by in the world. Is it enough? Am I enough? I look up. He's moved on. Patiently. Compassionately. Asking the same question, true name? True name? He asks without inflection…without expectation. No one knows the answer.

∽ 2 ∾

"How bad is the financial situation?" Howard is studying the draft agenda Michael and I prepared by for tomorrow's meeting. I focus on the first roman numeral, financial, and the spreadsheets that both firms provided, especially the pages that define the economic viability of his firm, Wyman Bautzer. The information is complicated: Prestigious client names and what's been billed to them; the hours that partners and associates and staff have worked on each matter; accounts receivable and payable; what's been written off; what percentage of each bill is likely to be collected and when; which partners are responsible for clients; and which employees are being hired, fired, reassigned. The attachments to the spreadsheets are lengthy.

I keep my eyes on the paper in front of us. A thorough understanding of the economics of the firm is both of our short suits. He doesn't know that I know he's uncomfortable. But, clear about my own weakness, I sense it in others.

He gives me broad brushstrokes, but his confidence wanes, and he pauses. I wait. Finally, he admits he's not as educated here as he could be. Shit, I think, not good. But say, *"Okay. Let's make sure someone on your team knows this, has this information… is prepared to answer."*

Allan and Michael are numbers guys, I tell Howard. Both are conversant in the objectivity of accounting and equally brilliant at the subjectivity of making numbers talk. They create strategy, uncover inefficiencies, find patterns that connect, and decide to support them or deconstruct them at will. They are dealmakers by vocation and avocation.

The best dealmakers know that as a deal wends its course, objectively and subjectively mutate. They change places, are interpreted to say "it's this," when "that" is all that is certain. The bigger the deal, the more that objective columns of debits and credits on a financial statement matter, and the less they tell the whole subjective story.

In law firm mergers, the keys are which clients will stay and who can be counted on to deliver them? Who and where are the lawyers that you can trust to make the sacrifices to keep and develop clients for the new team? The vague but critical future of those relationships determines everything from partner compensation and associate morale, to support staff loyalty, from taxes and overhead to liabilities and assets. The merger forces the issues, objective numbers and subjective relationships, to the forefront.

It is arduous work to quantify the extensive list of variables. In a firm like Howard's, with internal battles and the loss of a dozen partners, these are the issues that will add up to success or failure.

Will the numbers alone provide an objective standard that can be applied? This is not, after all, a toilet paper factory with so many sheets off an assembly line sent to so many stores at such and such price. And everyone needs some. Add the numbers up, and they make sense.

This is the delicate and complex web of relationships where the essential capital, the only capital, is human; it's only asset is brains and dedication and excellence. And every day of every week of every year it can and will walk out the door. The complexities are endless because this web is human. Flawed and perfect, crazy making and exalted, it is, we are, so very human.

"This client list is great, Howard, but do we know how many are real in terms of ongoing business? Which clients may go with the partners who are leaving and forming their new firm? Do we know who among the remaining partners has control of clients that bill the big numbers? Do we know in which specialty areas— litigation, corporate, real estate, entertainment—clients are loyal?"

Howard shifts under questioning, not from pressure I exert, but from his growing awareness of the land mines we have to traverse. It will take more than charisma or brains or tactics to get the deal done. Maybe for the first time he sees that the game is complicated, murkier in detail and nuance than he contemplated.

I never knew how close to bankruptcy his firm was. My bet is neither did Howard. His natural balls-out-for-life, for what he did everyday to breathe that drives into whatever presented itself probably blinded him to the immense downside. Did me too.

He doesn't have to do this, this deal at this time, I think. Like the partners in his firm who lost their bid to take over management and left angry, creating a wake of chaos behind them, he could leave unscathed. But some sense of responsibility for a partnership he joined only a few years ago, drew him in, and made him stay. His championing of his partners may be delusional, grandiose, or misplaced. But in a world of flimsy loyalties, it is admirable—maybe courageous. Remembering all that, I ease up on the questioning. Wait, silent. His enthusiasm builds as he describes his Wyman team:

"John is a competent executive director, good numbers guy. I have faith in him... and Craig, a great lawyer and businessman, too, has everyone's best interests at heart. His family is prominent in California. He has the kinds of contacts and loyalties that the KMZ leaders will recognize and that can hold a firm together. They know accounting, financials, the history of clients, a whole lot better than I do... they'll understand, articulate, explain..."

We are both relieved he has his game face back on. His confidence provides the subjective counterpoint to the necessity of the objective numbers. It is, perhaps, what will get this deal done.

"Anyway I'm counting on you too... you can direct this thing can't you, Bobbie?"

He leans over conspiratorially, breaks the stress of the confrontational balance sheet in front of us.

"Hey, I may be a decent director, Howard, but you're the show..."

We clink glasses, laugh, knowing we are both right.

* * *

Journal Entry, January 1990 Retreat Day 2: The dharma talk ends at 8:00 p.m. Unsatisfactorily. Why didn't he just give me the damn answer? Tell me my true name? Walking meditation back to the dorm through the dark. Silent, deliberate footsteps, slowed motion of meditation walking. Who are you? Who am I? Not the first time I've asked, but here, now, the question seems so simple that it is poignant in a way I have never known. Sister, daughter, wife, mother, mother, mother. A sob catches in my throat. Restricts my breath. Breathing scratchy and ragged. Breathe, breathe, I command myself, as if there is one me who is the guard of the breath, and the other unable to breathe.

The breath is the channel of connection from head to heart and back again. It is the most powerful link of mind to heart. They say this in retreat again and again. Calm the breath, calm the mind, ease the heart. But nothing works. Not commands. Not compassion. Nothing is right. Damn tired and burned out tonight. Irritated and guilty for being so irritated. So unmeditative. So raw. My mind fights with my heart and derails the breath. Who am I? Who the hell am I? Can

you swear on retreat? Well, hell, it is where I am today. Who am I? Definition. Defined. Labeled. Breathing into my life did I breathe these labels into the center of my soul, into the cells of my body, into my karma and dharma and back out again? Did I breathe them into existence myself in some exquisite process of self-creation or did I breathe them in from the out breath of someone else? Head to heart to heart to head until my true name is lost in label and definition.

This is what The Teacher questions, "Who are you?" Who am I without my definitions? Without labels? If your child dies, are you no longer a mother? Can you no longer mother someone, be mothering? I try to imagine my life without touchstones, without that which defines and by which I define. He asks who were you before your mother heard her own name for the first time? Before she even met your father? He goes on in this questioning way but he has lost me. I am still back here on this, mother, mother, mother. It is too close. I am too close to having lost my son. My heart and mind tired, distraught, stay fixed on having come so close to losing him. Forever… still not being in the clear. Where is there peace? Breathe, step, walk, breathe. All the way back to my room I have to command myself to keep moving.

"Breathing in I breathe in all the sorrow of the world, and breathing out I breathe out love." I say it in my mind to steady head to heart to head. Until here, alone in the dark, free to cry into this shallow breath into its frayed edges, sobs well up in my stomach. Taught early and young not to cry, dry heave tears are all I have. I do not want to give up. Do not. Cannot let go of any definition. Certainly not mother. Okay, I say to myself. Okay, just keep moving in the direction you are going. Stay on this path. There is nothing else to do. There is nowhere else to go.

* * *

The flight attendant brings lunch; I am relieved to lose myself in talk of people, persuasions, and opportunities. Howard and I are both believers in possibility—of creation and re-creation, endless vision of futures of our own making. Ones we are sure will be good for all.

Among the Katten Muchin Zavis client base there are sports teams and star athletes—familiar territory for Howard and the kind of celebrity relationships he can leverage. I focus him on that possibility,

"Right up your alley, and KMZ has some of the top business lawyers in Chicago—tons of experience in securities and real estate. They can extend your ability to represent your current clients. This merger will also give you access to major corporate clients you are unlikely to see at most other firms."

He agrees, the merger is an opportunity to do something radically innovative and that reminds him of a story. The master of stories, he settles into them, why he likes this partner or colleague or worries about another one. Enemies become friends in his storytelling.

As he speaks I remind myself that Howard became his firm's leader because he offered hope to the survivors of a bloody internecine battle. But Howard is not a manager, and he knows it. An aging athlete, he's still strong, agile, and vibrant; he's about ideas, magnetism, and the excitement of the moment. I try to assess whether that will be enough to catalyze the future of an entire organization. Nothing, I realize, is known for sure.

He speaks passionately for what could be built and compassionately for the careers of those caught in this maelstrom. He derides laggards, and has a natural eye for talent, but by experience, he is a hired gun for those with ambitions even bigger than his own. Can he abide the management, the time, and the thoroughness of the i dotting and t crossing repetitions of the merger process? There are disappointments ahead, I tell him, many of which will require the pain of change.

"To make a deal valuable, Katten Muchin Zavis has to be comfortable that they aren't diluting their own profits by taking you all on, and, Howard, it is better to be on economic parity, not to be seen as the poor cousins that show promise but are a sacrifice to have move in…"

To get there, some people, even partners, are going to have to be cut if they aren't immediately productive. Others may lose their status, drop from equity to nonequity partnerships, or have their compensation points readjusted downward. Which means just the people who rally around him now may stand to lose hundreds of thousands of dollars.

"There may be the loss of autonomy and power, too. Some who have grown used to having authority will suffer when they have to report to bosses in Chicago instead of down the hall."

He answers with gusto and self-confidence. Knows he is bluffing, thinks again, raising his strong suit: strategy. After all, he says, that's what a trial involves.

"But, Howard, the execution is so different." He reconsiders.

"Maybe, but trials, especially the ones I cut my teeth on, criminal, white collar, make you a realist, if you weren't one already. Okay, so I admit to being easily bored…but I think I excel at strategy and tactics to execute the plan. How different could a merger be?"

He smiles to himself, confident of his position. I cannot let him rest there, accept his own half answer, but I also don't know how far I can push him. Our relationship is only a few months old, and I am not sure that I know him well enough or that the timing is right to demand further examination. Clarity may be impossible to attain here and now. I must determine whether to risk the deal's viability by insisting on answers at this tenuous stage. I hesitate, reassess, then take a deep breath, lower my voice, and try to sound thoughtful, calm,

"At the end of a trial, it's you, on your feet, jury in the palm of your hand, where you can influence the verdict. This time there's a lot at stake that has to do with the performance and value of other partners and the firm as a whole—can't gloss over anything—or expect to control it. Numbers and the execution of strategies depend on all of the parts of the organization. This is not a one-guy star vehicle."

I gather confidence as I speak, look at him directly; I don't want either one of us to be surprised by a gauntlet thrown our way at the meetings tonight or tomorrow. I can't allow attempts to avoid personal weakness obscure an important question we should have asked ourselves.

His eyes don't meet mine. He looks up and away to his right, shifts the pages of the agenda, sips his white wine. He relaxes into another story; this one about his last trial, when Karen stepped in for him with a nervous client. He regales me with how precise and brilliant she was, how she *"aced the closing argument."* She is a natural leader and, while young *"makes decisions with grace and precision."* He assures me that she can handle the details that might escape him.

I am listening but thinking that in the world of mergers and acquisitions the three monkeys—deaf, dumb, and blind—lurk around the edges of deals. That's where the motivation is "have to get this done," to be next, newest, biggest, and best. But maybe or really "save my ass" or "make them sit up and take notice" are the unsaid, unheard ego obsessions that can take the deal down the path of delusion.

Unless someone is ready to point a finger at the truth. Of course that person often runs the risk of having the same finger bit the hell off if it's in the wrong guy's eye.

My job is to introduce possibility and believe in potential but not get captured by it. Not an easy task. The facts are sometimes clear and measurable, but more is intuitive and personal—who and what a key partner stands for and whether he or she is a standup "guy" who can be trusted to deliver the goods.

I piece together hints and clues drawn from anecdote weighed against dependable data and past lessons. I listen between the lines to learn who a person is in his or her gut, what he or she shows the world, and where the two differ. Truth and how to get to it, judgment, and hypervigilance count. It is also essential that I know my own motivations, what I want to think and see rather than what is there. I must remain conscious of my prejudices. I am not perfect. I have plenty of half-chewed fingers to prove it.

These thoughts alight and play through my concern. But for the remainder of this flight, I allow myself to be lulled from the deflation-inflation cycle of the merger that lies ahead.

Howard, the word magician, speaks of Hollywood, celebrities, and real life. His first wife, he tells me, now married to the Fonz, *"Great guy, all friends, after all, the children, two boys, one from each marriage,"* and then he speaks of cases won and lost. Horror stories of crimes and punishments are woven in a singular cadence.

* * *

Journal Entry, January 1990, Retreat Day 3: I no longer know why I came here. What I thought was lost–what I came to find. Hard work. I am drawn to hard work. I look behind me and cannot account for the confusion of my life, the stress of my mind. I look ahead and know the challenges inside and outside of myself are excessive, so I came. But I thought (did I think?) that there would be struggle, and then some ANSWER to cling to. But here they say DON'T CLING! And clinging is all I know to bring me something, something—what? Now I don't know even what the something is/

was that I said I wanted. But this keeps swirling in my mind, in my heart…If I'm no longer mother, sister, CEO, teacher… then what? Take it all away—then what? I am so angry that they are making me think like this, making me FEEL!! They are not me. I yell this out in my mind. LOUD. No one answers. They. Me. We. NO ONE. Did I put it all there, here—names, labels, identities—head to heart to head on this breath, to earn a life? To feel safe in the world, literally to ensure safety? If I'm not my labels, can I stay alive and cement a foundation to build a life on? Maybe, I breathed out and created my life—birthed myself. Or maybe it was created for me, labels and all. On the out breath of my mother, I became daughter. On the in breath of my children, I became mother. On the breath of life, at the end of a century, we women become CEOs and entrepreneurs and marathons runners to become what the world says we are, wants us to be, *have to be* to move the conversation forward. Then what of this, in each breath is possibility, in each breath is sorrow, and which will define me? In which will I find myself, in which breath? Breathing in all the sorrows and out all the love will I find my true name and where? And when? And where, when there is no peace. In this dark night, among strangers, far from my home I do not know my true name. If I find it, uncover it, open the right compartment, and discover it, what then? Will I know it and be able to claim it? Can I even see it, if I am without the defining boundaries of identity? Without my labels and my identities, will I recognize myself? If I remember my true name, will it be written in fire or ice or wind or earth? If I give up my old names, the ones by which I go calling in the world, who will know me? Will I be untethered to rise and fall on the whim of unseen forces, lose all control, all sense of belonging? And what of this… that labels are prisons. Control an illusion. And no one—not me—no one knows my true name anyway.

∽ 3 ∽

In bold, get-it-done Chicago, futures are decided in the past. Intricate owing systems, the geography of wards and bosses, injuries and gifts, are never forgotten and create a matrix that stretches back through generations of fathers, sons, and cousins from courtrooms to boardrooms to fire houses to the ubiquitous pols, the ever-presiding police fraternities, the Sons of St. Patrick, synagogues, and back rooms of back rooms. Michael Zavis and Allan Muchin are genius newcomers in this old game, that they plan to win.

In a city driven by deals, they get deals done. The Chicago Bulls and White Sox, downtown high-rise developers, bankers, investors, the artists and their benefactors, and civic leaders seek and take their advice. They are trusted, they are inside in one generation.

I love Michael and Allan for their bravado and brains. They pay me back with loyalty and respect. It is early for girls to play big-boy games. But to get to where they are, they've learned not to stand on any precedent. With enthusiasm and grace, they lift the curtain and let me see in; they tell it as straight as they know, expect the same back.

They're impressed with Howard, and have met him twice in LA— lunch first and a long dinner I attend at Valentino's, Howard's favorite Italian restaurant.

"Can't help but like the guy… great talent…But will he show up when the client isn't a California celebrity? Can he deliver for our key clients and build on the primary relationships? Will he be loyal or is he too independent?"

Their questions are mine. We are not neophytes. Howard is a star, but he's a risk. He is not institutional; will always play a game by rules he makes up as he goes along. Still, if you are managing a law firm from another city, and you want to land in LA on your feet, you need a guy to give you a running start. Howard may be that guy.

Howard and I arrive at the Ritz Carlton sky bar on the twelfth floor to join Allan and Michael and watch the sun's last vapors dissolve into Lake Michigan's waveless deep. City lights horseshoe the sandy strip, gather the energy of man's concrete boundaries to water and sky, and flicker point-lessly against so much natural darkness.

In their unsaid balance of alter egos, Allan allows Michael to take the lead. Aggressive, funny, Michael can be precocious or precise; delivers unnerving insights. He is keen on verbal dominance. Allan, self-possessed, balanced, a man of sensitivity and sensibilities, is no less incisive or tough but cloaks himself in a lower octave.

Michael opens by mentioning the names of friends and contacts he and Allan discovered that they share with Howard. We all note the crossovers and coincidences. No one says, "checked you out with the president of that company or civic leader, the one you said you knew," but they have. And all that talk, to and from confidantes, getting the skinny on someone, the feel, places him in the right compartment, shows if he's one of them. And plays itself out in what may appear to be about what they are saying. It is not. It is about posture, position, and power. These are the rules of this no-rule game.

These two men know Howard in all six degrees of separation. They drop names not to impress, but for the informing reaction a name will draw. The understanding is "We know who you are, we know people who know you. You can't fool us, not for long."

They ask Howard his opinions about different LA business leaders, pol-iticians, even the future of the professional sports teams and the weakness of their bench depth. Each repartee is spiced and counterpunched with the names of power brokers whom they know who agree or has offered a differ-ent view but all the talk is easy and loose. They listen to assess what mat-ters to Howard, ego full or egoless? Family man? A player? An apolitical watcher or someone whose politics will cause embarrassment? They ask themselves whether the line of Howard's integrity is straight and clear, or whether he redraws it in pencil every day.

Howard is adroit. Schooled by the world's largest egos, the ones mag-nified on billboards, he relaxes easily into Michael's half-joking.

Pretending to be consumed by the lights along the black lake, I think, "Dance, revelation, dips, and curves with no resting place." Composed, knees together, trying to be a lady, projecting ease, I am, nonetheless, hypertuned, vigilant. Every word counts, but no notes are taken—casual, remember? Just drinks, just us guys.

I absorb each sentence and inflection, sensitive to any drop in voice or rise in heat. Wait to practice what I have learned; step in sideways to ease conversation between drawn-in breaths and move the energy. Interrupt without interrupting. Specific words do not matter as much as cadence. The beat of possibility must continue. My job tonight is to set the pace, keep egos from clash or crash and burn.

They laugh at a story I tell—another deal, different time and city. The intervention breaks tensions and lets everyone know I am in the game.

I stay realistic, too. Remind myself that *no* deal is about me. Deals crater from narcissists ruining the soup, splitting have-to-have-my-way hairs. I speak in considered tones to support an argument, underline a point, loosen the grip of masculine score keeping through example and anecdote.

We order another round of drinks as Allan takes out tomorrow's agenda. I follow suit, compare his with the one Howard approved in flight. Minor adjustments are agreed on. I suggest we run through tomorrow's attendees.

Michael and Allan describe their team, the roster of partners, their roles and responsibilities. Because neither of them is a litigator, they have included litigation partners whose practice and perspective is crucial to the Wyman team, and the possible eventual fit between both firms. Michael tells us,

"They're young, proud of what they've accomplished in a short time. Should hear their story straight from them about how they've built their practices."

Allan agrees but adds that there isn't anyone from KMZ like Howard, *"Not with your trial record."* Younger partners at his firm can learn a lot from Howard, and they realize that, he says. His voice is not gratuitous and maintains the balance of equals.

Howard acknowledges the compliment, keeps it low-key without being humble.

We talk about the two Wyman partners who will join us tomorrow as negotiators for their firm. The first is also named Alan, an experienced business trial lawyer who has the loyalty of the younger partners and associates. Howard speaks with respect of his fondness for both of them but especially for Craig, the real estate lawyer who became the back room guy, galvanizing the firm through the recent difficult time and asking nothing in return.

Allan pays the bar bill, and as he does asks what we each hope gets accomplished tomorrow. Howard's response will tell us how serious he is—if he gets the tenor and tone of what tomorrow must be if a merger is to get done.

"Let's get the toughest issues on the table early and give them as much time as possible. We have *challenges everywhere, nervous partners, employees and banks wondering if we can hold the place together… hoping that we do. If this is going to be a* go, *why wait?*" Right answer, assertive not anxious, and realistic not desperate.

Allan proposes that we focus on the thorniest items: the Wyman debt; the current, and much rosier, financial situation at KMZ; and the sources of revenue needed to build a combined firm. Economic feasibility from day one will be our partners' goal, Allan says, we have to be able to address this with them in the room.

I am watching Michael watch Howard. He looks for slips in commitment, something in Howard's body language or response that will give away fear or hint at his level of honesty. Howard is steadfast, and agrees with Allan's points and to a finalized agenda. Michael finds nothing to red flag the moment.

Handshakes follow, smiles are sincere and relaxed as we stand to leave, and move toward waiting elevators. I sense shared relief as well as hope.

We head off to individual nights, none of which is over. Other matters and deals, calls to return, or crises to contend with that someone, somewhere, thinks have to be solved immediately, await us. Mobile phones, turned back on, start to ring, the hotel concierge hands Howard a FedEx from the West Coast. The movement of business-professional-personal streams together with blinding effect.

* * *

Journal Entry, Chicago, October, 1990: Tonight, exhausted and enlivened, merger talks continue. Been on this road before - can't get overexcited. Have taken other mergers down to the wire and have them bust apart. But, so far, there's reason to hope this one is different, all positive, right vibes. Crazy day… travel, anxiety, totally cool, on-the-brink timing, near disasters; I had to stretch to keep up.
BUT… last half hour on the plane, Howard wants to talk next steps, asks, should we meet back in LA, end of the week? No, I say, have to be in economic free fall-hell, NYC, meet with clients, none of whom are too happy, won't be fun but have to go… He asks, then how

about my place on weekend? New house, love for you to see it, meet the wife, BBQ with friends, mentions top CAA agent, Ronnie Meyers, and superstar Clint Eastwood... love you to be there, good for you to know them. Wow, sounds great, I hesitate, he continues his story about the house and wife, Margie I think, remodeling something? Don't know what really happened next, how I got to the place to tell the truth, his words and enthusiasm and companionability swirled around me, and I slipped away from them, him, from the attendant refreshing drinks, offering pillows into a space from which I continued to see and hear but am isolated, breathless. Don't remember assessing or making a decision, only remember gathering myself into a slow-motion shift, a no-lies-no-mask space, not *all*_truths be told—not ready, not necessary anyway, but a space nonetheless held me, no lame excuse rescued me.

Can't, finally said, have to be in Atlanta. Something about Howard, his streetwise, no-judgment persona is safe and I let my guard down, boundary wall between public face and private ache becomes vaporous in his open acceptance, directness whither my resistance.

Atlanta? He laughs, I just gave you an invitation to a star-studded LA party... what the hell could be so important in Atlanta?

Rehab. I say it directly into the last breath ending his sentence... Rehab, my son, alcohol and drugs. There's a moment's pause. His laugh is replaced with a flicker of what I read as knowing, as empathy... can't be sure but can't take anything back either.

He asks about police but knows, says kids don't go to rehab, especially across the country, without cops and courts. Yes, I say, hope he doesn't ask more. I say whatever is said carefully, forcing myself to sit back, relax, loosen my arms, and hands, breathe yoga-belly breath, and release my tight tummy. True is true, no blame, no holding on will make it better, remind myself that I have made enough progress to tell a truth straight and know I will be Okay.

Howard says, don't judge your son, it's hard, what he's going through, too hard. The drugs have a life of their own, are powerful in their own right, take even the innocent over, are demanding and controlling... willful. He does not flinch or dramatize his words, is careful to hold my attention.

I nod, yes, afraid more words will bring tears…He waits as I pull myself together, finally I say, yes, I've thought all this too, come to understand, but also know it is not enough to free me from the pain of guilt (I think but don't say shame…) certainly not from responsibility… try to keep my voice steady not deliver pathos or seek sympathy. Howard sees, hears it all. Then tells me, the drugs don't care who they hurt, including mothers… try not to judge yourself either; it's not true anyway, the guilt that is.

Yes, I say, maybe I think. I do not say, "He was slipping through my fingers like blood slips through an open wound, soaks towels, and gauze bandages because you hit a main artery, and there is no way to reach in with trembling fingers to tie a knot and stop the hemorrhaging." I don't say "I thought my son would die, and I could not reach fast enough or deep enough to keep him alive."

Howard continued his leveling eye contact, says again, the drugs don't care much for mothers. I don't respond. I tried to square my shoulders, keep my back straight, counting out steady breaths to stop the shaking that leapt from my legs to my chest to my throat. He waits and then asks, what are you doing for yourself? For yourself? For myself? I had no idea what to answer and pause too long. Terrible time for you, he says still direct, not overly sympathetic; he repeats what I have not heard, "Can't be responsible for all of it," loud enough that it demands response.

Yes, I say, not convinced; guess what you say is true. Drugs, even alcohol, like a demon tapeworm, demand feeding, take over, have their own call to survive, to keep the sickness going, and to take all prisoners. I thought, but don't say, the only thing I know that is true is responsibility… if not me who? I have loved this boy without limitation and cannot let myself off now. I am the one constant in his life, the one who stood next to him, and the one who should have been counted on to keep wolves from the door. His disease is my disease. *Responsibility* is not a strong enough word for this, blood of my blood, flesh of my flesh.

All of this arrived as a jumble of words in my mind that must have played out on my face. I see Howard watching me, finally say to him, well I know… 12 steps…family therapy…support groups and workshops. I know the theory is that responsibility is shared, but, still, Howard, he is *my* son. I stop there, choke feeling back to my stomach... refuse to cry... boundaries between personal/professional weaker than I can bear... afraid I've gone too far.

Howard then asked about Justin's dad? How is he taking this? I pulled back as I know I always do when asked about Bill, hesitated, until Howard must see the confusion between loyalty and truth, so he said, "Everyone takes these things different ways. He's not there yet right?" I am glad not to have to offer explanation. Right, I answer, not there yet. He doesn't ask again, says instead something comforting in strong words, what men say and more, but I know what mothers know—unbroken strings, unbroken rhythm, heart to child to self to heart.

The attendant's "Buckle up, seat backs up, ready for landing," saved me. Howard shrugged, patted me on the arm, it'll be okay, he gestures.

I am glad to have said it and glad not to say more. To bleed in public is forbidden in a long line of secrets. But just the act of telling the truth, to simply, one human being to another, outside the sacrosanct anonymity of programs and process and in rebellion of family loyalty dogma and not die of shame is okay when okay is good enough.

* * *

That night, dreams of papers with black dots in white columns give way to black limousines. Three in a perfect circle, accelerator pushed-through-the-floor speed, spewing exhaust, throwing up gray dust on repetitive cruise control. Space collapses between them until they appear at full-tilt vertical to the ground. The power of silent force is exhilarating, heart pounding, the cars become an indistinguishable black to gray to black like a smear of Japanese watercolor.

The dreamer, I squint through the flaying emission, and between the wheels and whirl, see a tree in the center. It is standing but ragged, dying, last year's leaves, crackled yellow, falling. Looking at the sapling, I wonder have fumes killed it? Or was it weak, then made more ill by the swirl of dust and exhaust? My dreamer's eye is drawn to something else, a bud—not one but three. Despite the vision of imminent death, a few green buds refuse to be denied. Life finds a thin branch.

The symbols are uncomplicated but wake me. Sadness and hope fill my chest. Do not cling to either, I remind myself. I write to :not forget; life, my life; I am all of these pieces.

But questions remain; must something die for aliveness to bud? Can a dying tree birth new leaves among commotion and adrenalin dust? Can one be an accelerated engine and a surrendering tree at once, so that bud-open-grow can come forth? Can anything flourish in the midst of concentric circles of steel, glass, leather, and polish?

The tree is universal symbol, center pole of mythological man, worshipped in ancient oak groves of ritual and magic. Tree serves practical life too, holding up tents, tipis, yurts, and homes for flying spirits.

The life-giving tree is also the tree of death; the Lakota, chests cut to the ligaments with buffalo bones, tie themselves to the trunk that drips with their sacrificial blood, and dance for days, praying for release from the only enemy that matters—the one within oneself. Christ, who suffered for the promise of redemption, dying so others live, carried the death tree. The cosmic tree shelters the Buddha, where, after seven years of seeking, he surrenders to the mercy of the moment, *svaha*, and is enlightened.

Awake, rested, and alive. Rushing to shower, mascara, unwrapping plastic sheaf of pantyhose, blow-dry hair, dress, role of the day ahead, I think again of my true name. Wonder whether it is a name in a roll call of the dying, or one of baptism of desire or fire. Whether a true name holds true in circles of birth and death where the start and closure collapse together in endless unfolding.

❧ 4 ❧

When I graduated from Gonzaga University, class of '67, I thought myself far too interested in scholarly pursuits, the study of American history, the Civil War and its influence on American politics, to teach elementary school. My plan, if you could call it that, was to teach while my husband finished his MBA, and then go back and finish grad school myself. Three weeks into teaching fifth grade at St. Brendan's parish school in Los Angeles, I was hooked. I fell in love with the kids, their inquisitive minds, developing characters, and with the possible impact of teachers for good.

I reasoned that the determination of the young might guide us to a better, safer, and saner place. It was the era of peace marches and the civil rights movement. Upheaval filled the air, and positive change spilled into the classrooms.

Assignments took me from private to public education, from teaching preschool in a federal housing project, to the politics of integration, and to working in a big city hospital with childhood cancer patients. But as I became a business woman, the world as I had imagined it to be, balanced among myriad disciplines and interests, rapidly appeared to have been an illusion.

The further out into the marketplace I ventured, the clearer it became that business rules the world. From Columbian drug cartels to the coffers of Mother Teresa's charities, in micro- and macroeconomies of scale, to globalized, televised "money lines," and NASDAQ ticker tapes streaming under political debates, business is ubiquitous. It dominates what we see, who we hear, and what we think.

While extremists of every stripe argue tribal justice and national boundaries, French water companies buy American entertainment conglomerates. McDonald's sells hamburgers at the bottom of Rome's Spanish Steps, Hindus living in Bangladesh handle troubleshooting for American computer repair, and bikinis on the beaches of Brazil are sewn by peasants in northern China who will never see Rio.

If business runs the world, deals run business. They are the engine, the combustible driver, of growth, the creation and byproduct of change.

Business is vision, mission, strategy, research and development, leadership, HR, marketing, distribution, production, sales, technology, and teamwork. It all counts but takes a backseat to merge and acquire. To grow and compete as fast as possible, M&As became the ultimate, keep-the-stock-price-up, the profits-per-partner competitive edge guarantee, in a world of no guarantees. Everything else is a fungible commodity.

The deal world is man-made of adrenalin and muscle, and show-no-weakness. It takes powerful leadership to balance fierceness of purpose, focus, and intent; to seek what others want and make it one's own. It requires steadiness of hand on the management wheel of fortune and boldness, as well as clarity in plot and plan, precision in execution, and the occasional intervention of brilliant intuition just to make sure you leave them panting for the next move.

Conscientious leaders balance a talent for foresight with duty to detail. Voices along the watchtower rise and argue, persuade, justify, and lead astray for accurate, selfish, or downright stupid reasons. Leaders must weigh truth, fiction, allies, malcontents, numbers, odd, and even. They have to tease reason out of the grasping jaws of voracious appetites and don't-dare-change scaredy-cats. The very best of them know not to get delusional, ego bound, or blinded. They act in the organization's interests rather than their own.

They know that economics can't be separated from culture and that the system overwhelms mere product. *"Unselfishness is the mark of great leaders."* I don't know who said that, but it's true. And rare.

The M & A territory is treacherous at every turn of its serpentine road from idea to completion. Concretized beliefs are blown up in a minute by new information or by a change in the wind of fear, in the complexity of loss or gain.

Deals can be decided by whims of personal caprice; they can shatter because a CEO will lose his private jet or ski chalet. On the other hand, deals can close in spite of thousands of employees who will be fired. Lives are thrown up in the air with no soft landing for any except key executives granted golden parachutes of stock options that open with millions of dollars.

Even the white hats can lose their grip on reality when fear causes self-absorption to rule over best intentions. Don't take any of it lightly because no one else who counts will. Hope of a safe harbor can cloud the professional judgment on which others rely. And safe harbors themselves are often found to have sharks swimming in shallow waters.

Deals throw out wide circles of possibility where villains, heroes and just plain folks emerge and surprise by disappointing performance or thrill with selfless genius. Unexpected heroes put a stake in the ground for integrity or voiceless constituencies or core mission, and original principles are easily trampled by galloping greed. Guys in white hats and black hats often change headgear.

As old structures are thrown into the air of investigation and reassessment; voices have a chance to be heard that serve the unfolding dynamic. Some shrink from the challenges; others rise with disquieting speed to tackle tough decisions. The lives of real people, without parachutes but with hopes and mortgages, rest on the courage, creativity, decisiveness of a few. It is hard to call ahead of time which players will stand at the close of the day, and which will fall.

We ended 1987 on a sour note. A few firestorm years of hostile takeovers, "poison pills," and multibillion-dollar deals changed the American landscape forever, collapsing entire industries into new, larger beasts. But the ultimate questions: long-term good or bad for the economy, for the once substantial, now diluted middle class, for reengineered employees, for the dominance of stock price at any cost is rarely addressed. Truth is argued, weighed, and measured without conclusion. Pundit speculation is all we have for good sense.

Law firms lag corporations in merging, acquiring each other's assets, offices, talent, clients, and global influence. But, the move is on. And the rules of the M & A game will be applied and negotiated in a way unique to the legal profession. Law firms will explode in one decade from an average national heft of less than one hundred lawyers, to five hundred and then eventually to over a thousand. This expansion is in response to the amoeba-like growth of business in a global community that has no patience for slow and rewards risk.

But, there is a fundamental difference between corporations and the law firms that serve them, for lawyers carry a responsibility beyond the bottom line. Wherever they go to promote the fortunes of their clients and themselves, they define and often create the law of the land.

From business meetings to criminal courts to global finance in first and third worlds, they write and test the rule of law. The fingerprints of

America's lawyers are on every deal that creates wealth, highways, high rises, entertainment venues; cures or cripples debt. The mergers that unite law firms extend that influence exponentially.

In Chicago that day, the momentum of merge and acquire is unfolding but far from custom. Wyman Bautzer is hanging by whitened knuckles on a precipice while Katten Muchin is flexing success, brains, and muscle, are both trying to create a future yet unformed.

∾ **5** ∾

In the theater of merger and acquisition, the boardroom is center stage. I've learned to arrive early and take the middle chair on the receiving side of the table. I avoid the seats at either end. They don't allow the breadth of vision to catch slip of tongue or furrowed brow. Head and foot of table emphasize authority, draw too fine a focus when subtlety and balance are my roles. I empower this middle kingdom, gathering energy in allowing it to flow out, opening and expanding understanding. As a woman who is fully willing to be one, I create alchemy from this position. To offer or challenge opinion, my voice rises from the deep well of that which no one can take away: experience.

Katten Muchin Zavis can afford to be generous with corporate luxury. The expanse of glass that fronts the boardroom looks out onto the reception area, warm in earth tones and leather. I take mental notes of who enters the boardroom, their order, confidence, ease, and tension.

Michael introduces a number of them to each other who shake hands, while others pass last minute instructions to the reliability of assistants.

Details are arranged to confirm expectations and encourage efficiency. Coffee urns and silver water decanters, cream-white china on lacquered trays arrive and are placed on side tables. A stack of yellow legal pads, pens, and pencils are arranged distances from one another but in easy reach of those who will claim the upholstered chairs.

Allan Muchin arrives second to last and assesses the arrangements. Michael Zavis has plopped down notebooks to mark his place at the table's head. Allan leaves one chair between the two of them, two between he and I. He takes out his ubiquitous cigar from a vest pocket, rolls it unlit in his mouth, tilts back in his chair, looks like a man waiting to be entertained.

Michael finishes making the rounds, shares one more laugh and walks to the end of the table. I am eyeing Howard, the last to arrive. He was summoned to an emergency phone call in the reception area. He is standing, trying to end the conversation. My antennae are up as others may judge his dedication to the deal, and thus the deal itself, on such details. Just as Michael settles his place, Howard hangs up and arrives through the last open door. He asks around the table for permission to assume the opposite end from Michael.

Everyone looks up as Howard extends his hand to the few he hasn't met, apologizing for the interruption by the international film star he won't name. His partner, Craig, says the celebrity actor was,

"Panicked, insisted he had to talk to Howard, no one else would do. We probably have a conflict... probably can't represent him anyway, but he broke from shooting in Rome to get Howard's advice."

Howard smiles at the flattery, but assures us that everyone here understands the demands of spoiled clients.

"Especially you, Bobbie... after all you have all of us." He waves his hand, takes in the group. He's good, he's on.

"Yes, of course,"

I smile, leaning back, no hesitation, no need to spring forward.

"And all of you lawyers... the most temperamental stars."

Soft laughter follows, and I know it's the most that can be said with this much macho in this small a space.

The energy of the group then settles and focuses on the agendas set at each place. Michael is brimming with his unique intensity. We are in the belly of his whale. It's his domain, and his ideas that count, at least today. The wit that dominated as we assembled, changes to all business as he calls the meeting to order, rising to stand in front of the chair he won't occupy for the rest of the session. He reads aloud the agenda, asks for and acknowledges every participant's acceptance.

Within minutes he is pacing, orating, taking us through the Wyman financial statement line by line. Michael loves numbers. He jostles and caresses them, takes on all comers to his conclusions, interrupting challenges to their validity. The scrutiny of capricious numbers are his personal power chip. He plays out the cards of his knowledge like a seasoned poker player dealing from a stacked deck. Howard is kinetic. But Michael is kinetic on high-octane fuel.

Commanding attention, he strides up one side of the forty-foot room, down the other, growls and frowns, jabs the air to make a point while laying bare Wyman's financial distress. His voice rises to embellish disgust. *"Why the hell would we want this deal?"* he demands. Only Allan is not caught off guard.

Michael jumps to a laundry list of bad news. The numbers speak for themselves. His disgust morphs into anger, then despair that such high-level professionals could allow this. He wrings his hands, throws them up and open in the air. He lets his tough words settle, but just slightly, enough for held-in half sighs to be audible, then he starts up the mountain again. This time he changes tack, relaxes into sympathy, effectively drowning out the scattered murmurings of the Wyman partners' protest. He recognizes, he tells us, that the three Wyman partners at this meeting are all *"stars, team players... more than that, HEROES!"* They've held the firm together, taking heat from the press, the banks, their fellow lawyers without any chance of recompense, all to preserve the firm they love.

"Hell, statues should be erected in your honor." He demands in their defense.

But, he concludes, they can't carry the entire firm. They must face the realities of the losses, including jobs, necessitated by the departure of their former partners, and the resulting upending of their financial health. KMZ won't save everyone by committing to a merger, he ends. Feigning exhaustion Michael collapses in his chair quieting the room, allowing both his support of the three men on the one hand, and the defense of his own firm on the other to sink in. But, in seconds, he jumps up, resuming his pace, grumbling to himself.

The Wyman partners begin to protest form over substance: were the numbers added up properly? After all, they argue, losing those partners wasn't all bad, they represented costly overhead that is now eliminated. And, how about the renegotiation of the lease? It's not finished, but it will take a huge chunk out of the monthly nut of the firm. And then there are the staff cutbacks, and the perks and extras that were trimmed. Were those factored in? Do the numbers reflect the painful changes that were made?

Embarrassment and defensiveness at their weakened condition and of not being in control of all the facts bleeds into their voices as they attempt to explain the unexplainable.

We all wonder how much of Michael's exposé is theater, a negotiating posture designed to cut the best deal for his firm. Or, whether he is on to something we hadn't grasped; something we need to analyze and take responsibility for. The Wyman lawyers want to understand, don't want to appear negligent, but no one from their negotiating team is ready to declare Michael champion. No one is willing to deny him either.

Accountants are called in, *worst-case* scenarios are sought. If the merger doesn't produce the kind of bottom line that will assure an abundant future, what then? And, what is the *best-case* scenario? How will the combined firm perform if all the practices gel, if the economy grows? How will the numbers change in three years, in five?

We discuss every Wyman partner and some of the more senior associates. The California team argues and advocates for each. KMZ lawyers pepper them with questions forcing them to think and rethink strategy and synergy; they must consider how individuals will contribute to a merged firm that has new demands and procedures. Allan sits back allowing Michael to run the show, only leaning forward to correct a misunderstanding or redefine a misconception. He contains Michael's fire with his clarity and breaks rising tension while rolling the cigar about his mouth.

Howard stays alert and relaxed, doesn't show strain like others, never tries to upstage Michael; he gives him his due without giving up an inch of game. Howard agrees with Michael's assessment of the numbers, is not afraid to lose negotiating points by saying so, but argues persuasively to the entire room that they are predicated on the unusual problems of the past year and don't reflect the firm's historical excellence. He does not relinquish his belief in what brought him to Wyman a few years ago, the firm's distinguished name, its position in the LA entertainment community, and its professional reputation. He is convinced that Wyman's best days are ahead and that the right merger can rekindle the storied past. Everyone is glad when lunch is announced as none would admit to flagging intensity.

We are deal warriors, no front burner heat can cause us to flinch or pale. But we are due for a civilized moment, and the meal gives the Wyman team a chance to meet additional Chicago partners who have not been in the negotiations. KMZ is my client, so I am assigned to host a subgroup introducing the chairmen of the real estate and corporate departments to Wyman's managers.

A sprinkling of new faces, and their enthusiasm in meeting potential future partners, eases the morning's tension. The KMZ partners are enthusiastic, their firm is a work in progress built on a culture of sleeves-rolled-up innovation. They delight in showing it off.

∽ 6 ∽

The last three hours can make or break the deal. Private caucuses form after lunch in the hallways leading to the boardroom. Both sides quietly wrangle next moves, searching for alignment and coherence. Presenting a united front to the other side is essential.

The three Wyman partners are men recently in their fifties—men of accomplishment, of local prestige, but today they are at the helm of a sinking ship that they never planned to command. They ask of each other, what must be given up and what to retain at all costs.

They return to the boardroom refusing to be bullied and insistent on recognition of the firm's reputation and their personal integrity. They deliver impassioned and in-your-face arguments that the deal must include the entire organization, from its stakeholder partners to the messenger boys. They are desperate, too, knowing they need to get a deal done, but insist on one that inflicts the least amount of damage and protects what human assets remain.

But the numbers are the numbers. Sliced and diced twice and again, they consistently come up short. Michael is past badgering, and the accountants have made their points. Now the KMZ team repeats the data from different perspectives: yes, you save money when ex-partners aren't taking a salary out of the firm. But, you also lose the revenue they generated. And, those who left were some of the biggest generators. Yes, we considered the new lease, and the reduction to the original obligation, but at the same time there is a tax bill due that wasn't factored in and an employee insurance policy that must be paid off.

In the long run the overhead reductions will help, the KMZ side agrees, but in the short run there are severance packages and vacation time and other financial drains that will add to an immediate cash crunch. Allan approaches the question of the day with dignity and respect for Howard, Craig, and Alan:

"Is Wyman a viable business? Consider this carefully—can you make it on current numbers without this merger?"

The Wyman partners don't answer. From their group sigh, the slumping of shoulders, the lifting and dropping of eyes, I know that they see now that to get a deal done that secures the future of as many as possible, and saves the historical reputation of the institution, more cuts are inevitable. The dismantling of careers they helped to create in better times is an invisible dark cloud spreading out, sponging up the fresh air of the table.

Gone is the belligerent *"Screw you, Michael. We don't have to take these terms, your deal, or you. We may be at a low point… but we are still US… the number one entertainment, and good-at-a-lot more-than-that-too law firm."* The barrage of financial data and pointed inquiry has taken its toll. Silence seeps through the room. Chairs are pushed back; eye contact is avoided.

We stay like that, uncomfortable, for minutes. But Allan and Michael are not going to leave the situation tenuous. They are problem solvers they tell us, not in gusts of hot air but in considered sentences laced with concern. Allan says for both of them,

"We're worried and still interested in the concept of a merger, but we have to give it legs… make it a solid economic proposition. Otherwise it won't be right for anyone."

A damaged asset may still be an asset, he reminds us, but it's only valuable if management is unafraid and realistic. And, they don't say, but imply, if that asset is purchased for the right price. They praise again the sacrifices of the few who are making contributions to the firm's solvency. They talk about the rightness of saving the strongest contributors, and rebuilding relationships. Revival could turn tragedy to trophy. Ambitious vision is an asset.

In the margins of my copious notes I write *"I am squirming in my skin for them."* The Wyman partners are being asked to analyze their organization and its people as a business asset, devoid of personal promises, when personal is their guiding principle. I note increasing lines on faces, folding and unfolding of arms against the strain of newly oriented responsibilities. After a long silence Craig says,

"This is a business, and as a business there are a set of choices and decisions that must be made. We get it, of course, but this is true too: I will be the one who has to say you don't have a future here, a paycheck… sorry about the sick kid, ex-wife, all your obligations and lengthy service to the firm. But you'll have to go. You're not asking us to sell off a division of a company… to repair a leaky faucet… to remodel

an old building, for Christ's sake... you're telling us to sell off lives and relation-
ships... to forget history and friendships."

His partner from Wyman, the other Alan, adds, *"We're not the kind of*
people who make promises easily or forget them when they are no longer convenient!"

Michael says, his voice contained and decisive, *"We wouldn't want you if*
you were."

In the deafening disappointment that follows the silent subtext screams:
there was a time, just a minute ago it seemed, when their lives meant something quantifiable. Among the best, acknowledged by peers, big enough
and small enough to know their import.

They graduated from Harvard, top 10 percent from Yale or Boalt Hall
or the University of Chicago, Phi Beta everything. They played the game
well in the universe they knew—top this and top that. It was safe, foundations felt solid and trustworthy, and now what? Will their place and position no longer give them meaning in this crazy world where the rules they
thought were carved in stone have become liquid? New and bold rushed in
with mind-twisting speed, global complexities of ethnicities, geopolitics,
and changing technology; tectonic plate shifts delivering new hierarchies.
All before the beginning of the next business day.

Over every gate is a sign that reads Hurry. There is a rush, a need to
define, earn a name, a right to be, and a place in space. What was laid out
carefully by generations—graduate at twenty-one, earn this partnership or
promotion at thirty-five, executive privilege at forty-five, title and comfort
at sixty—and decided over golf, country club lunch at the alumni whatever, can now be decided without you present, in a foreign office thousands
of miles away, by a guy or maybe a gal you don't know.

I write *I am squirming for myself.* It is painful to watch and harder still
to strangle my instincts to fix feelings and dilute anger. I want to pipe
up, rebuild trust, diminish animosity panting behind the stress that carves
grooves around tight lips. I know to swallow those feelings, make space for
the unease, remember The Teacher says be with all of it and deny none of
it. It is the only path to consciousness.

To stay present I write *It tastes like sawdust in my throat... my eyes burn...I*
hate this part. I force myself to stay engaged no matter where engagement
takes me. I know this too: the tension of revelation, though miserable, is
necessary. Problems need to surface, be evaluated, simmer even seethe for
reality to be examined; to burn away what is no longer necessary. Delusion

must be revealed for true and real to take its place. It doesn't make it any easier to sit here knowing that.

Distress exists for both sides, is experienced differently. The Wyman representatives are fighting for some semblance of preservation, knowing their options are running out. They do not want to go back to LA with the wrong deal, and they can't go back with no deal. But they have fewer chips to negotiate with than they thought. The clamor of dashed hopes and shaken egos is palpable, sad, and disarming.

The KMZ leadership is required to keep the pressure up, to cut its own best deal. It is a mandate that comes with pressure—not to dilute what they have built by acquiring a distressed asset that proves damaging to the whole. They have the better hand to play, but it is not without risk.

Chairs are pushed back, ties loosened, jackets taken off, shirt sleeves rolled up. We all hope for the right outcome on this chessboard of live pieces.

"We are compelled to assess the businesses we are in, will be in together if we go forward, and who among us, all of us, adds value that can be built on, creates synergy in the marketplace. We want to be fair… but we want to recognize who works hardest, who has cared for your firm when times were tough. Reward those people now. Don't let the organization fail trying to protect those of lesser contribution."

Allan is clear, direct, and unemotional. It has been said before in the course of this long day, but now his words are heard. They must determine what each individual lawyer brings to the merger in terms of clients, hours worked, practice viability, as well as the importance of each department going forward.

Howard, restrained and calculated, agrees but says that he's not the right person to evaluate partners, instead compliments Craig and Alan, credits their integrity, as he turns that responsibility over to them. Craig and Alan listen to him without comment but are opening the financial statements before he finishes.

"Alright… you've said this in a manner that makes good sense, that is good for both firms going forward. Ultimately, that's our constituency, the partners who add value, and our shared responsibility for the whole entity demands our obligation to the truth of that evaluation."

With the Wyman partner's acceptance of their task, people breathe and start to move again, stand and stretch. Enthusiasm is restrained but easing back. With just over an hour to go the task that has eluded us all day is agreed on. The Wyman partners are no less loyal, but their focus is changed. They take the lead in discussing the construct of putting together the two firms, of creating a partnership based on combined strength.

The KMZ partners wait respectfully as the other team gets comfortable around their developing strategy. And, when they do, both sides join in, discussing business development, marketing, and growth.

Someone notices the time and warns of scheduled plane departures. People begin to stand, stretch to shake hands across the broad expanse of table, and declare the meeting a success. A KMZ partner takes charge, promises to call everyone and schedule the next round of talks. They assure each other it will be soon.

The West Coast contingent is buoyed by KMZ's interest. Their work is not done, and the deal is not closed. But, they are relieved that a merger is possible while acutely aware of the sacrifices that lie ahead. They understand the bigger picture now, and see that reality and its vicissitudes brings crisis and opportunity.

I shake hands, smile, and am relieved, too, but not fooled. We are a long way off from a done deal.

My professional loyalties are to my client, KMZ, but to influence any outcome, I must stay close to both sides. Sympathy and compassion come easily when I see all the men not as heroes or villains, but as human beings trying to do their best.

I take a place by the door, express my support to each of the California lawyers as they depart, assure them the choices they are making now, difficult as they may be, are the right ones. I wonder privately at my confidence, if I am right, or whether the hope of the future, the excitement of getting a merger done, clouds my judgment.

Allan says nothing until the last elevator doors close, *"Can you stay over tonight, meet tomorrow? We have to go over some ideas with you that came up during this meeting…talk about some of those younger partners and where they fit into the plans."*

We walk around the corner to his office where Michael, who left the boardroom ahead of us, is waiting, perched on the corner of Allan's desk looking tired but satisfied. *"You have to stay, Bobbie. A lot went down today, and I want to go over these people with you again. We have to look at them as if we have a deal done. What do you say?"*

These are my sweet spots—the strengths and weaknesses of practices, how they fit, who fits into them, why you would keep them, and why you wouldn't. *"Can't…have to catch a plane in an hour to La Guardia for meetings in New York."*

The tone reflects my disappointment. It is obvious how much I'd rather stay than go on client rounds in New York where the markets and the law firms are in deconstruct.

"Clients waiting… have to face the economic misery with them… won't be fun but they are counting on me being there."

Michael quick as a cat to his feet, demanding and incredulous says,

"Clients? We thought we *were your only clients!"*

"Well," I say. *"You are in my heart."*

"That was too fast, Bobbie," Michael laughs, *"but I'll take it anyway."*

* * *

Journal Entry, Chicago, 1990: The Teacher says, stress is the space between what life is and what we want it to be. This deal is stretched between reality and could be (hope so!) So too, all of us, wanting a deal that will make things 'right,' whatever that is… worth something, the saving of one firm, the exalting of another, and is filled with promise. Wanting permeates the room. And me? Not so different… Halfway through the morning, I wonder what I am doing here? Once again as the only woman in the room what do I have to offer? Haven't felt this way before, but this deal is different in size and difficulty, and maybe it was also the accountants sitting on my left for a good part of the day. They were zinging numbers back and forth to Michael and Allan, filling in blanks with answers I didn't understand, and maybe it was the overwhelming feeling I couldn't influence, the quick breaks from friendship to deal posturing…Maybe it's none of that, maybe it's just where I am, questioning everything that got me here to this point of my life, everything that once felt so reliable. Late in the day, in the margins of my yellow legal pad I write "do I have a right to be here?" I question the power of my mind, courage of my heart, strained and sensitized. After a while in scribbled doodles of notes, am surprised to see, that I have been unconsciously writing the names of kids I taught in the projects and barrios, in the oncology ward at children's hospital, my darlings at

Friends' school, Arthur, Bryn, Katherine, Jennifer, Matthew… takes me minutes to realize I am writing a record of sorts, a history lesson (?) maybe to make me feel safe… identify myself as having done SOMETHING of value "convincing myself of my worth," I write that too… The wide lines on the main part of the paper hold a different record, the details and opinions, corporate sophistication of the time I am in. Wondering at the notes tonight while flying to NYC, I realize later it is also "proof" of what I have to offer; an understanding of life gained in the way women of my generation gained knowledge— from experiences that marked our work, teaching, nursing, caretaking of all sorts. Caring about and for causes, community volunteering and building… raising consciousness and money with equal fervor. And then we recreated ourselves, believing it was the promise of our time to do so, move forward, make a stake for the future of women. There wasn't any time to prepare, we used who we were, pushed past barriers, used life lessons about commitment, professionalism, credibility. Empowered our enthusiasm, revved up competitive juices, "Work harder, think clearer, take nothing for granted, use all of who you are." We did, we got it! I shrunk and rose under criticism and praise, failures and triumphs, large and small victories. The market place presented opportunities to explore myself and the world that I could only guess at as a teacher… And I went at it head on, most of the time for the sheer adventure. At every turn I pushed forward. Indomitable. It was the only way I knew to be in a man's world of no-holds-barred, high stakes competition. Now sitting, wondering about my value to this deal and what got me here? Do I belong? I look at the list of names and realize they mean something else to me; a verification that the deepest lessons, wherever learned, have value. The numbers may confuse me, the deal points at times are inscrutable, but I know what the looks on these faces mean, where the twist of their minds, bent on rightness and responsibility will take them, what they will force themselves to compete for even if the only reward is the saving of face. And, how none of that will be clear to them. I began finally to relax, knowing I am all of the past, proud of it too, but not captured or determined by it, that I am " here now," having won a right to be here by my hard work. I think this too *not so different*! Refereeing soccer games of middle school boys, splaying themselves on asphalt for the possibility of a moment's dominance, and a boardroom of men in full-merger negotiations. After a time, I return to the Zen moment of "no preferences," where "objectivity" is complete acceptance of just what's so. Not captive of left or right columns of hope or desire or partial pasts. It is the space where wholeness is holiness, the place where objective and subjective become one. Where the value of being fully human is exalted by just being alive and awake to the entire catastrophe we call life.

❧ 7 ❧

Tommy Fallon is the type of character who is at once unique and yet so typical of New York that if he didn't exist, you'd have to invent him. A beat cop whose proudest moment was making lieutenant, he was forced to retire early after two gunshot wounds. The second, in his back, resulted in several surgeries, honorary medals, and a hated desk job.

"It was hell," he tells me when we meet in 1987; listening to the conquests of others coming in and out of the squad room all day while he shuffled and filed official reports that no one would see again.

"Shit for brains," he barks out and quickly apologizes. *"Sorry ma'am,"* he says in the way a cop would. But hell, he says, carried away by the offending memory, that's what it takes to do monotonous paperwork.

So when he's eligible for early retirement an ex-cop friend offers him a job driving limos for investment bankers, uptown lawyers, visiting dignitaries. Five years later, he has two Town Cars of his own, doesn't have to drive for anyone else, and has the limo at his disposal should he need one.

"A regular watcha-call-it? ENTREPRENEUR! Self-employed, just like you, missus. It's the American dream ain't it?"

A self-satisfied smile widens his Irish-American freckled face, assured of my answer.

When I began representing New York law firms in the early 80s, traveling coast-to-coast, arriving at odd hours, a client warned me to pay attention to safety, lectured me on the naiveté of non-New Yorkers. He insisted on having Tommy pick me up when the next impromptu meeting required taking the red-eye, getting into Kennedy at midnight.

Baggage claim was filled with angry, tired commuters, all of us having spent hours circling over the city in snowstorm turbulence. I was happy to see my name on the large card Tommy waved above the heads of the crowd. With spare introductory words and surprising gentility, Tommy planted me safely to one side, dove into the midst of the conveyor belt and jostling patrons, elbowing and grabbing his way to my bags.

A giant dervish with red hair graying at the temples and the confidence of a streetwise smack talker, he glared people into good behavior, dressed down an incompetent baggage handler, assisted an elderly couple, and got back to me in under ten minutes.

Quite a performance, I whistled to him as we exited to the car. He laughed, all part of the job, he said, relishing any action. *"Bronx?"* I asked, hearing his heavy accent, thinking of movie stereotypes. He dropped my bags on the frost-covered sidewalk.

"Brooklyn!" a sideways glower punctuated my offense. After my quick apology, citing my lack of familiarity with the social and ethnic politics of the city, he picked up the bags.

Collecting himself, he educated me on the history and importance of the boroughs, the Irish here, Italians there, the Polish, Germans, recently the Russian and Israeli émigrés, where they lived, and the importance of the neighborhoods. Forgiving my trespasses, he said, *"Hell, ya' couldn'a known."* From then on we were buds and, on occasion, confidantes.

There is a rumor he carries a revolver in the glove box with his old badge. I don't ask, and he never tells. But we do share family stories. I am familiar with his four kids and know the eldest son is training to be a firefighter earns extra money driving for Tommy. One daughter is getting her bachelor's degree in the military and wants to work in logistics. A second one, a high school all-American basketball player, is finishing teacher training while juggling a baby, and is married to a rookie cop.

"Broke her mother's heart." She wanted her daughter, the prettiest one, so talented, to marry a banker or lawyer not end up a cop's wife. Like her, I said to the back of Tommy's head years ago when he told me the story. Yeah, he sighed, like her and her mother before her. But, what can you do? They fall in love, and what can you do? There was a long pause in this story as he told it. I imagined he was wondering why his wife thinks her life has been so bad she wouldn't want it repeated.

"Florida," he finally said, My wife thinks life would be better if we moved to Florida. Leave the neighborhood, the kids, friends made over a lifetime? It's crazy thinking, Tommy is sure of it. What the hell would I do in Florida, *"Can I asks ya' that?"* he barked at the steering wheel. In seconds he resumed his humor.

"Can you see me playing golf in them Bermuda shorts they all wear, dealing canasta at night with the retired folks? And how about our youngest son? The kids a friggin' genius, top student in an all boys Catholic Academy... know it's braggin', don't care... What the hell is Tommy Jr. going to do in Florida?"

Maybe make us rich, Tommy credited his wife as saying, maybe there's better opportunities away from the same old lives in Brooklyn, she insisted.

We laugh together about the pretension and foibles of the New York elite and wannabe famous he occasionally drives around town. He's a street philosopher and no one's fool about who he is, where he fits in the scheme of his town's hierarchies. He believes in the balancing equations of life, has dozens of stories to prove what goes around comes around.

On this particular trip, October 1990, meeting me at Arrivals, 10:00 P.M., he reaches over the reception lines to grab my carry on, says.

"Ya' look exhausted. Ya' gotta ease up ahm tellin' ya'…when was the last time you ate? Bet it was lunch, come on we're getting your bags then I'm takin' ya' to eat at a great deli I know. That's the trouble with all your fancy schmancy meetings, no real food."

I let myself be led, happy for the distraction of Tommy's humor, the unusual pleasure of being cared for. After I order, kick off my heels under the table, and try to shake off a fifteen-hour workday, Tommy telling me *"Try this and try that,"* I inquire after his business. How is it with the slow down on Wall Street, I ask him if he's feeling it?

"Worst on the stretch limo business," he sighs. "Expense accounts all cut out or back, and that's what paid for it. Rides they get booked months in advance, like the proms, have been canceled." The day-to-day meeting rush, guys going uptown for a meeting, or downtown for lunch, well, he explains, that's down too, probably by a third. But, he cheers up.

"I got 'mainstays.' Ya' like that word? Got it from an investment adviser I drive, mainstays, yeah, like you, they're still steady."

His brow wrinkles with concern. He slugs down another gulp of coffee. What else is going on, I ask; these conversations always give me more insight on New York than official sources.

He thinks a minute, looks around, lowers his voice, says, "Hey listen to this." Two years ago he gets a call for the stretch, it's already out, so he has to go through hell to get another one because it's snowing.

Tommy says he finally found one, but he had to borrow it from a guy he doesn't like owing favors to, *"If you know what I mean, another ex cop but no pal."*

Anyway, he tells me, he picks up these young investment bankers downtown whom he had driven a couple of times, and one of their dads was in the Police Academy with Tommy. *"So the kid treats me like we're old friends. They're coming from a watch-a-call-it? Oh yeah, a closin' dinner, that's right ain't it?"* I nod, yes.

"Yeah," Tommy goes on, some big deal they did closed, they were proud of themselves, wanted to party. " *It's okay by me, hell, they're young - hey, they done good. They deserve to celebrate,"* he is excited now, waving the coffee server away.. *So's I pick 'em up and shit-for-brains if they don't start doin' lines of cocaine in my friggin' backseat. I don't wanna embarrass the cop's kid, but hell I ain't gonna be drivin' around New York with coke I can see for Christ's sake, in a borrowed car… I find an excuse, pull to the curb, get the kid out, yell 'are you shittin' me?' at him."*

Animated and louder now, people in the deli turn around. Tommy excuses himself, lowers his voice again, apologizes, but says, he was, *"pissed and the kid was drunk, hyped up too, 'ya know the usual."* But he lays into him anyway. Shit I seen it all, Tommy assures me, *"I ain't no babe-in-da woods."*

I say, yes, I'm sure that's true, and he laughs with me. He says, hell it's a compliment, but, jeez he says, *"lines in the car?"* And me, he adds, *"with my badge on me and packin,'"* he hesitates, blushes slightly, tells me I don't need to know about that, but the point is, he says, that he yells at the kid that they either stop or they are out of his car.

Another time I might have laughed or commented, but tonight with Atlanta on my mind, I see addicts, drug dealers, cartels, leeches with squid tentacles behind every bush and heartache; I stare into the restaurant preoccupied.

"You o.k.?" Tommy asks. *"Me, yeah, o.k."* I lie, *"Tired is all."* Then I add that I'm just surprised how much drug use there is and by whom.

Tommy laughs, wow, he says, could I tell you stories, but you asked how's business, well that's what I'm getting to. *"This same kid, the one on coke, well he calls me last week, don't ya' know. He needs a job!"* Tommy barks out a gasp, can you believe that? *"Do you want to know how the market is?"* he asks me. *"Whether New York is feeling it? Big-time guys, one minute up and comers, above the law, the next time I talk to the kid he's calling to see can he drive for me?"*

The young banker told Tommy that the whole damn bank was in trouble, laid off dozens of junior guys. Some come from rich families who can give them help, but this kid has a wife and a mortgage, needs cash, and has no resources. Tommy says that the kid begged him,

"Don't tell my dad, it'll break his heart to learn his Ivy League son has been laid off."

Do you believe it, Tommy asks, doesn't wait for an answer. And you know that night with the coke, he continues, you know what the kid did when I gave him the business out on the curb? No, I say, expecting the worst. The kid unrolled the hundred dollar bill they were using to sniff coke, *"unrolled it,"*

Tommy is incredulous even now, *"and stuffed it into my lapel pocket."* Can you believe that shit, he asks, apologizes again and says *"I gotta watch my mouth, but jeez the gall,"* he finishes still awed.

He leans back in the booth, says, that night with the coke he kicked them all out at Fifty-second and Lex, told them to grab a cab, knowing they'd have to end up walking blocks in the snow.

After a reflective moment he adds, *"I'd a given the kid a job drivin' if I still had the limo… told him that, and said hell kid we're all in this together."*

We sit awhile, and my food is served, Tommy drinks another cup of black coffee, uncharacteristically subdued. Finally, he says that his sister volunteers with Catholic Charities in New Jersey; their aunt who's a nun and runs a soup kitchen across the river got his sister involved years ago. She comes home last week blown away by the number of homeless, he says eyes drifting away from me. People with kids living in shelters. *"It's a crime,"* he sighs, adding,

"Ya' know me, I ain't no bleedin' heart. I think them bums in cardboard boxes in the doorways of Manhattan should be rounded up and dumped somewheres, bunch of crazies most of them. But, hell, she seen abandoned mothers with little kids livin' in backs of cars."

Well, he says firmly, without apology, that it makes him damned sick. But what can anyone do he concludes, *"it's the system."* They don't like it much, he assures me, but in New York they know it's always been this way,

"We're all tied together in the goddamn system. One big part falls, we all come unglued."

Crime rates are up according to Tommy's precinct pals whom he sees daily, jumping higher as the markets dip lower—right on cue, he adds. The mayor is inept, over his head, cops are caught conspiring with Wall Street crooks worried the feds are after them. It's pathetic, Tommy sighs. Says, *"Hell maybe the old lady is right,"* maybe Florida is better. *"Hey,"* he says to me looking up, *"Don't pick at your food. There's people starving out there."*

"Tornado," I say, dutifully taking a bite. I saw this documentary film about tornadoes, and it's stayed in my mind; cows and cars and clothes off backyard lines all tossed together as if they are one thing, as if nothing is special.

Wind gathers on the heat of an unsuspecting thunderstorm that comes up suddenly on an otherwise cloudless day. It creates a spiral that lariats wider and then wider still until entire homes, lifted with all their contents, are riding over the plains, across roads and bridges. It tears up fence posts like a string of pearls breaking in a straight line, then wraps electrical wires, laid in exact formations by careful men, into the Christmas ribbons of a giant, invisible Grinch.

I can see the documentary in my mind's eye, mesmerized by the power of the tornado, the indiscriminate pulling up, ripping apart, laying back down, no thought to purpose or history. No care for the dreams of mortals, for whom things are tokens of stability. In the end, when the tornado finally exhales one last time, trash and treasures jumble together. No respect for dreams destroyed, for futures unrealized.

I say to Tommy that California's earthquakes can be devastating, and more surprising, less predictable. At least with the tornado you see it coming. Yet the image of that roaring spiral tossing trucks along with their inhabitant chickens, horses flying alongside church steeples, left me shocked, amazed.

I don't tell him that my first reaction to the film was, *"This is my life,"* this is how it feels to me, where sacred things become unidentifiable, torn and twisted until old names don't fit the object of my longing.

I tell Tommy I was impressed by the randomness of the mad swirl. How it tossed everything up together, not knowing who or what will ride, survive, be saved, or even recognized.

Yeah, he says, sharing the analogy, it's how New York feels. Maybe not so sudden for those in the know, but for the rest of us it came out of nowhere. He speaks with respect for the mystery of it. Like your tornado, he adds, it just carries us all along. None of us know where we will end up. We sit a moment each watching something on our personal screens until Tommy laughs, *"Ah hell!"* New York's still New York.

"Ain't nothing gonna bring the ole gal down for long. It's just us, her humble servants, gonna suffer in purgatory awhile. But you know somethin'? Ain't nobody leavin' her either… Florida… can you imagine me in Florida? Take more than a tornado."

∿ **8** ∿

Bobbing and weaving on the edge of a personal tornado, I came to sense that any status of place or definition I valued and clung to would be uprooted like so many cornstalks.

Part of me yearned for a surrender that could destroy all that was untrue, anything that tethered me to false realities. But most of me wanted a rock as anchor, a foundation that wouldn't give way.

I am looking back now, of course, to that day, those times. Backward looking has its advantages. Insights develop with experience. Reflected knowledge, benefited by more information, meditation, and the distance of time can bring understanding. The very reason for maintaining illusions may disappear with passing years.

Like the river we cannot step in twice, memory, too, is fluid. Flowing freely in its natural course, it creates eddies of immense beauty each containing myriad microscopic life dependent upon each other for survival but able to give themselves up to the river with ease and grace. Stagnation occurs only where debris blocks and logjams.

Memory is shaped by currents of consciousness, by the time and force of psychic hydraulics. The part that I am most confident of remembering true is the constant ache of division, the splitting of my external, high-powered life, divided and pulled by emotional and spiritual change. My questioning of the outer world's significance—does it matter? To whom? How much? Challenging the need to deconstruct all that defined me.

The external world of risk/reward that based victory on achievement and well-defined goals, argued with an inner journey where rules are not articulated; where every answer opens to a paradox.

Progress along The Way is not marked by gold stars, is mysterious, circles back on itself, producing a test, another question. An internal journey is always about exploration, is never about destination.

Wakefulness itself being both bliss and burden. I could see my oppositions but not reconcile them. Healing left to right, dark to light, true and not true, joining poles and fragments, appeared impossible. My choice was to be taken by river and wind, to allow the forces of change to carry me.

Often into a frightening darkness where memory was not my friend - control delusional.

By 1990 I began to recognize that I had run from my demons; mollified, organized, denied, ignored, or created success out of them. Compartmentalized them into the challenges of the present. This was not all bad. Success as a teacher and in business was greatly served by my just-keep-truckin,' positive, energetic push away from dark memory, from limitations of any kind. Nothing stopped my full-throttle engagement in life's responsibilities and adventures. At least not until the fear of losing my son brought me crashing to my knees. At that point, a tornado seemed a blessing.

Foundations I counted on and trusted in, especially my ability to succeed, vaporized. The part of me that wanted to believe in recognizable self-definition and stability put up a hell of a fight. Until the external spiral itself drove me deeper into crevices of howling internal space.

The foundation gone, I could no longer lie to myself, prop up the old concrete pilings of family, loyalty, and good-girl excellence. And so I forced the contradictions at every turn. Teetering illusions became so many sacred cows waiting to be thrown into the inner vortex, out to the farthest wind.

* * *

Journal Entry, October 1990: New York is as I've never seen it before. Gone is the glamour of only two years ago. A pall has fallen over Wall Street. The reign of the new billionaires from the 'greed is good' gang, the hostile takeover, junk bond kings, is tarnished and tawdry, brutal actually, as thousands of regular folks are out of jobs. Two days and nights in New York, the best city in the world, seemed like a week! The crackling onset of fall no match for somber gray moods. The "be, do, have, Masters of the Universe, dream, make a dream come true" is gone in the M & A crash, replaced by a thinly veiled desperation. The era that fuelled the law firm's push to new markets (LA at any cost!) is also gone. Partner profits in NYC plummet when deals die. Any delusional thinking of ever expanding business has been destroyed. The client base of the leading law firms, investment banks, corporate America, is just starting to pull out of stagnancy. But it will take another year before the law firms fully recover. Two years ago the NYC firms, my clients, couldn't grow fast enough, with me their chief sales person and proponent. Today, every meeting's mantra is "save the very best but as few as possible, cut back," or even, "cut out, GET OUT, close the office, save face." Yesterday's LA dream has become a liability.

The NYC business cycle we all enjoyed and prospered from has gone from rapid, sometimes buoyant construct to deconstruct in a blink.

I was part of all this... Now what? In each meeting we spend only a few minutes reevaluating the bright ideas that created the California offices, then lots of time discussing how to change the direction of LA strategies. It's a euphemism, of course. To change "strategy" means changing lives, exactly the ones to whom we made promises. Where does integrity lie: in the promises to a few or in maintaining the organization for the largest number?

The questions are weighty and real, posed by mostly good, well-intentioned, and sometimes courageous men... But "truth" is never so simple to see and harder to act on. None of us, not the most sophisticated law firm CEO has found himself in this situation before.

The LA offices were an experiment, a response to the growing needs of national and global clients. Do you keep them open when they are no longer central to those same clients? When markets are down? Do you keep promises made at a different time, under different circumstances? Do you maintain old strategies when all growth looks too expensive for leaner times?

Throughout the day my own role in all of this plays through my mind. Collusion or collaboration? How do I add value when value itself is beat up and looks different than it did? When construction was the only agenda item? Who am I in this role… what do I take responsibility for? I expect answers and find myself lacking.

The Teacher's instruction to ask who is your True Self and what is your true name?" alights to wander in and out of tired thoughts. I hear only my mind's dilemma... "I thought I was this or that, but little makes sense right now."

Safe labels elude me, but who am I without them?

Most importantly: what was the illusion that got in the way of knowing the whole reality in the first place? Is it the same barrier to knowing True Self?

* * *

When the New York law firms came west, I built my business and reputation on their expansion. It looked real and solid. In 1987, the wave of corporate M&A, hostile takeover, and leveraged buy-outs of that generation came to an explosive close, and by 1990 those heady days were memories.

But as I traveled by cab up Park Avenue, shuttling from one meeting to another, I could see that New York was down but not out. It is the great bubbling hub of financial power worldwide, destined to fight for survival and win.

For its law firms, to stay on top of the national scene meant national layoffs, and serious cuts into all overhead. Starting with leased space and fungible perks, the least painful nicks and cuts were followed by slashes into muscle: employed staff, nonlawyer professionals. Eventually the young associates fresh from law school were given walking papers. Finally the most sacrosanct group, partners themselves, were reevaluated with many forced to leave organizations that had been their home for thirty years.

From cities afar, LA, Chicago, San Francisco, Dallas, and Houston, to the upstart tech market of the Silicon Valley, we watched New York's ongoing woes, believing we were not vulnerable to the same economic downsides. In the breach left by New York's momentary demise, law firm managers see an opportunity to take over territories New York's firms have left behind. My company, with all the experience that New York had provided us, again played a pivotal role helping to create an entire new community of firms that has come to be called the national law firms.

In LA we were particularly arrogant, believing we could become the next best business city. But New York proves to be a harbinger of bad things to come, and by 1991 as the Big Apple begins to stabilize, economic pain will spread to LA The defense industry, stalwart of California growth and robustness, will suffer cutbacks and then closures. The savings-and-loan crisis will rock the real estate markets and commercial banks. Eventually even the entertainment industry gets bought, sold, and claimed by foreign companies and different owners.

In October of 1990, however, we don't understand this connectedness. Separation is a tough illusion to give up. Most of the time it takes reality banging down the door, unleashing hinges before we see things as they are instead of how we want them to be.

My company's motto *We are in the business of creating opportunities* didn't fit easily with the deconstruction. It certainly didn't align with my image of myself, the Eveready Energizer bunny full of motivation and solutions. Undaunted positivity.

Deconstruction takes different muscles and skill sets, is dicier to egos and identities framed by possibility and expectations of success. It is anathema to strategies initiated in growth and expansion cycles, and to the dynamism of American business itself. Old timers like to raise the hairs of initiates with boom-and-bust depression stories. But the truth is when you are caught dead center in the middle of a freefall, the natural tearing apart, the consequences of broken dreams and promises, undoing of careers and lives is greater than can be imagined in the metrics of change models.

Fingers are pointed outward looking for someone to blame. Collusion with failed plans and lost revenue would admit defeat, or at least expensive error. There would be a price to pay. Corporate heads are down. Only the most honest don't run for cover.

Eventually I would discover that the deconstruction cycle paralleled my life. That, in fact, parallel paths of construction/deconstruction, brought lessons in courage, were natural cycles of death and rebirth from which torn and tattered gave rise to beauty and wisdom. But, in 1990 it all felt, most of the time, like hell.

* * *

Journal Entry, October 1990, New York: If I was willing to believe in growth and possibility, then I have to take responsibility for its opposite. Isn't that the essence of being a grown up, showing up? It is ironic that New York is in a tailspin and Chicago, LA, the followers who looked to New York to mark the future, are now stronger, bullish, and maybe will become the leaders of the next growth cycle? I am pulled between extremes, believing in the what could be of LA and Chicago, and the what can't be of New York. I'm wary now of believing in booms, but still excited by the future…worried about the busts, but wanting solutions that will work for the majority. Can I live and work on parallel paths, suffering with New York, celebrating with LA?

There is terrific pressure everywhere in NYC, and it's reflected on everyone. No meeting is completely comfortable. All relationships are at least slightly poisoned by the smell of defeat.

And me?? Confronting it all is both good and miserable. It keeps me focused on people speaking the hard truth, on the objective realities, on decisions and consequences. Keeps my mind from wandering… 48 hours to Atlanta…

36, now only 24…

If I lose my concentration on immediate tasks for even a moment I am pulled into my own process, distracted into worry, questioning.

The documentary stays with me. I recall that within the tornado's outer spiral an inner vortex forms where light is smothered, at some point all mischief is sucked into the twisting center. It is quieter and cooler there, but little else is known about the core because nothing drawn that deeply within survives the force.

Is this true for me? Do I care? Is destruction of all things known, being pulled into my interior, such a bad thing? Or will loss compound loss? Early in the morning on my second day in NYC I rivet my mind on the Serenity Prayer – use it to ground myself. The simple repetition of vowels and vows steadies the restless mind and nerves, prepares me to be fully attentive to client challenges; it keeps me from being attached to either tension of external concerns of the marketplace or compulsion to go within and avoid what must be done in the outside world.

So I say, or think I say, over and over God grant me the serenity to accept the things I cannot change; the courage to change the things I can; the wisdom to know the difference."

* * *

Taking my seat on the plane to Atlanta to see my son, I exhale the grime and disappointment of the city with my own grief. Then I realize, listening to the words in my head, that I have been repeating only the first line, *"God, grant me serenity."* I laugh at my fragile humanity. I thought I was pulled together, able to bear opposite tensions with the bridge of this humble prayer only to realize it took me eight hours to hear the four precious words.

"Present, I wasn't even present to my own voice."

Ah, well, maybe it is all that is required, the essential part of prayer, to be serene, to call on God; and to accept the devastation of living in a time of things falling apart.

❧ 9 ❧

Landing at the Atlanta airport at 4:00 P.M., picking up a rental car, and heading to a suburb called College Park. I am shocked by the profusion of nature. A complex of hotel-motel, fast food, and neon rises unchecked at the freeway off-ramp, for suburban College Park. Logos and beckoning signs compete with the randomness of trees and shrubs refusing to be limited by chain saw or forced into landscaping.

Accustomed to the intrusion of city noise and corporate demands, my spirit accepts and rejects at once the rabbit-warren driveways and parking lots attaching Marriott's to Days Inn's to drive-through food chains and bars advertising their BBQ ribs. Fresh from the deconstructing-restructuring New York economy, I wonder at the urge to develop this jungle in favor of the promise of commercial prosperity. But College Park, squeezed between the airport and the capital of the "New South," Atlanta, its rich neighbor, has no choice but to strive.

"I understand," I say aloud. I have to admit it's my world too; *"achievement, success, purpose, goal."* Checking into the Comfort Inn, I alternately drag and heave my bags to the room, and I strip off the restrictions of big-city suit and heels. I allow myself a long shower, wrap into a kimono, and try to unwind, watching the sun go down over the Delta Airlines hub that dominates Atlanta's tarmacs.

Thoughts, scattered by travel, lack of sleep and threading disparate ideas, question the promise of creation, both material and that of God. *"Or is it one and the same?"*

My thoughts turn to my child, to all that is at stake, and contrast it to the week's many challenges. My stomach sours, feeling the tug of competing anxieties. I ignore it and try to stay conscious. *Here and Now.* I command my mind to focus *Be Here Now.* I sit half lotus, take cleansing breaths followed by a counting pattern, ten in-breaths, ten out. Repetition does not keep my eyes from wandering to my watch or checking it against the validity of the hotel clock. *Be Here Now.* Saying it aloud gets my mind's attention. *Now,* do not escape into hope. Do not attach to what could be; to what you want it to be.

I hear the determination and authority in my voice. Calming, I say the entire reality aloud. I am in Atlanta, Georgia, College Park. I am here to see my son. He is in rehab. I am scared. I don't know what will occur. I cannot control it. It's okay. All okay as it is. It is what it is. Acceptance. Acceptance.

The Teacher says *to expect nothing.* I remind myself that expectation creates a picture of what must happen for happiness and peace to be possible, to feel safe. Fulfilled. When mind clings to just one picture as the only acceptable option, I am not open to whatever presents itself, to the whole truth.

I will long for something different than the conflicts inherent in knowing the entire reality. *Expect Nothing.* Be awake to whatever occurs, here and now. Anything less is delusional thinking; leads to illusion.

I am a beginner. This is not easy. I want to escape but long for truth. It is a paradox. The edginess of hope perspires off fingertips, pounds in my heart, shimmers against the tension of shoulders squared to resolve. Hope restrained makes me light-headed as it tries to force its way in. *Hope is okay.* But clinging to hope limits knowledge. Understanding will elude me if what I hope for is preconceived or concretized. I note all of this in the way I have been taught: notice the body tenses, wanting a safe answer, then releases. Gives in. Fights back.

"Stay Present." I repeat the command aloud twice more to control my shaking mind and body. Minutes pass until my breath is even, body still.

I cannot rest for long. With three quarters of an hour left before I leave for family night at the rehab facility, I stand and reach for the phone. Check voicemail at work. No messages.

I try my husband's office number. It's still early in California, and he should be there. An assistant answers. She says she hasn't seen him all afternoon, and he was going to look at a new real estate project with some people from the office. She say that she thought he'd be back by now, but she hasn't heard from him. I feel a swell of loneliness wash over me, and a chill I can't name.

"Okay," I say, trying to keep it out of my voice, "Just tell him I called and that I made it to Atlanta safely. Ask him to call when he can." I vow not to bother calling again until Sunday, not to have anything, anyone, distract me from being present here. Then question my sincerity.

Moving client files to get to another layer of clothes I wonder, which life is real? Which is illusion? Does it matter? Do I care? I change into slacks and casual shirt, flat shoes, and take off all jewelry but wedding ring. No pretense of the outside world should distinguish me, I think. Add only a cotton sweater in case the heat drops off the sweaty southern night.

Assembling the little I need, my journal, a small stack of inspirational books, the Alcoholics Anonymous "Big Book," I try to settle on a quick read to galvanize me. But in the end I give it up and instead watch the last fire-rays of sunset over the distant scream of an arriving jetliner. I sink into the passion of the colors, into the heat and light it reflects against the room's plate glass window.

Finally something warm like grace, like confidence, or maybe faith wraps me into a cocoon embrace. Calmed I create a mantra *Breathe True Self. No false identities, no labels or illusions will help me here.*

$$\backsim 10 \backsim$$

—Rehabilitate/re'ha bil' i tat/ v.t., :1. restore to effectiveness or normal life by training, etc.; especially after imprisonment or illness. 2. restore to former privileges or reputation. 3. restore to proper condition. n. {related to re-ability}

To start over, as if time can be peeled back. As if we are sure who needs restoration or know who among us is in "proper condition" and can pass judgment on a "normal" life. Whether those out of the institution can determine the restoration of those who are in it.

I drive to the Anchor Facility for the first session of the Family Weekend; thoughts distract me and the twelve-minute drive has to be retraced until a low-rise maze of industrial buildings pops out of the darkness. I check the directions and assure myself of the address for at least the hundredth time. The Anchor Program is divided into two parts. Phase one is a compulsory lockdown at Anchor Hospital lasting two to four weeks. There the protocol of detox, no privilege, hospital gown, and slippers isolates and breaks down arrogance and rebellion. The message is the same for all who enter: this is a sickness, and you are the patient. The cure takes radical measures.

The second phase is a halfway house arrangement. In recovery terms being moved to the halfway house means the patient has earned enough points to have some privileges restored. For all of them, including my son, it means freedom from hospital isolation. But it comes with a new set of requirements. The first rule of reentry is having to live in apartments with three roommates they don't meet until the day they move in. For the teens, there is the special challenge that their roommates are all adults, strangers from around the country. The only thing they share is addiction.

In addition the teens have an especially disciplined and enforced lifestyle. They continue their high school educations along with group, family, and individual therapy, Twelve Step participation, constant surveillance, and monitoring.

The adult patients who share the teens' off-site living arrangements and rigors of healing are, at Anchor, all health care professionals, primarily

MDs. Their detox hospital stays have often been more difficult than the kids'. They come into the halfway house apartments emotionally exhausted, more compromised in health and mind due to their ages and the extreme fall from careers that others admire and emulate.

The presence of adults, whose addictions have devastated lives, often caused injury and even death to those in their care, is an additional reminder to the young that nothing is guaranteed in life but the consequences of their choices. Addiction is blind to status and doesn't absolve for position, stature, money, family ties, or community standing. Addiction swallows up piece by piece, sometimes whole, whatever, and whomever succumbs to its trap.

Tomorrow we will meet the roommates and see the apartments. Tonight we gather at room 101, Anchor Outpatient Clinic Facility. It is a weekly "community" meeting for the teens and their families and is part of the Family Weekend of educational and counseling sessions.

Occupying three large warehouses of an industrial development at the edge of College Park's entrepreneurial zeal, the teen high school and rehab is pressed in next to "Lang's Fans and Refrigeration," "Ron's Metal Works" and "While Away Sports." This is not the Betty Ford Clinic in the sun and sand-washed expensive desert. There are no rock stars here; no celebrity tell-alls will come out of this place. No tenant is impressed with anything but hard work.

The bleak surroundings, tangled vines strangling a high concrete wall behind the line of parked cars, blocks of gray uniform spaces, does not discourage me. I sit in the car watching a few parents gather under the interrupting glare of bulbs strung sparingly between standard brown doors.

I am nervous, yes, but eager and excited to see my son. I want only to hug him and tell him I love him, miss him, and am so proud of him. Now that maybe he can hear me again.

"I am ridiculously excited." Why, I ask myself, this is not a trip to Maui or a Harvard graduation. Hell, he is nowhere near being home free. But my cautions are useless. I want to be here and nowhere else. I am ready to call addiction by its name, to not hide, not be afraid, to do anything, anywhere for the slimmest chance of his survival.

I pray for courage as I turn off the car, watch my hands tremble, breathe deeply to quell them. I've been in Program, in the work of recovery, my own and Justin's for three years, long enough to know depth charge surprises, confrontations, the vast range of emotion that waits to pounce in every new experience.

But, I smile to myself. It's why I came, isn't it? To do this next level of work, to strip away lies, and to understand? I allow the smile to loosen the tightness across my chest and heart. I wonder about the conflicting feeling, all the emotion I didn't own that is now close to the surface. Be here now; contain all of it. Whatever it takes. Wherever it leads.

"First his survival, God. My son's first and then mine. All of the truth, even this, especially this."

∽ 11 ∾

On the last syllables of the survival mantra, I join the parents congregating on the sidewalk. A father is putting out the brown stub of a cigarette, says loudly,

"Guess I'll have to ask the kid how to quit cold turkey… he'd love that wouldn't he?"

After nervous laughter, someone says there's nothing worse than advice from a reformed addict especially to a parent. We all agree.

I step forward and introduce myself in the silence that follows. I'm Bobbie, I say, Justin's mom, not knowing whether his name registers.

"From where?" someone asks. *"LA"* I respond. *"Louisiana?"* A voice queries back. *"No, Los Angeles."*

The smoker's voice echoes my own thoughts, says,

"Wow! That's a long way from home… afraid if he was any closer that his friends would bust him out?"

These people know the risks and realities. The counselors who set up the weekend told me the families are mainly from Georgia or near southern states. They are here for weekly private family therapy with their children, mother or father support groups, and monthly community meetings such as this one.

They know the ropes; each other's lives and stories.

"Actually, yes… a couple of his friends traveled across the country as it was, said they were coming to surf the southeast coast, and thought they'd just drop by."

I roll my eyes to the preposterous notion, laughter follows, and a collective headshake.

"Must have been a popular kid."

This from the smoker, respect in his voice. I know from meetings in LA with other parents that this isn't always the case. Many kids turn to drugs for the opposite reasons: unpopular, outsiders, no-siders, friendless souls. I keep this in mind, say, yes, he was the life of every party, *"Unfortunately."*

The laughter that follows is looser, all of us trying to keep a proper cordiality, but we are nervous too, guarded, embarrassed. We are, after all, here for the same purpose if not for the same reasons. We are held together by fear of being made wrong and fear too that if someone *doesn't* make us wrong, if we don't admit and pay for all wrongs, another and worse mistake will happen. We are afraid of failing the tests of recovery. And afraid of losing the game in life, parenting, we most wanted to win. But, in the end, the fear that haunts this quiet gathering the most, is the fear of loss. *"Forever,"* whispers across everyone's heart, *"lose him, lose her... forever."*

If we don't understand the elusive beast of addiction, of disease, we will lose our child. We have heard other parents' stories, had more than a taste of it in our own homes. Unlike any other disease, whether it is true or fair or not, this loss will feel like our fault, our failing. That fear clutches at every throat; even those who want to scream out their innocence.

In the shadows of one bare bulb, we catch sideways glances of each other. We're so different, our children too, special, unique, except, of course, in this one crucial way. They are here. We are with them. A father, trailing wife, two preteen children, breaks our reverie in a conventioneer's booming voice,

"Well here we all are again... sorry to be late don't 'ya know... have the weekend schedules with me... this is the one we all helped the staff revise after our session on Wednesday... thought I'd be here early enough to welcome the newcomers... traffic... gets worse every week, don't 'ya know."

He rambles about how the schedule should be accurate, but things change here, laughs too loud about that, then stops momentarily as he meets me. Justin's mom? They all know Justin well. Hell of a kid, he emphasizes, *"dynamic, charismatic."* Doesn't look at me as he says that Justin makes them all laugh; pushes the envelope in these group meetings.

"And that's a good thing, don't 'ya know... we all need that, don't we? It's what the Program is all about, isn't that right?"

This is a three hundred pound man of average height whose reddening face is visible even in the night's dimness. No one answers or agrees, but the smoker, Charley, says, "It's true. Justin won't let anyone get away with anything, but he can *take it as well as dish it out."*

Charley turns to the schedule keeper, calling him Fred, and asks, *"Isn't this your last Family Weekend? Isn't your kid's time up?"*

Fred is happy for the change in topic, says, yes, loud, enthusiastic. Says his boy comes home next week, end of the month actually. The entire family is here for a small vacation. The counselors have agreed to have his eldest son, the Anchor patient, join them in Atlanta for the weekend.

"Dr. Morrison arranged for us to stay in a real nice hotel in that fancy Peachtree district… first family vacation in a long time … a kinda celebration after all these months here and apart, don't 'ya know."

His southern accent is syrupy, but his words come fast and punctuated through a tight smile.

As he moves around the circle a second time, his children, without looking directly at him, move adroitly away so that at all times they are opposite him, heads down. The mom, wan, hair stringy and fine, wears no makeup, a thin worn rain coat hangs to her ankles. Her absent-minded brittleness is a counterpoint to the father's joviality and sheer size.

I wonder, without judgment, who is the real patient? My heart opens to the children, the "well ones," who look lost and embarrassed, unable to speak up for themselves. I try to force the issue, turn to them, specifically ask their names, repeat mine.

Their mumbled answers fall away into the night, as the smoker's slow exaggerated drawl interrupts,

"You have a strange vacation plan, Fred. This isn't exactly Disney World now is it?"

He lights another cigarette as he speaks, inhales with a slight smirk. Fred's kids smile to each other, then down at the asphalt. In doing so they miss their father's move around the group and over to them where he stretches his portly arms, envelopes them and his wife. They strain against his grasp then go limp.

Fred says that they all have learned a lot in the Anchor Program, that they're *"pulling it together,"* that he for one, sees lots of positive changes. The mother, shoulders folded in like a sleeping bird, head hung low, the kids following her lead, are silent. I recognize his ramble of blind hopefulness; think to myself that I've practiced it too.

Fred says, it's what they all needed, a reminder of the importance of family. That's what this place and his son's problems have brought them. In a voice tentative but loud he says, "Maybe it's what the scriptures mean when they say, *"'and a child shall lead them.'"*

People shift around and neither agree nor disagree. We strain, instead, to read the schedule he's handed each of us, distracted by the lack of sufficient illumination.

∾ 12 ∾

Just as people begin complaining that we are past the 6:00 P.M. start time, Don, the head counselor arrives. In his three months at Anchor, Justin has written home infrequently, but Don has been in each letter. He quotes Don's advice, repeats his lessons, and writes of his admiration for the man's tender toughness, and honesty. He is the authority figure all the kids trust.

Like most of the counselors in the Anchor Program, Don is a recovering addict. He spent college years philandering with drugs, never losing his grades or his cool. But, a few years after grad school he sent himself into a four year binge when he got home from work one day to find his wife and three-year-old daughter dead. Their bodies and brains splattered across the living room floors and walls. He doesn't know to this day if it was a random burglary gone very wrong or some druggy he met who knew he could find a stash hidden at Don's place.

He wanted to die, to join his family wherever they were. Heroin was as good a death as any. One day he ran out of money and dealers, ended up in jail and forced detox. In delirium, soaked in vomit and sweat, he dreamt of his wife praying for him to live, to get sober; telling him she loved him, and it was not his time. Six years later, finishing up advanced degrees in psychology and addiction therapy, he helps other people's kids stay alive. I am grateful to his dead wife.

Don is unimposing. Swarthy-skinned, short, athletic with large, liquid brown eyes. A self-contained calm is his most distinguishing feature. He shows none of the dread and anxious expectation that glistens in the dampness of the rest of our skins. He is humble and kind and has no trouble taking charge. He apologizes for being late as he unlocks doors, and switches on electricity.

An emergency in the lockdown facility kept him at the hospital late is all that he tells us. We can interpret for ourselves. Some kid has gone bonkers, hit someone, threw things, or worse, attempted suicide. Don doesn't gossip and no one wants more information. We follow him inside, blink at the rush of fluorescent lighting after the darkness of black asphalt and moonless night.

Don stands just inside the open door, greets each of us as we file in, ruffles the heads of youngsters, returns the hugs of parents who extend themselves. Keeps his comments private, short, meaningful.

Don clasps both my hands, his smile warm and intelligent. Tells me he loves my boy, that Justin has told him that we are close, that he is sorry I have had to wait three months to see my son, but that he thinks it will prove to be worth it; worth a trip across the country.

I mumble something. Surprised by the quality of his love, I want to stay right there, bask in it awhile longer and have him tell me again that he loves Justin. It is a balm to the wound, I say to myself, as I move into a pre-fab makeshift high school classroom, not saying the thanks that forms a lump in my throat.

❧ 13 ❧

I am struck by the haphazard starkness of the room. To my left are lockers, closets, library tables piled with textbooks, loose-leaf papers. Desks of all sizes lean against the lockers or are strewn across the linoleum floor pock-marked by black smudges left by the metal of cheap folding chairs, easy to stack and slide. None of it is matched or coordinated for color or ambience. The three front walls are covered in green chalkboards. Not one is wiped clean.

Don standing at the front of the room, says that the vans carrying the Anchor patients, our children, will arrive soon. While we wait he asks for help purchasing some writing space. Excited siblings from eight- to fourteen-years-old, volunteer immediately. Laughing to each other they compete for the few erasers and cleaning rags, making a game of it. Don teases them, says they are welcome back any time. He needs a better cleaning crew than their brothers and sisters.

A mother chimes in, says don't expect much, they are certainly not this helpful at home. I turn to see a woman, curly hair, frizzed by humidity, leaning against the door jam, half out of the room, stamping a cigarette with the heel of her shoe. I notice the young girl at the front board who must be her daughter, turn to frown, then catching her mother's eye, smile sweetly only to return to the board, redness in her cheeks; determination in her scrubbing.

Don addresses the assembling families, reminds everyone to form the usual circle. And please remember the list of discussion protocols that he writes on the now cleaned board: no cross talk, respect silences, and tell the truth.

But there are no rules for ice breaking. Most parents are tentative, smile shyly, a few reach for a hug or cling to an extended hand. I overhear one mother thank another for her supportive phone call during the week. No, she says, there isn't any improvement in her father's health. No, they haven't felt he was strong enough to hear the news of their son's *"confinement."* But the old man is also confused as to why his favorite grandson hasn't come to visit him on what they all know might be his deathbed.

"I don't have the heart to tell him. I don't have the heart." The second woman assures her she does, and that she is strong and doing all she can. The first woman appears not to hear, her attention taken by a child pulling on her hand, demanding a chair of her own.

No communication is complete. Sentences of understanding, support, concern are left half spoken and partially answered. The room, painted a washed-out institutional yellow-green, feels stretched tight against the threat of unplanned emotion. Even encouragement has a stick up it. Creating a seating arrangement is the closest we come to intimacy.

I watch from a distance, assessing the unsaid rules of place and position. Deciding that families have found one another, moved near friends made in past sessions and that I am free to choose what suits me; I take an oversized desk that is one of fifteen or twenty strewn about. Some face in the direction of a board or an open door. Others appear to have been tossed by students in eager escape.

I listen to the last of parents' demands to restless kids. *This is a family weekend and we are a family, aren't we?* And *No you may not sit over there away from us with your friend. Sit here with me, with Dad.* I realize we're all pulling courage together and looking for allies. Why? To face our own children? To help us cope and deal and learn and be challenged?

Most sit with backs straight, rigid in anticipation. Others slouch, sucked in at the stomach, shoulders rounded, false smiles, and stiff necks. Breaths held in are shallow, others are forced out, exhausted from worry and the pretense of pride. I am glad The Teacher said to stay present to everything God brings. In the end, he assured me, the questions answer themselves.

～ 14 ～

Sitting alone in the haphazard circle, I turn my desk around to face the front board, write down in my journal the last of Don's familiar instructions: *"Use the language and Steps of Alcoholics Anonymous, and of Al-Anon. Follow the Traditions of the Twelve Step Program. Remember to 'Take what you want, leave the rest behind.'"*

Reading it I hear what is unsaid; leave all pretense of place, time, identity at the door. Any false act that works somewhere else, won't work here—or won't for long. Don't try to be someone. That someone will be outed, rousted from her safe place, and turned back on you.

I know the overt, covert expectations and rules. Therapy, group sessions for families in crisis at a hospital back home in California, and AA and Al-Anon meetings have all preceded this evening. I know that the elusive enemy I have come to engage defines all relationships within the boundaries of this space.

Addiction makes the rules, forces us to show up a certain way, meet it again, face to face. It doesn't matter what masks we desire or fit well in our other lives, this is the territory of worst fear, where none of us is sure who we are anyway. The words on the blackboard are human attempts to put boundaries on addiction's power—to rope it in and draw lines in the sands of its grasp.

I am riveted by my need for engagement, quelled by the challenge of the enemy who would take my child's life from me, but determined to know it without blinders. Without excuses. Feeling adrenalin's course, I am awake, afraid of loss, yes, but alert and hopeful that the rules and traditions that work for others can work for me, for us. I am confident too that tonight will bring me understanding I couldn't gain without being here.

My big desk and I remain turned toward the front board but not so I am outside the meeting's circle. Bang! Heads whip around, conversations end in midsentence as the heavy metal door pops off its pneumatic seal, slams the wall, thrust by youthful muscle, childish zeal. Boom! Justin's voice fills the room,

"What did I tell you? There'd be my mom, sitting up front... right under the teacher's nose!!"

Don shoots him a settle-down, no-nonsense look that forbears more than forbids. Behind Justin trails the Anchor teen group, about fifteen of them, glad to have him absorb the group's focus and break the tension of arrival and apprehension. They laugh and adopt versions of Justin's "gotcha" look and swagger.

Justin possesses a magical ability to pierce the heart of unease. His sunburst flamboyance throws open windows and doors locked against fresh air. He deals with his own anxiety by breaking up the density of pretension, including mine, with his big laugh and teasing. It is hard to ignore him; he's the child who pushes back until his own tender skin stops crawling. The one who cares and does not care at once about the results of his actions. He can expose common guilt that is marked and tagged in a society of lies. It makes him dangerous company if you wish to save face.

Tonight he calls out the fear of every adolescent child, an embarrassing parent. Outrageous and alive, undiminished by his weeks in rehab, he is calling me on my good-girl peculiarity, is not unhappy to draw attention to himself by busting me. The room exhales into nervous laughter then half inhales anticipating my response.

They don't see that I am ecstatic to hear life again in my son's voice. I calculate response for a second then ceremoniously lift my desk and thud it smack-dab in the front and center of the classroom and blackboard, directly under Don's watchful gaze.

Laughter and a number of "touches" come up from parents and the room changes. Families, freed for a moment from the grip of worry and expectation, greet one another. In three strides Justin is at my side, I stand, wobbly, limited by desk top and shaking legs as he wraps me in his giant hug.

I am astounded by his beauty, so male, so young, and all pounding energy. At six feet three, once again clear eyed and vigorous, he is a force of nature. Amazed, exhilarated, and shaken too, to see him whole, I have nothing to return in greeting but gratitude that springs to my silent lips, "Thank you, God. "Thank you."

Justin helps pull my desk back into the circle, Don waits and then says that we'll start by giving every family the opportunity to report on last week's progress in the AA Program, a *"what worked"* and *"what didn't work"* check-in. This will take about an hour given the size of the group. Afterward the Anchor teens will go to AA or Narcotics Anonymous meetings outside the facility with their adult roommates. Parents and siblings will remain here for a short intro of the rest of the family weekend activities.

The kids in Program groan over another meeting. Don ignores the protest and says nightly meetings are compulsory, and everyone must be there on time unless, of course, someone has a *"burning issue."* It's an inside joke. Worse than nightly Program meetings are the parental issues that focus, "burning," sometimes obsessively, on one person's problems.

Right away Justin pipes up, *"Don't get any ideas, Mom!"* He points a finger at me and tilts his head the way one might at a naughty pet. Says in mock defense to Don's reproving look, yeah, okay, but she'd be the one.

Don winks at me, understands I am not offended, only wish I had a comeback, and turns to a parent to begin the meeting with the traditional opening with the Lord's Prayer.

The father recites thoughtfully familiar words for us to follow aloud. Don asks a short, thin boy who looks not more than fourteen-years-old, along with his mother, to recite the Serenity Prayer. The two of them look back and forth at each other as they invoke tender phrases. Silence descends on us, as if the words *"... Serenity, courage,* and *wisdom* can sink into us and remind us of our shared vulnerability, humanity, struggle.

Turning to the Program manual, Don chooses a teenage girl, Sarah, to read the Twelve Steps. She resists, shakes her head defiantly, and blushes. A weak "Can't, please no," squeaks out as she keeps her eyes on Don who answers with an encouraging smile. He has his reasons for wanting her to push the boundaries of fear, I think, but the pain of her shyness is palpable.

We squirm with her and send silent strength. She offers up a sigh, finally begins in a small halting voice.

"Step One... I came to see I was powerless. Step Two... that only a Higher Power could restore me to sanity.

Sarah's parents, sitting on either side of her, have an infant with them, Emmy, a nine- or ten- month-old I guess. Meeting them earlier I assumed that it was a second family situation. But realize now the petite teenager balancing the manual and the baby precariously in her lap, is the mother.

Reluctantly Sarah shifts the baby to her mother's waiting arms, adjusts her own clothes, makes sure the baby is comfortable, reads on. *"Number Three, made a decision to turn our will and our lives over to God as we understand*

Him." She stresses the last phrase, looking at the teens around her, pauses, then looks down at the book. Gathering courage, Sarah swallows hard, clears her throat, and reads, *"Number Four… we made a searching and fearless inventory of ourselves."*

She speaks in halts and starts, eyes drawn back to the infant squirming to be with her. *"Five, admitted to God, to ourselves and to another human being…"* she shakes her head to focus. Don moves around the circle, stands behind her. Sarah looks up at him; she appears grim and tense but continues. *"The exact nature of our wrongs."* The last phrase cracks her voice, and Emmy responds, cries her mother's sadness in soft hiccups.

"Number Six… were entirely ready for God to remove these defects of character. Seven, humbly asked Him to help us. Eight, made a list of all persons we had harmed and became willing to make amends to them all."

Sarah's tears are now catching in sobs, but she straightens her back, forces resolve, and says, *"Number Nine… made direct amends to all we have harmed."*

Someone hands her a tissue. She wipes her eyes as if to blot them out, blows her nose, stops, takes a deliberate breath, tries to start again. But the baby holds out bare arms, keens for her mother in an indignant and injured cry, refusing the grandmother's comfort. Sarah, unable and unwilling to ignore her rushes to finish.

"Step Number Ten, continued to take a personal inventory. Eleven, sought through prayer and Meditation to improve our conscious contact with God… pray… knowledge of His will… and the power to carry it out."

"Step Twelve," Sarah sighs, pushing to finish. *"Having had a spiritual awakening… message to others… practice."*

Without stopping at last words she exchanges the book for the baby who nestles into her, thumb to mouth, eyes searching Sarah's teary face until sleep overwhelms her, tiny fingers closed over her mother's in determined possession.

The grandmother, a small woman who looks so like her daughter and not much older, except for worry lines that crease her brow and trickle crevices between damp eyes, tries to accommodate mother and baby. Earlier this evening, Sarah had been solicitous and eager for help with Emmy. But now, she is rattled as the older woman whispers advice, tucks the baby's blanket around her, offers Sarah a bottle just in case the infant awakens. Instead of listening, Sarah tightens her arms about Emmy and tries to move herself as far away as her chair will take her in that tight circle. The grandmother is left to sit in all that goes unsaid between them.

Moved and disturbed, unexpected tears, hot as the Georgia night, flame to my eyes. The memory of my babies, the press of their sleep in my arms, their downy heads tucked under my chin, comes back in a rush of smells and sounds. I look down fighting back enemy tears. When I look up, Justin is watching me, a question in his eyes and arched brows. I don't attempt an answer, instead I force a smile that he returns, a question still on his face.

How do I explain to him, to myself, the strange victory of being here with him, with all of them? He is alive and well. Love has prevailed, as it has in this moment with Sarah and her child. But there is also a profound grief. They rest beside and within each other, pushing, shoving for dominance, in the clench of my stomach; the fire in my throat.

Don's voice breaks my thought. Al-Anon is a Twelve Step Program to support the family and friends of Alcoholics, he is saying. Designed by people who share lives with loved ones afflicted by addiction, Al-Anon gives strength and hope and, we have come to see, needed healing and recovery to the extended community.

"We believe that alcoholism is a family disease and that changed attitudes, patterns of behavior and observing the family as a system can reveal ways to heal all its members."

He takes a considered pause, and lets us absorb his words. He knows they are confrontational and wants us to observe our reactions. No one looks around for relief or acquiescence. Arms crossed against chests, and eyes cast down and away for relief. Some buy the philosophy and the Program whole, if for no other reason than the hope for answers. Others reject or accept it in part, according to what suits their personal beliefs. All of us have heard "family issues" before and know we are going to have to hear it again before this weekend is over.

Don has someone read the Twelve Steps of Al-Anon, which are almost identical to the ones Sarah just read but written with the families and friends of Alcoholics in mind, and the Twelve Traditions written as support for the Program itself. I fight to focus, not get lost in crosscurrents of emotion that threaten mindfulness. Commanding myself to stay present, breathing comes in short gulps. I begin a series of counting breaths, calm myself, finally feel my eyes cool, the tightness in throat and chest loosen and relax.

The Teacher says to abide it all—victory and losses together; that it is The Way. It is the only way.

∾ 15 ∾

Don directs the check-in process, reminds us to report our family's progress since last week to the group. Stick to the Twelve Steps, he says, to the principles and process of the Program that guides all activities here and in the recovery community.

No stories, he says, making sure he has everyone's eye. Hard to do, he acknowledges, but keeping to what worked, what didn't, is enough. It helps keep judgment at bay and reminds us that in a process of recovery, the personal story is only a context for something more essential.

Without waiting for volunteers Don calls on the family closest to him. It's a good start. The father, Henry, tells us he is a recovering alcoholic of many years. He knows the ropes, speaks the Program language with conviction. He says the hardest part is to stay *"lovingly detached."* He wants to control his son's behavior and, he laughs, *"force the Steps on him."* Knows this is crazy, that obsessive control is "my disease, my *insanity,"* and that it was long before alcohol became its manifestation.

But now, he tells us, he wants to reach in and force his son to accept the entire Program, on his timetable. He stops here, smiles, says his years in Program have convinced him no *"alchy horse"* was ever forced to stop drinking. But there it is, he says, my own insanity, control, there it is in my face again, after I thought I'd conquered it.

He wants to scream at his son, *"Look at my life,"* don't spend years doing what I did. But he has to honor the work, the process of sobriety, and let go. He knows that *"but don't like it much."*

His wife, stately, composed, tilts her head first to her husband on her right, then opens her smile to her son on her left. Says she, too, has found herself insane over the past two weeks since her son left lockdown. Crazy is a word you hear often in Program, she acknowledges, not just the alcoholic crazy, but also the Al-Anon crazy. *"Couldn't control my husband's drinking all those years,"* she says; also knows she can't control her son's. But it didn't keep her from pacing floors waiting for a call to tell her he had left the halfway house, gotten into a terrible accident, was injured, maimed, or worse.

The great thing about lockdown is you know where they are, that they are unlikely to escape, get hurt, or hurt someone else.

She turns toward her son, Jeremy, says his name reverently, then tells him, the hardest part was realizing she had let him down when he was younger, had not been there for him when she was chasing his dad around bars trying to stop his drinking. She let herself believe that her son would be fine as long as his dad was sober.

"Should have known better, should have known that my obsession actually left you isolated, and that I didn't attend to your sadness and confusion."

She says she expected the boy to understand an adult world and be grateful Dad was well. She stops, runs her hand over Jeremy's long dark hair. He lifts his eyes, and I see tears mixed with embarrassment, discomfort but no rebellion.

Don asks him if he would like to respond. Jeremy shakes his head no but reaches to grasp his father's hand who leans to meet him. They rest entwined fingers in the mother's lap.

Other families take their turns and are not so fluid in language or clear in intent. But everyone tries to navigate feelings and stay within respectful limits. Tell the truth as they see it.

When Don calls on me, I push up against the surprise of shyness to say my name and that of my son. What didn't work for me in the past week, I say directly to Don and then Justin, was my anxiety about coming here—both the expectation of seeing my son and fear at not knowing what I would find. What worked, ironically, was finally being here. I leave it that way and am not asked for more. Don smiles at me, though, says again, thanks for making the long trip. Responding, you're welcome, seems ridiculous so I shrug and smile back. Is it enough?

❧ 16 ❧

It's a significant event when Anchor patients have earned enough credit to leave campus and make their first trip home. It's a hopeful and difficult time, Don says. Old memories of drug days linger in the relationships and in the history of the home itself.

On the other hand, most families long for healing. A homecoming, even if it's just a day and night and then back to Anchor, carries the promise of better days based in sobriety.

Last week the Jenkins family shared their conflicted feelings about preparing to have their son Tim home for the weekend, Don tells us. Family disruptions are rare since Tim left. With him home, they feared a return to patterns of rage, police, and, of course, drugs. Their dilemma is common. No one wants to give up the peace in the house, but no one wants to give up on Tim either.

Don has left them for last to allow time for their progress report. The Jenkins are easy to pick out by their familial squirm. Don asks, who would like to start?

The redheaded mother who spoke at the beginning of the night, hair illuminated by humidity, putting out her cigarette in the doorway, gives no one else a chance. Edgy and impatient at Don's modulated explanation, she interrupts his last syllables, wanting to *"set the record straight,"* she says, a stream of anger and frustration popping her out of her seat.

Her husband, shorter in height and lighter in weight to her, has both his hands on her left arm and shoulder trying to hold her still.

Don regains authority with a voice raise, asks the woman, Doris, to take her seat and repeats the instructions: no talking out of turn, no interruptions. Controlled strength in his soft west Texas accent, without drama or opinion, he asks the Jenkins again who would like to speak first.

Unembarrassed, unbowed, Doris stands, shakes off her husband's hands, growls that no one seems to understand how hard they tried, "she tried," to make Tim's first weekend home, *"fun."* She says the word as if it has three syllables in the middle. She gathers steam saying the weekend was about,

"My sacrifices... My work for Tim... My considerations, trying, always trying, to do right by him, and HE, well, just who does he think HE is... when I did so much to make it right in MY house."

Biting and gnawing on the bone of self-righteousness, her first-person possessives are lost on no one. But these families also understand how living comes to a crushing halt, needs and wants shatter when the 10,000-pound addiction gorilla sits in the middle of the living room. Few sympathize with Doris but fewer still lack empathy for her. It is like this here, contradictions, complexities, no one sure of easy demarcations of black versus white; no one choosing sides.

Don takes in all that transpires, does not support or reject anything except each person's right to speak. Doris runs out of steam, threatens to draw in another combative breath and rant on. Don takes advantage of the pause to ask the father and siblings if they have anything they'd like to say. The girl, Diana, eleven- or twelve-years-old, who blushed at her mother's remarks while she helped clean the board, sits on the edge of her chair, knees together and hunched up close. She leans on her father's right side, fingers laced around his forearm. Shakes her head "no," winces, drops her gaze.

The father leans across Doris, asks if Danny wants to speak. Tim's younger brother sits between Tim and Doris. The middle child, his smile and fidgets betray ambivalence about whom to please: his rebel brother, so wrong but so cool, an antihero icon or his parents, who have elevated him to favorite son. He avoids risk, doesn't shy away like his sister but says, *"not me!"* with enough emphasis that he draws appreciative laughs from other kids.

The father clears his voice. No, he says, so subdued I have to lean forward to hear, *"things did not go perfectly."* He stops to look at his wife's open-mouthed scowl, aghast at his conciliatory tone and careful words. He rests his hand on her arm to assure her and when he resumes speaking his voice is stronger. He has learned that the patterns in the family are partly responsible for the disease. And so it seems to him, when things don't go well, they need to look at the whole family and what could be done differently the next time.

Doris' fury ratchets up with each of her husband's few words. Don moves in, does not allow her to overwhelm the others. He questions and prods each family member gently but with authority, asking for precise words, insisting on participation, meager as it is, from the siblings, all the while holding Doris' barrage of protests at bay.

Tim is a dead ringer for his mother, with too much uncontrolled red hair; he's kinetic, itching for a fight, sitting sullen with bony legs strewn across two folding chairs arms snaked around his tall body.

When Don turns to him, asking his opinion, he jumps to his feet. This is the way it has always been, he says, through clenched teeth. Imitates his mother's whine perfectly,

"'Who does he think he is in MY house.' Face it, Mom, you don't want me home. You want a robot—somebody else you can control. Well, I'm not like any of them. I'd rather stay here every weekend than in Mommy's house being perfect but never perfect enough."

Don walks over to him, places his hand on the boy's shoulder, asks him to sit. We hear him add faintly, be respectful, remember it's the truth from your point of view.

Doris sputters a riff of "I told you so's," he is so ungrateful, so uncaring. She talks to Don's back then to the rest of us. Her husband tries to hush her, gives up and pulls her down to her seat. Tim, eyes fixed on Don, gathers himself. He hangs his big curly head in his palms, rests there before saying, in a whisper to the counselor, that it is only her house. *"It is never anyone else's home."*

Our collective energy rises to stifle Doris's retort. We wait, knowing this boy is close to a personal truth worth fighting for. No one looks away as Tim clears his voice. With maturity he pours out pain and purpose together, says he knows he has to earn their respect. Don moves then, next to the father and mother, signaling Tim to speak directly to them.

Tim repeats himself, does not flinch from the close contact. He apologizes for all the trouble he has caused in the past, says he has come to understand the pain and terror of his drug days, and that he doesn't want to hurt himself or the family any longer. Repeats he has to earn trust by good behavior, but, he adds, he needs them to trust him enough to prove it. *"Done my time, doing it still,"* he says to them, *"can't do it at home too."* He says that at Anchor trust is a two way street.

Don trusts me and that makes me trust him too. *"If home is just another jail, well, it's not much of a home,"*

Choked up, unable to say more, Tim nods at Don, yes, that's all. He folds back into the chair, done in from the effort.

Doris is unmoved by her son, blasts a defense. Don cuts her off, says, it's only important that everyone got the information.

Then looking only at the father, asks, John, what did you hear? John repeats Tim word for word, one arm tightly around his wife's broad hunched-up shoulders, eyes riveted on the boy.

Good, Don says at the end, let's have that sit awhile. The private family session on Saturday will give us time to explore this again. The important thing tonight, Don tells the rest of us, is to understand the commonality of the issues. Each story is different, as are family dynamics, roles, and characters, but the themes are universal.

It is both discouraging and edifying, to be so like the insanity of others. Everything in me wants to resist the notion. But to be different may mean never being understood here, let alone in the rest of the world.

Tiny prickles of heat and cold rise, fall, and dance under my skin, over the hairs of my neck and arms. Tensions of engagement, voices of judgment, pull at me from inside my tired skull. I want to separate from these people. Doris, so enraged a woman, is impossible to warm to. And the rest of the family, I think, dispossessed, at jagged right angles to each other. It is easy to categorize and assemble all the pieces of their history and pain. As usual I empathize with the children, grow protective, and want to leap forward, guard them against her. It is irrational to dream of grabbing the innocent, taking them home, and making things better in some nebulous way.

Chokes in my throat, tears leaping to my lower eyelids remind me why I am here. Looking across the circle to my son, I know I cannot hide in the drama of others. I drop my head and meditate on blue ice, cold waterfalls until the heat eases and the desire to throttle Doris vanishes. *"Compassion,"* The Teacher's voice in my mind says.

When I open my eyes, I look at her again. She's still fuming and frustrated. Her husband is trying to buck up and be the man he needs to be to bridge the gaps in his family. The children squirm in their range of injury: best loved, least noticed, misunderstood, rebel, princess, sick one, or hero. Each knows without knowing that neither parent can come fully to their rescue.

What more could my judgment, cast from outside the direct suffering of the system, add? More suffering. Don is right. Think commonality, look for connections because otherwise we never learn. We, I, string out illusions of differentness, "better than," "not like us," for safety and control. Intellectual superiority, comparisons and pecking orders keep us isolated, alone in fear.

The Teacher says *that all your education, all your knowledge, and even your wisdom keep you from deep understanding.*

If I open to all the suffering without comfortable labels, "this bad mother," "that sick child," if I pull all the shared suffering into me, being in it but not of it, will the jewel of compassion flourish? Will I see suffering in its totality, in the space of No Space where we are all One?

I don't want to think that I am them, and they are me. I flash on all those I have loved who, in this hour of my sadness, want to forget that Justin and I are so like them and that we are friends and family. I remind myself that humility opens the door to empathy and to compassion. The slightest tug at my chest tells me to take full breaths, to expand the chest and heart and allow more life to swim through. Without judgment, without attachment. I repeat, *"Serenity, courage, wisdom,"* remembering separation is the greatest illusion of all.

* * *

Journal entry, Anchor, 1990:
On Monday I leave my office. I'm nervous and excited by the possibility of the first big merger and bringing to finality a couple of years of trying to make something happen for Katten Muchin Zavis—really for Michael and Allan, great clients who I've become fond of. After Chicago, it's onto New York and then Atlanta, College Park, Anchor.
While I waited for Howard to show up, I turned to look at the sun and the thought *"I can't live like this anymore"* pops out of nowhere. Stunned, I stare across the quadrangle from shadow to light, past Century Park East, already loud with cars, into the innocuous buildings on the opposite side where the morning light is just now evaporating the dark and repeat the sentence, consider it, roll it around my mouth and mind, let it come to a resting place and put myself through the paces of dialectic, rudimentary as it is, of what I've learned. Who is the *"I"* that can't, that won't? isn't able to? refuses? *"To live like,"* like what? like a business person? like a mother? or wife? like a person striving for two opposite goals? inner transformation versus

outer success? *"Anymore?"* Evermore? why now? The dissection rests there because to analyze it would likely lead me down wrong roads of more thought and no answers, so I let it sit.

Split, fragmented but equally powerful forces drive me inside myself and drive me out into the world. Can they be one? Can I be one with both? Today, this week, they struggle for dominance, demand attention. Sometimes I am left feeling like a fraud in both realities, untrue in either life; at other times, they weave together. I can step back see inside/outside manifesting the other, then they split, I split again, and one appears the enemy of the other. I am left confused, frustrated, and not at peace. Peace, is that what I seek? Is it peace or appeasement because I'm too much the scrappy mover and shaker to be happy with a tepid peace!

Inside me the sentence lurks all week, when I am committed and thoughtful, scared or joyous, and I know I will have to reckon with it. I also know I am not ready. And there is something else; I know it was an epiphany moment, and the demand, *"not-live-like-this"* came from within me and is mine.

❦ 17 ❦

Before daybreak a siren wails. If I question the sound, my mind will chat up the darkness, making sleep impossible. I peek at the green digits of the hotel clock, 5:30 A.M., slam the pillow over my head. Four hours of sleep is not enough, even for me. The whine starts again, *"fire alarm."* I am unmoved.

Fire alarms go off in hotels more often than anyone admits. When you are on the road a lot, you know it is rarely a real fire. After years of this, you don't panic. But later in the morning, caffeine and alert, facing another day, you wonder at your foolhardiness and whether there is danger in habitually ignoring the sound. You promise yourself to come up with a safety plan the next time you check in somewhere, and to pay attention to exits at least. But then the cab arrives, the suitcase gets loaded, you check out, tip the bellman, give the driver instructions, the cell phone rings, and you forget your concern. Until the next alarm.

"Do not get up," I command myself, realizing rest is rare. Before my eyes close, the alarm shouts one more short scream. Enough to end resolve. I roll over and scrunch wrinkled papers under my arms and right leg, laugh at having fallen asleep on top of the covers and last night's homework: Personal Inventories of Behavioral Patterns. Gathering the loose papers, disarranged from tossing and turning through the night, I say aloud, *"I am pathetic."* Possessed

I sit up, trying to remember order and placement of the unnumbered pages, and read " In a Family System everyone plays a part. What part do you play?" There are options to consider, categories explained, choices given. "When I am in control I feel…when I am lonely I may act out this way."

My abbreviated answers, for personal consumption, are squeezed into boxes and columns separated by thin black lines and numbered inquiries. In the left column are the questions. Running across the top of the papers are choices by degree—how much, when, where, and with whom? My answers take up all available space, trailing off with little arrows and parenthetical overs to the backs of pages. So many words, so little time.

It is 5:45 A.M. I am alone in a strange town made stranger by the circumstances of my visit, the desperation of my love, and the fear of loss piled on loss.

I am content too. *"Crazy,"* I think, pulling a sweatshirt over well-worn travel pajamas, moving to the window to watch the tiniest glimmers of first light over the distant airport. Crazy how at peace I feel, being in a place so wrought with tension. But sharing the struggle with other parents and with professionals who refuse to accept lies or deviations from the Program's demands, consoles my sorrow.

This is a life-and-death battle. I can't let myself get delusional, call it by the wrong name. Forget. Peace and war and joy and sadness are all here together. I accept this without heaviness of heart or mind as I stare at the rising pink clouds across the fading night.

"I am at my personal nexus." Here in Atlanta, I am at a juncture of the grime and grace of life. A moment that negates pretense perhaps necessary in the outer world. I have a great need to be one with it all.

I return to bed with coffee, the two-cup version provided by the hotel, made in the Formica bathroom on the tiny space next to the sink that sits just below the hair dryer. I tell myself I have to break this caffeine habit after downing a Pepcid to quiet my stomach, which is still tender after the emergency-ward ulcer two years ago. But my resolve is half hearted in the face of chronic aches behind my eyes and in the connecting muscle and tissue of shoulders and neck pleading for the jolt one strong cup can provide.

I gather last night's papers and review what I wrote. For half an hour, I force eyes and mind to focus and recognize familiar thoughts. Then am shocked by the purity of unedited honesty; by the outpouring of emotion long held but never acknowledged.

Without warning, the poignant words and raw memory, ruthlessly cut through patterns of denial, and demolish what I have left of defense. Even here, alone, I am embarrassed by what I have written; assure myself a breakthrough is worth any personal ego price. Command myself to take a breath, hold back tears, and reread it all the way through. With inconsistencies and even contradictions taken into account, I have not spared myself. Self-flagellation is not beyond my comprehension or habit.

No one else is blamed or castigated. My mission, redemption, the life of my child demand courage. To hide now would keep denial and delusion in place; spread lies in front of me and poison the well of recovery.

At the top of the last page we are reminded: "The progress of recovery is the same as the progress and process of disease." And this: "You cannot cure anyone else's disease. Work the Program as it unfolds naturally, heal yourself; keep your eyes and mind on your own recovery."

What is the intent behind these words? Why do these simple instructions seem baffling without the cool analysis, strategy, and execution of the business world, and its reasonable, if demanding expectations? Frustration cascades up from the pit of my stomach, fear warns that the instructions are palliative but not a cure.

"*I want my son to live… to be well.*" I roar into the emptiness of no one to hear, collapse on the bed, pull knees to chest in a fetal position. I don't care about the implications. Shake off cold tears, wipe them away with angry fists, scream into the scratchy white pillow case until my throat goes dry.

"*Step One: I am powerless over alcohol and drugs, my life has become unmanageable.*"

I say it aloud forcefully but continue holding the pillow just for the sake of clinging to something. "*Addiction, no control, powerless,*" I say each word to convince myself, to understand what is not understandable, what I am up against. In Al-Anon they tell us that the Twelve Steps are the same as in AA because whether you are the addict or not if you are captured in the web of addiction insanity follows.

I pray, please God, please help me surrender to this truth: I have no control; I can only be responsible for my own recovery and sanity. I say it so it will sink into the marrow of my half-believing bones, the body's cells, the electrical circuitry of my brain. I say it so I will let go into faith. So my head will stop hurting, and my body stop shaking.

I lie there several minutes knowing a better person would meditate. But I am agitated and drained from the tension of self-exposure and too much emotion. So instead I pull on running clothes, put a dharma talk tape into my Walkman, hoping someone else's enlightenment will enlighten me. I hear the warning of the grasping mind, wanting to distract me into more worry. I ignore it.

Outside I welcome the shock of cool, morning air. Running a circuit of sidewalk to parking lot to short stretch of dangerous highway and back until sweat and pump of muscle remind me that even here, even now, I am willing to be awake to all that is within me.

"Powerless." None of the irony is lost on me. We work so hard to have power in the world, especially now, especially women. *Empowerment*—it's a glorious word, a strengthening promise. And here I am, I say to myself, walking through the lobby, taking the elevator back to my room, praying to accept powerlessness. Knowing it may be the only way to fight the enemy I fear most, the one who can kill my son.

* * *

Journal Entry, College Park, Atlanta: If I am not my identities and descriptions, even mother, then am I my emotions? Am I defined by feeling? Are they another false self or are they gateway to True Self? Because, God knows, we are asked enough about them… how do you *feel* when? What comes up for you when? No "why" is asked, no verifying or validating story is called for, only feeling is pulled from the cauldron of experience. If True Name/True Self, authentic being is what I am to search for, and feeling is the gateway, then where can I go and what more can I do to strip away the barriers to feeling to dig into emotion and reveal its secrets? What more is demanded, how much can I bear of feelings I would rather NOT know, NOT feel? Here and now I am alarmingly emotionally exhausted in ways that I have never known myself to be. *How do you feel?* The questioning becomes tedious, then painful, too confrontational, and then dull and boring then painful again.

But when I stop fighting it, when I admit, "I am torn and worn and achingly sad," and when I collapse into it, I do not die as I thought I would. After deluged by waves of grief and oceans of sadness, a kind of truth reveals itself, and then, again, not right away but after a time, a tinny, fragile, newborn kind of courage, wells up in me, untested but present. Recognizing it but knowing I don't know how to maintain it, I do the only thing I can, return to meditation breathing and yoga patterns to calm me, to look into the experience without mind chatter. What do I find? Most of the time my body is tensed for another blow to my ego or is tight and controlled from too much of just *too much*…

When I stay disciplined this happens; hard feelings rise in me, rise and fall away, rise again, fall again, and dark sorrow rises until I feel I will be consumed, disappear in it. But if I stay there and breathe, allowing all of it to be, then as surely as it rose, it falls away. If I don't chase sorrow, it falls away. When I refuse to let my mind attach to solutions or get lost in story, seek escape of any kind, then a small miracle happens, and it comes and goes, rises and falls away. The Teacher said that it would; sorrow, sadness, grief, and rage fall away as surely as they rise. So, I come to this, if True Self is not my identity, then it is not my emotions either because I have seen in those rare moments of detachment that feeling, the hardest and worst, rises and falls away. Yes, eager to catch me and make me cling, to attach and make me suffer, BUT only and if I allow it. Maybe to find an authentic self, I should study my actions, choices, and decisions. Will that lead me to the center of understanding? But I know that being and doing are not the same and that action has too often led me away from, not toward an interior light. The Teacher is right, "not this either." Frustrated with the inquiry, I settle for this much, a prayer said both in longing and jest. "True Self, True Self, where are you when I need you most?"

❧ 18 ❧

No longer confused by last night's opening jitters, I drive to the Anchor Facility and notice the distant outline of Atlanta's skyline. Not as vast or tall as New York's or as busy as Chicago's, but in juxtaposition to the unassuming complex that houses Anchor, it is startling. The rehab, I think, is a far cry from the sophistication of corporate America, its sleek composition of steel, glass, marble.

Pulling up to the squat buildings that form the facility, sitting in my rental car, I reflect on the hard work that goes on here without pretension. Weighing that against global economic pursuits, so dominant and often without intrinsic value, the dichotomy is obvious but confusing. Is it possible to be true in both worlds? Does conflict between inner search, the quest for personal truth, and the outside world make one pursuit wrong? One right? Can truth, reality, understanding, and happiness exist in both? Or do we compartmentalize to keep sane but in doing so never become whole?

These thoughts do not pull me one way or another, they stream through unobstructed and unclaimed, marked by a promise to pursue them later. *"Stay present!"* The command makes me eager and brave with the prospect that today will take me beyond spaces easily defined. I center myself by running a breath of energy up my spine, feel the stuck spots, run it down and up again. Note the shiver of anticipation, shrug off the desire to be a *"perfect something,"* yogi, meditator, or saint. Instead I plunge into my too human condition as the only one that is real, that is me, sigh, leave the car, and enter the facility.

This morning's session is for parents only, so the clutter of classrooms and offices are quieter than last night. A few mothers and one dad are in the cramped kitchenette brewing coffee, opening Winchell's donut boxes, chattering softly, subdued, trying not to step on each other's toes. They greet me smiling but guarded. Everyone bears a brave face given away by a noticeable strain in voices, forced laughter, reaching for comfort and community. The intimacy of last night's sharing and confrontations and the uncertainty of today's session prickles up against our resolve to stay positive, engaged—to be socially acceptable in this unacceptable moment of our lives.

I look for a job to do, end up helping make pots of coffee in forty-eight cup aluminum containers. A father says that we'd better make one pot of decaf, though no one will be looking for it except maybe counselors and Martha Morrison. Better put that fruit out too, he adds. Martha is turning into a regular health nut, she will frown on all these sweets. I help him display feeble-looking fruit on doilies we peel off from one another and place next to sugar bowls, creamers, cups and spoons, all in plastic or Styrofoam.

Plain white cardboard plates and thin napkins are stacked nearby on the folding table we carry into the classroom and push against the back wall as the rest of the parents assemble. When we finish kitchen chores, I choose a desk again knowing there will be notes to take. I sit close to a window hoping to attract whatever natural light is available.

❧ **19** ❧

At precisely 9:00 A.M. Dr. Martha Morrison strides into the meeting with the gliding ease of a high jumper or hurdles champion. Arms swinging loosely at her sides, steps deliberate, she is tall, lean, and as elegant as one can be in cobalt velour pants and jacket. Silver stripes run along the seams of her workout clothes and match those on blue and white running shoes. Among the bleary-eyed parents, the backdrop of unadorned corkboards, and paltry breakfast offerings, she is a robust gale. Composed, her large eyes of unfathomable depth, clear, unapologetic, she introduces herself.

"Hi, my name is Martha, and I am a recovering alcoholic and addict."

She recites the standard AA greeting not to shock or beg for mercy.

"My drug of choice was pure methamphetamine hydrochloride, which is better known as speed. I shot it into my veins, inhaled it, craved it like mother's milk, washed it down with Southern Comfort, tempered it with large doses of marijuana, or drove it up with cocaine and prescription pills."

She tells us that she started using as a young teenager, continued through college and medical school, where she graduated at the top of her class, and through the requisite internship program, where she also enjoyed the highest levels of achievement. A hospital, she tells us, is a treasure trove for junkies. She saw it as an opportunity to increase her use, which she did throughout the time she served as chief resident in psychiatry. She pauses a brief moment, says,

"And, since with speed I couldn't sleep, I volunteered to head the night shift in the emergency ward." She pauses, smiles slightly, adds, *"It took me many years to realize I was the real emergency."*

No remorse or melodrama creeps into her voice. She is a woman standing in a clarifying truth, unafraid of reaction or response.

When I got sober, she tells us, it was here at Anchor in the physician's Program. Eventually she got advanced certification as an addiction specialist and eventually became the chief of staff for anchor. The more she explored the history of her addiction, the more interested she was in the issues around her early use, and that became the impetus to start the teen program.

Martha writes the words *roles, parts, labels* and *definitions* on the board. Psychology, she begins, slowly walking across the front of the room assuring herself of our attention, accepts that people play roles first in their families, later in the groups and societies they join or form. Martha writes *star child rebel hero smartest shy person, problem solver, problem creator, victim,* and *martyr* on the board. Recognize them, she asks innocently, with a wry smile. Embarrassed laughter floats through the crowd as we acknowledge the labels, apply them, discard them.

Here's the one most teen addicts play, she writes *identified patient*. It's a tricky one, maybe the Trickster itself. No one has to question the sanity or illness of the relationships when one member is identified as the patient. She makes slow eye contact from parent to parent.

"Because the 'sick one' carries all the negative and undisclosed illness of the family into the world and is the scapegoat for what is hidden," she says.

We know she is talking about herself, too, and about her own family but still there is a drawn-in-breath from the lot of us. Did I do this? Identify my child, my son and cast what could not be acknowledged, sin or illness, grief or unhappiness on him, so that the system could continue without questioning what else lay underneath? Is the addict the 10,000-pound gorilla or is he the diversionary tactic so the real gorilla can duck and hide?

Martha waits for a half a minute, she knows we are processing that our minds twist with internal debate. She assesses us for damage, sees none worth the distraction, and then writes *family systems* in a bold cursive on the front board. She tells us that to understand the addict we first need to grasp the influence of the systems that give rise to addiction and keep it operating—the primary one being the family.

Whether that family is traditional, an orphanage, extended, split up or unusual in any number of ways, it is the foundation of heritage and the genesis of continuing patterns. Ironically, she asserts, the main function of any system, including the family, is to continue, to survive. *"To keep going just to keep going."* Consciously, or more likely, unconsciously, behaviors and the roles or parts we play are supported in order to sustain the system. *"To ensure its survival."*

She doesn't ask if we are with her, but she takes time, speaks with care, and says that in this model we come to see that we are defined by the system's culture, socioeconomics, anthropology, and by what it believes about itself. And, she adds, the things *"it refuses to believe in."* In some families continual failures keep the family together, and in others, only success is acceptable.

"All family systems define us by the things the system does well." For instance, compete, study, and excel. And by the things it may not do: express love, support, or confidence. Or, she stresses *"do too well":* invoke its judgments, prejudices, hatreds, or conceits. But, in the end, she says carefully, walking from left to right gathering us all into her broad gaze, it is more than a collection of attributes, it is a living system.

She watches us for squirms, for questions unasked, waits a few moments, and turns again to the board, where she writes Everyone plays a part; what part do you play? She stops and looks at what she wrote, turns, and smiles; she reads our minds when she says that there is no blame or finger pointing when you truly understand systems. Each of us came from a system of relating that we bring with us to each new engagement. Those systems came with labels and definitions of who we are supposed to be. Until we comprehend where we are stuck in self-defining patterns and how we can make different, though difficult choices, we tend to play out roles that have been assigned, which are comfortable and familiar. *"In our comfort zone... Where the strokes we think we need are guaranteed."*

Even negative feedback like young addicts often get, is a sign that the system recognizes us and that we belong. And belonging is safe. *"Safe, even a sick safe, keeps away the fear of not belonging."*

Dr. Morrison wonders aloud whether we all get this? No one raises a hand, responds in any way. She reminds us that we have been sent materials, written by professionals inside and outside the Anchor community to educate us. But, she admits, the concepts are difficult to grasp and apply. After all, it doesn't line up with the tenacious American belief in the rugged individual, the Lone Ranger, or even with the brave notion that *"one person can make a difference."* Our cultural indoctrination rankles against new explanations premised on relating and relationship.

So, let me be clear, she says, stops again and looks around.

"Systems are now understood to be the essential building blocks of psychology, environmental and biological studies, also of sociology, political theory, even business and economics."

In all these disciplines the key term is *"interdependence."* Here we study interdependent systems through the lens of addiction and its relationship to the family.

There's no blame, she repeats, because "roles" and "parts" are established unconsciously from early years if from not birth. They make sense to us because the relating of the entire system supports them. What systems thinking brings to this *"old list of labels,"* she continues, pointing to those she's written on the board, is the deeper understanding that although we may change roles, even reverse them at times,

"The relating between the parts is what defines the community, in this case the family, and keeps it balanced."

I imagine at this point that she senses our confusion and denial. She asks for questions. The few she gets have a unifying theme; are we this crazy? "Why would we keep a system going that makes us sick and that supports addiction?" Are we robotic, programmed, without free will?

She takes several minutes to think through her response. Says, let me explain it this way, a newly married couple brings to their relationship labels and roles that they learned from their families of origin, that they have refined and practiced in society under many guises before they were married. As they have children, they start unconsciously defining those children—Jane the responsible one, Johnny the follower etc. Before long the kids are acting out those roles, relating to each other and their parents through those roles, and the system is in place. *"Once in place, it builds its own momentum."*

The system creates patterns, feedback loops, rewards, and punishments. It is a complicated series of verbal and nonverbal cues that balances, organizes, and institutionalizes relationships until the system knows itself. Until everyone in the system responds according to said and unsaid codes of behavior. Roles are set up for repetition, for the maintenance and longevity of the system itself. And, yes, she answers, *"There is always free will and choice."* After all, that's why learning about systems helps us be conscious enough to choose.

To change the system so that it doesn't support insanity, in this case addiction, the roles themselves have to change, and the system supporting those roles has to change. She stresses the last phrase.

"At Anchor, we ask of ourselves, our families, eventually the world, 'what is your part?' because to understand the system we have to understand the relating AND the parts. Without understanding, we cannot make new choices," she says.

This time the questions that follow are less shame based: what do we do, can we do, now? Not everyone wants to know, some heads shake in disbelief, some turn away in denial of any culpability. But no one wants to take Martha on, and she doesn't encourage argument. She has waged successful battle with all demons including intellectual snobs. Her task is truth; ask questions but don't bother with diversionary tactics. No time, no interest.

"No one stands alone in their sickness—no addict or alcoholic, no well person, or 'getting-sober-not-there-yet person' either. No one recovers or refuses to recover alone…BUT, and this is the hard part… all of your children, indeed all the Program participants are taught, system or not, they are wholly responsible for the choices of addiction AND sobriety."

Understanding systems is vital in educating us to the building blocks of relationships, she insists, *"But, they are NOT an excuse.."* The patients, and the entire Anchor system and community come to understand that even if it requires exclusion from family and friends, sobriety is their prime responsibility. It is "our" series of choices, she says reminding us who she is, why she's here, " my personal choices," that lead to a sober or addicted life.

The support, understanding, love or rejection of the family makes that fight for the right choice easier or more difficult. But, the choice is ours alone.

She waits to make sure she has the attention of even the recalcitrant. She emphasizes that most recovering addicts have to leave everyone behind if the systems they are part of can't change to support their sobriety.

"It is the single biggest recovery challenge your children will have."

She wants us to see these two, systems and choice, not in opposition to each other but as one dynamic. What is the part you play? What choice will you make? Systems understanding allows us to see where and how we were influenced, validated, made crazy, loved, and reviled, she tells us. But it doesn't absolve us of our choice to use and abuse or of its consequences.

The room drops off my line of sight. I feel suspended and alone in the center of her words. I don't disagree. I've done my homework and accept, if not completely comprehend, her conclusions. But I also know they are in conflict with my own patterns of behavior and responsibility. In the way I viewed "my part" Justin's issues were mine alone; hell, I was happy to be found guilty if it meant a cure for my son.

The idea of a system should bring relief from self-inflicted blame. But widening the context, adding other relationships, questioning the family is threatening in ways I have avoided and that I fear.

Martha's answers aloud my internal quarrel. *"There's no blame,"* her voice cuts like a diamond through dense thought. *"There's no shame"* because blame, shame, guilt don't bring healing or change. *"They keep us in cycles of suffering."*

I cannot accept her viewpoint with peace. Will questioning lead me past blame, past guilt, or will I find myself in an even darker place, uncovering circles upon circles, unable to influence, let alone control, the consequences?

"Control." I note the word. If I admit faults and mistakes, I stay in control? Is that the payoff for continuing on a path of self blame?

"There isn't any guilt," real or imagined in the Program, she assures us. This is a process of examination about relating, relationships, the cause, effects, choices and counter-choices of the system as it manifests itself always, *"always,"* she stresses, looks around for our attention *"to assure its own survival,"* even when it is dysfunctional, even if it's a loony bin. After all, it may be a crazy family but it's *"my family."* Safe. Knowable.

"Change feels like death to the system; transformation like total devastation."

I try to refocus, to comprehend my uneasiness, hear her use the vocabulary of systems: "feedback loops," "causation," "principles of structure," and how we can "discover internal contradictions."

Darkening rain clouds throw shadow spikes across the length of the room. Someone turns on overhead lighting, and someone else closes the window near me, nodding to me for agreement as the slash of horizontal rain seeps on to the floor. I look around, notice the same questions, confusion, and embarrassment on the faces of other parents that I feel. I catch myself wondering if she can see my part in the system? Does it show?

I realize this is the very guilt she is trying to dissuade, that my thoughts are familiar ones about myself, perhaps used to hide something else. I have to fight myself so as to not separate in any way that will draw her attention or lacks courage.

A parent asks if the child brings the system to rehab? Yes, Martha says. They repeat the roles that are familiar and comfortable. If they are the passive member of the family, they try passivity in their new surroundings; if their role is angry child, they try anger. If the behavior works, that is, if the Anchor system supports their role, they keep repeating it. Remember, *"crazy or not it's the comfort zone."* Change looks like death, she repeats, *"is death,"* to the continuity and consistency the system craves.

I listen but know I am not getting it all. Martha cracks open a door to a blameless world where responsibility and accountability reign and leads us to further dimensions of understanding.

Let go of old stereotypes. Reconsider the sinners and the saints, the victims and the victimizers. Strip away labels. Ask instead, what has been assigned to me? What have I assigned to others, in the process of creating and maintaining relationships, that leads to sickness, to separation, to blame, to addiction? She challenges us to accept, maybe expect, something greater.

But when I step back, attempting to take in the beautiful dance of relationship, see the threads that connect one to all, and I feel fear rise. *"Of what?"* No answer follows. Am I myopic, disabled by a system? To challenge the systems, the family I created, the one I came from will shake things apart.

Chaos. What will I do, who will I be in the chaos of things falling apart? The open mind I pride myself on, that has led me to other successes, that is whole and accepting of grace, doesn't answer.

Rather my fragmented mind, chasing after worries, stuck on personal history, afraid of tempting the fates of examination meets me at every questioning corner. I see how attached I am to labels and definitions. I yearn to understand for the power of truth to emerge, for release but fear the chaos change will bring. Split between who I am and who I long to be, I feel confused, alone.

The Teacher says that whatever comes do not push it away. Alone comes up for examination, I tell the invisible teacher in my mind.

Stay in aloneness, breathe into aloneness, without judgment; follow the breath and do not change the subject. Do not run away into thought or action. Do not attach to feeling or story.

Parents are asking questions openly now. But I sit and look at *alone*, and a knowing comes over me: expecting much of myself, less of others, perfectionism, striving, prevents me from seeing the whole system. Is that it? *"NO! That's a lie!"* I stop myself and get more honest. *"No…alone is a safeguard"* against feeling dependent, needy, abandoned. Alone, I am in control of all the faultfinding; Alone, I am the only responsible party. *"Separate and in control."* Sad, scared, powerful, successful, a failure, but completely self-reliant.

Illusion, Martha is saying; The Teacher says that *"separation is an illusion."* There is no alone. If you don't know the system and how all the parts relate to each other, then you don't know the truth.

Martha's voice breaks my meditation. This is a Program of progress, she says, not of perfection. It's a Twelve Step mantra, one of many: *"simple truths for complex minds."*

Seeing the truth, "getting" it, and then acting on it to first change ourselves and later to influence the system, well, she smiles, that takes a lifetime or more than one. She cautions us not to get discouraged, indicates the five professionals who have quietly assembled behind her at the front of the room, and turns to welcome them. She says they're also in the process of understanding in their professional and personal lives. One of the reasons they choose to work together at Anchor is to stay out of delusional thinking.

This place, she says, and the work we do here, especially with your children, reminds us it takes a lifetime of examination, of seeking truth, of digging for courage, to stay clean and sober. To be authentic. To understand. *"No work, no change."* No change makes transformation impossible. So be assured, she finishes, *"We're in this process with you…you are not alone."*

She turns to her colleagues, they nod agreement and offer supportive comments, smiling at Martha and at us. We want to join in, feel the camaraderie, relax into process, unstiffen our backs, laugh at the nonsense of ego and the flimsiness of self-defense. Let go, get real. But instead a parent asks for a ten-minute break, and the group sigh of relief is so audible that the staff, readying themselves for participation, laugh sympathetically in unison.

∿ 20 ∿

"White coat," the teen's derogatory name for the first panelist, fits him. Starched creases squeak against his collegiate tie, knotted under a collar that squeezes a slack-skinned throat. It's a risky environment in which to cling to symbols of status. Busting egos is part of the unsaid code of conduct. He nods stiff and uncertain, launching into his resume, tells us that he serves on the executive committee of medical boards, and is on staff at one of the South's prestigious teaching hospitals. *"Academic research and statistical analysis"* are his specialties.

He turns his attention to a volume of notes and a slide show on the statistics of addiction. Before he can continue Martha gives him a wise half smile that says the impressive introduction isn't quite complete. He blushes, raises his eyebrows at her, coughs once, lifts his head so that his eyes face us, and says, *"Hi, I'm Bob, and I'm a recovering alcoholic."*

My judgment softens. He becomes human in his shyness and in coming out from behind the shield of his labels. He pauses a moment as if to say more, flushes again, shrugs a small *"sorry"* to Martha, and begins his lecture. It is a litany of bulletproof facts and dry analysis, of charts and numbers drawn from police blotters, hospitals, rehabs.

"If your child is an alcoholic he or she has less than a 5 percent chance to be sober before a thirtieth birthday. If he is addicted to marijuana, it is more likely that he will spend the rest of his life lighting up than coming clean."

Crime statistics; morgue body counts from car crashes; and dropout rates from schools, marriages, and life itself are arranged in neat lines and columns. Suicides are commonplace, he tells us, often disguised as accidents or as overdoses. Numbers support that information, too, no stories; no commentary just the lengthy presentation of black digits projected on the wide silvery pull-down projector screen.

He spends time on the destruction of brain cells from glue and gasoline sniffing, a favorite of southern teens he tell us, especially those who can't afford more costly highs. The damage is permanent. Loss of synapse connection can be experienced from prolonged use of inhalants and also from hash, marijuana, or opium smoking. *"Safe drugs are a teenage delusion."* He looks up at us, plays with the knot of his tie.

The data might give one serious pause in any context, leading one to question a nightly glass of wine, but here, with the faces of our children vivid from last night, they strike cold and hard as nails in coffins. We hear what he wants us to hear: stay realistic, know the facts, and know the enemy.

The most alarming rise in abuse statistics, he tells us, is in the use of prescription drugs. Vicodin, Percodan, Valium, and a growing list of pharmaceuticals for sleeping, pain, or anxiety have become acceptable solutions to problems unsolved. We see the greatest rise in prescription addiction in college kids, he tells us. He stops, looks around, and adds also among middle-class housewives, where, it is safe to say, there is an epidemic. Teenagers steal them from the medicine cabinets of family and friends.

Adult addiction impacts each subsequent generation; he removes his glasses, wipes them clean with a folded white handkerchief, and looks at us directly. I wonder if he is thinking of his own children, ones he has or plans to bring into the world. He doesn't say, sighs, refocuses, and goes on.

"Family systems are the basic building block from which we spring, but when we study the national statistics of addiction, we realize the import and influence of the expanding spirals of society and cultural influences…from football beer commercial, to the comfort of the local bar or the bosses' wine cellar, alcohol consumption is not just supported, it is celebrated."

There's an expectation of imbibement, an encouragement to party on. It's in our advertising language, in our movies, in popular music. Why suffer? Here is a pill, a drink, a toke, a blow, or a snort to make it okay. There's only one problem, Bob, now agitated, losing his professional detachment tells us. His rising voice surprises me, and then his head is up and off the sheaf of papers, his bland face reddens as he says, when you are sick, an addict, you are bombarded with stimuli that makes you sicker, that is more difficult to turn down.

"Is it any wonder that the teen statistics are so damning? Is it a mystery why kids use? Why many fall into full-blown dependency, injure their minds, their bodies, and their futures?"

In the timber of his voice our collective anger frees and flows. Stuck in our private hells he releases us out of the tight box of family drama into the larger system—society as the enemy. It would be too easy to blame the world, I think, moved, but not tempted into agreement. And, in a moment, Bob calms, sighs again, and says, there's a lot we could focus on, including how business, political, community, international politics, and even medical systems collude to keep us addicted, sick.

"And, in the end," he says, *"knowing societal issues can't help us get sober unless we are willing to do all of our personal work first."*

Bob sets out a new round of numbers then shakes his head as if reminded of something, moves closer to us, narrowing the boundary of his authority. He lowers his tone, confides that he loves his research, but it can leave him overwhelmed. There are success stories, he says; there is some hope. *"But it's a battle, and no different than any war. It would be an error not to know the facts and what we are up against."* He opens his mouth to say more, drops his head, reconsiders, smiles to Martha, and thanks us for listening. She nods acknowledgement to him, does not ask for questions, and turns the floor to the next speaker, a clinical psychologist, Anthony, who introduces a film on family systems.

As interior lights dim and shades are drawn against the receding sunlight, eyes close for a moment in defense or rest or both. Some couples move closer together and hold hands, a protection against a bleak future the stats predict. Others move apart, the threat of confronting old injury, of tearing flimsy bonds, inducing solitude. I am relieved not to feel responsible for anyone else's feelings. Know I am too raw to extend myself or pretend to be strong, clear, in charge or just okay.

The film, is an institutional documentary, with marginal acting and thin story line, but its eerie realism denies our efforts to dismiss its lack of professional quality. Within a few frames we are convinced we know this movie family, how they interact, who's to blame for the disruptions, the violence, the equally devastating silences, the miscommunications, door slamming, and name calling.

But, cleverly, the cards get turned and turned again until a complex web plays itself out and makes us pause, reconsider, if not discard, our original judgments.

When the film ends, Anthony, says, yes, I am a recovering alcoholic, *"among other bad habits,"* and seven years sober, thanks to Anchor's professional health providers program.

"That and Martha's insistence that I stop blaming the world for my issues."

He smiles through this intro, then turns serious, says provocatively, hitching a thumb to the last credits on the movie screen, aren't so different from us are they? There is silence, followed by a barrage of objection.

"THOSE people…in THAT film."

" THEIR children…Not like mine, like me, like ours…"

"We never would…" *"It's preposterous… maybe like someone else but NOT US!"*

"Too violent…too crazy… too much."

Anthony, assisted by Martha pushes back. They probe rather than argue with parents. They ask leading questions: Are you saying these patterns, this film is not realistic? Not familiar in any way?

They listen but don't agree or disagree. Parents settle into quiet congratulations on their insights and refusal to be categorized. Then a father calls Martha's name from the back of the room.

I turn and recognize Sam, a late arrival of the previous night. He begins thoughtfully, saying the film is not a masterpiece, says parents are right, the characters are stereotypical, the plot contrived, maybe too violent, yes, certainly in comparison to his family. But, then again, he says he can hear and see pieces of himself in both the mother and father figures. Like them he enables his son's behavior by forgiving breaks in honesty and making excuses for him. He has come to see that he accepts less than what the boy is capable of. He takes a breath, clears his voice, and adds, *"I think I do these things because I fear that my son will reject me."* And then, like the parents in the film, in desperate moments, switching to anger and retribution, he finds himself piling on his son's mistakes from the past and punishing him for all that he, Sam, had chosen to ignore. It's not pretty, he says, *"it's not what I want to see about myself,"* but it may be true.

A silence follows until, without standing or raising my hand to be heard, I turn to look in Sam's direction. I say for me there is a certain undertone, almost a rhythm, a blend of sounds in the conversations of the movie family, and *"how they act and react rather than actual words they speak, that is familiar."* And their body language too, how their backs turn to each other, their mouths hang open or sag in disbelief, redden in anger. These things, sad and even stupid, exaggerated in the film, I've seen and heard in my own home. *"No, not exactly the same way, but still too close to deny."*

I don't say more. To do so would be to pretend I know something. My throat freezes. I notice it; don't know why it is there or why my hands tremble. No one responds, although a few parents nod in agreement. Martha allows my words and Sam's to simmer among us. When no one else contributes she goes to the board, writes *enabling*, *body language*, and *familiar*. She waits a moment, thanks Anthony, turns to the panel and says, we have three speakers left, so let's hear from them now.

Seated at the folding table are Warren, Bob, and Anthony, plus three more staff members, two women and a man. They are of different ethnic, racial backgrounds, and professional standing, have various degrees, and status in their communities. But all start their presentations by acknowledging their status as a recovering alcoholic or drug addict. What they speak to us, the parents, they say to themselves, to each other, and to their families. They are all dressed appropriately, hair combed, nails clean, and eyes clear. The stories they tell, advice they offer, is crisp, certain, and unequivocal. Their group posture is composed and straight. Their voices don't waver as they spell out truth and reality as they have experienced it, as they practice it now.

New evidence, the psychotherapist, Jeanine, tells us, shows more than an occasional risk of the sudden onset of schizophrenic symptoms in even a onetime user of LSD, cocaine, speed, or crack. The onslaught of information makes us twist in our seats and stare into space, imagining the worst. When I look at Martha, knowing she's abused all of the above, her eyes don't give away alarm or self pity. I am relieved to know they are as unmerciful, and as tough on themselves, as they are on us.

The director of the continuation high school that all Anchor teens attend speaks next. Heavyset, warm and empathetic, Marie says she's *"proud"* to name both Al-Anon and Adult Children of Alcoholics as primary Programs. The teens tease her plenty, she laughs, accusing her of being a classic do-gooder, first child of drunk parents. *"It's true! They got me!"* Unembarrassed she says it's why she works at Anchor in spite of low wages, and the teen's *"constant harassment."* The work reminds her how much she needs a continuous process and the consistent language of the Program to live her life.

The complexity of getting sober, the physical and emotional stress, trying to catch up in school, live in a new environment, and with adult *"recovery roomies,"* attend to lessons with brains and bodies in overhaul, she sighs again, *" it's a terrific challenge for them."* They are young, and they can learn and adapt, but it is foolish to expect algebra to be their first concern.

They are rebellious because they are in the pain of sobriety, combined with teenage angst.

"A schizophrenic teenager is a redundant statement."

She laughs shyly, quoting a friend with a PhD in educational psychology. The kids are making an effort, she asserts, and they want to do better. As they sober up they are shocked and saddened by how far they have fallen behind. That alone can cause them to start using again. Feelings of hopelessness, unfortunately, are common. Part of her job is to keep them believing in themselves and their ability to make up for the past.

She fumbles a moment, not wanting to end at a low point, overwhelmed by the endless list of challenges. But she just thanks us, briefly sits, then stands and signals Martha that she would like to say something more. *"Your children are all precious to me, to us, and that's the other reason I stay—the kids and the staff."*

A short, round man, prematurely semi-bald, shaggy wisps of hair fringing his ears in a bowl cut, takes the floor, introduces himself as Warren, a recovering alcoholic and the Anchor resident internist. He is impressed with science and appears delighted to lecture on the effects of addiction on a growing body. *"Brain synapse injuries are common."* Changes to the cerebral cortex, to the kidneys, liver, and even the heart *"can be expected with prolonged use or heavy dosage in short spurts."*

Recent findings, he tells us, indicate that a lowered immune system response is almost guaranteed. When kids start sobering up, they generally suffer bouts of pneumonia or bronchitis. Autoimmune diseases such as arthritis and lupus, often start to show up, according to long-term studies. Of course, he says, there are always new street drugs making their way into society. Each carries different effects for different people.

He darkens the room again to show slides, first an ulcerative liver taken from a middle-aged alcoholic who died in a car crash. And here, he tells us, flourishing gruesome pictures in a row, are cadavers of individuals who overdosed on drugs, and a pumped out stomach of a pill addict. Then two slides, one taken from someone with normal brain tissue at death, the second from a multidrug addict shows lesions and unusual forms of scar tissue.

"He was a breastfed baby." I don't know why this thought comes to me. Then *"I made his baby food before there were food processors."* Jars of assembly-line, salted, sugared, mass-produced, not good enough for my babies. *"Broccoli."* He ate raw broccoli when others had junk food. I do not see the

screen or slides any longer. I see only tiny hands and bowed mouth, my earnest, intense mothering, my toddler's fat round cheeks and belly.

I look down and count the holes in the institutional linoleum. Bite my lower lip until it swells to keep from crying, from shouting out loud, to not think of liver, kidneys, brains, injured, damaged. When I come to, I find Warren's information as disturbing as his lack of eye contact.

Muffled groans escape from other parents edging towards hopelessness. He is an easy target for the disquiet we've contained all morning. Parents go from anger, to dismay, to overwhelmed and frustrated, back to grief, then defeat with the clinical weight of it all. A father challenges Warren on an arcane point of science declaring himself to be a chemical engineer with *"some knowledge of such things."*

Martha interrupts and suggests Warren wrap up his segment. He flusters, wanting to set things right with the engineer, shoots Martha a pleading look which gets only a head nod in response. So he gathers his slides, asks for lights to be turned back on, gives us an embarrassed small bow, and finds his seat.

Martha takes a purposeful walk around the beleaguered assembly, suggests we all stand and stretch, get oxygen to our brains. Everyone complies, a few get beverage refills, others walk to the windows for fresh air, wishing, I think, for any way out.

∽ 21 ∽

When Martha begins speaking all sit again and focus on her. What we've heard today, she says, no inflection, no apology, is true, real medicine; in fact it's *"the best science has to offer on the subject, that research, analysis, knowledge can teach us."* We have the benefit here at Anchor, she turns to the panel, deliberately focusing on them, *"of direct experience,"* as our acid test after all the science is considered.

Returning to face the parents, she says, we also know full recovery can occur. The human body is a miracle, surprises us with its resilience, and often with its will to be alive and healthy. If kids get sober, even if they go in and out of using before quitting altogether, they have time left to rebuild bodies and heal.

"It would be comforting but wrong to ignore the information you've heard today, to delude yourselves into thinking that the price of addiction is not high, but defeat is not a helpful attitude either."

Parents begin to thaw, raise hands tentatively, and ask questions. Some are unable to stay composed. One mother, tears streaming, no attempt to wipe them away, wants to know the long-term effects of a seizure her son had in an emergency ward with a near overdose, high levels of crack in his bloodstream. Others nurse disbelief, shaking their heads, dropping voices, wanting to know the possibility of epilepsy, of psychosis, of brain aneurisms from this drug, that drink, from the accidents that have followed. Martha chooses one or another professional to respond. Their answers are medical, precise but not distant or cold.

"This is hard-core stuff, painful to hear," Sam says, from the back of the room. But he can't help asking about future defects. *"What is the effect on the next generation, on the child of my child?"* After all, he says the teens are not so far away from becoming adults, with children of their own. It is not a thought anyone else has dared to conjure. A collective in-breath stops the movement in the room.

The panel remains still as Bob stands. He drops his clinicians' detachment, says that these are the questions he asks himself; the ones that keep him up at night. Have we, he asks rhetorically, waves to include his colleagues, condemned our own children, our grandchildren? Not all the answers are known, not from science, medicine, or sociology. Long-term studies take years to verify and may help explain certain patterns of illness and the repetition of addiction in subsequent generations that are observed but not scientifically proven.

Anthony agrees, says, the most reliable, if disturbing information comes from systems theory studies. The generational effect of abuse, drink, drugs, emotional, sexual, on lives well removed from the original source, the so-called first mover of disease, of addiction, is documented; is known. Research confirms what we have discussed before, Martha says. Clearly, we all contain the whole system not only in our physical and personal DNA but in the endless spirals of psychology, sociology, beliefs, and habits that pass on unchallenged.

"Just as the 'wave is the water and the water the wave,' there is an inseparability that has to be reckoned with."

The hope, if we can call it that, she says, lies in being able to identify the patterns, and stop them here and now. If we own up to the past, not condemning it but recognizing it and taking responsibility for it, then maybe we can open a door for the next generation to understand in a way we could not. Only then, she says unequivocally, will anyone create new and positive patterns not determined by the past."

If we are delusional, if we deny the patterns, they will, they do repeat."

My eyes burn from the fluorescent lights, from held back tears and exhaustion. I am strangled by the somber density of the room. So much information, no easy solutions.

I think, *"vision, strategy, execution,"* the three part code of business success, is nowhere here to be found. I glance around at the other parents, tired, nerves frayed; egos trampled. I want to tell them what The Teacher says if you heal an injury, you heal it for the seven generations before you and the seven generations yet to come. But my throat is dry, my heart subdued, and, with the others, I sit silent.

* * *

Journal Entry, Anchor, 1990: *"Oh the night that Paddy Murphy died I never will forget, the whole damn town got stinkin' drunk and they're not sober yet and the one thing that they did that night that filled my heart with fear they took the ice right off the corpse and put it on the beer, oh honey, that's how they showed their respects for Paddy Murphy, honey, that's how they showed their honor and their pride, oh honey, that's how they showed their respects for Paddy Murphy on the night that Paddy died…on the night that Paddy died!!"*

When we lived in Chicago with my beloved grandparents, the parties were every weekend and included the extended family and their extended families. The Italians were still all from the old country, and they made sausage and even wine in the basement during the summer. We went to bed showered with kisses and anisette cookies in our hands; every adult loved us, or at least it felt that way, and kids were expected just to be kids. But when we came across the country in the new Hudson Hornet, and we had only our parents and the other parties started, and there were no real adults in the room. No one to rescue or trust.

"Cocaine Bill and his morphine bride came walking down the avenue side by side… oh my honey, honey, honey, have another on me, snort, snort, on me, on me…"

If I was six, Randy was five, and Nicole was four. We'd be awakened at, I don't know, midnight, one or two in the morning, dragging stuffed animals. Nic with her ragged piece of pillowcase because she had to "nip" even while singing; we'd walk robotically, dragged from the paralysis sleep of the young, into bright lights, but we sang so often we knew to line up by age and sing on cue. *"Oh they walked down Seventh and they walked down Main just looking for a sign that said 'cocaine' oh my honey, honey, honey have another, snort-snort, on me, on me.*

"Family Systems." They say it with such authority, a certain, I don't know, formality, but at our house, it meant a lot of things not bounded by the language of study and application, by statistics and professional opinion. *"Take it off, take it off yelled the boys in the rear, take it off, take it off, that was all you could hear, but she's always a lady even in pantomime and she stops, and always just in time."*

It was Nicole, I think, but don't know-have to remember to ask her, who sang the stripper song in a classroom show and tell and was sent home. I just remember being dissolved by embarrassment, when the nun told me, staring at me as if I had something to confess. I just remember being so angry at Nicole for not knowing the appropriate place and timing for my dad's songs. She must have been in kindergarten at the time, maybe first grade, so I would have been in third or fourth. Babies, we were babies.

Bobbie loves a party, that was the family story when my parents found me asleep behind the couch in the living room after many a long night. But it wasn't the party I loved; it was the chaos I feared and to stay close, vigilant, hyperaudient, and watch until sleep captured me, made me feel safe, made me feel I could jump up and sing, dance, intervene when glass broke or my mother cried or doors slammed. It worked before, it would work again.

Family Systems. Years later, Nicole and I go to see the same chiropractor, Liz Bernstein. She says, "Wow, it's so interesting you both have the same neck and trapezius injuries and trauma." We laugh, tell her, yeah it's from all the bobbing and weaving. Nicole says, imitating our young girl voices, "Hey watch out here he comes again," together, on cue, we duck to avoid the imaginary blows, and we laugh and high five each other. Liz gasps, draws in a breath, hand over mouth, then catches herself, pushes back her glasses with an index finger, and, blushing, tries to laugh along. Family Systems. Dysfunction. Enabling. Codependent. Words never convey the entire reality, but it's not undiscovered territory. We talk about it some, my sisters and me; Randy never, ever wanting to remember or to join in, and Traci, not there for the first years in California, has her own stories, some worse just by the fact that Nic and I were mostly out of the house by the time she was in elementary school. We talk from our heads, "Wow! That was something, that day, the other time, that night when… remember?" But, for women given to heart-felt conversations, we never speak to each other about the past from our hearts or with emotion. And we always laugh, manage a joke, or say "Whew, dodged that bullet," when we share a story, a memory. We say to each other, "no repressed memories here, hell no, our parents were so obvious."

We speak from our heads, and we laugh, humor marks all of us. So does courage, stoicism, and loyalty. Hear no, speak no, and see no evil. We keep truckin,' when the going gets tough, the tough get going, we wear nothing on our sleeves. We tell no one. And why should we? The past is the past, what doesn't kill you makes you stronger, and we are strong. Besides, Dad used to say, "Are you cry-ing? Better shut up, or I'll give you something to cry about!" We don't cry.

And now, all these years later, in a strange place with strangers, Mar-tha Morrison and her gang challenge us, me, to connect the tendrils of memory, past to present. Someone asks, what is the effect on the next generation and the next. I force myself to listen, but I know no answer is good.

❧ 22 ❧

Hi, I'm Heather…" The door opens, and a freckled, vibrant young woman bounds into the room. She apologizes for being late, tells us she was representing Anchor at a National Conference on teen addiction, and on the recovery protocols of *"our"* facility.

She's oblivious to the mood of the room, and we're all drawn to her light-hearted chatter. The panel immediately shifts attention to her, a group smile spreads among them. She is a favorite, I think, as I watch her wink at Martha, saying, *"Wait until you hear what they said about YOU… you will decidedly blush from the UN-qualified praise."* It is said with practiced Scarlet O'Hara flair. Soft chuckles escape here and there and in spite of ourselves. We find comfort in her casual manner and girlish glee.

Still looking at Martha, Heather laughs as she would privately with a girlfriend, ignoring the rest of us. *"If only they knew,"* Heather exaggerates. Without understanding the innuendoes, we laugh with her, and for the first time all morning, breathe deeply, relax, happy to be included and charmed.

As she speaks, she loosens the grip of the of the way-too-many props, charts, handouts, notebooks, she has in disorganized possession. Grimacing apologetically, says she is not used to two performances in one day. Three men rush to her assistance. She brushes strawberry blonde hair off her face and behind an ear, thanks them, only to have errant wisps appealingly misbehave as she gathers materials in a two-arm scoop, plops them on the table behind her.

Martha uses the interruption to warn us not to be fooled by Heather. She is a competent and responsible staffer whose main function is ombudsperson for the teen program. She coordinates the teens' schedules, the feedback and cooperation of assisting professionals, and then reports between them, to the teens and to the parents. *"Not that you would guess it now,"* Martha adds with mock disgust at Heathers disarray.

Heather bounces on the balls of her feet throughout, notwithstanding her low-heeled alligator pumps. Energetic, impish, charismatic, her presence lifts spirits, reduces our overwhelm and sorrow. She is a relief, I think, and we all feel the need for it. She won't bludgeon us the way the others have done. Hope springs from her humor and generosity; we are convinced she is "different." We forget ourselves.

Heather begins with a quick thanks to Martha for the kind words, returns our smiles but with her natural voltage dialed down several notches, she begins.

"Hi, I'm Heather, and I'm a recovering cocaine addict. Last week, I celebrated my sixth "birthday" in AA and Narcotics Anonymous. Before I got straight I robbed my parents of their savings using forged checks. And I stole their safety deposit box key. When I turned to crack, I unloaded the box into a paper bag. I pawned all of it, including my grandmother's heirloom jewelry. She died two days later of a stroke. She died clinging to the last treasure she had... an antique locket with my baby picture in it."

She pauses, digs for the strength to go on, shakes her shoulders, eyes cast down. When she looks up she is resolute, takes a step toward us, speaks in a crystal-clear voice, doesn't spare herself.

"I would have stolen that too, but they buried her with it... I didn't go to the funeral. I was in jail. I was nineteen-years-old at the time and had been head cheerleader, which still counts for something in the South, as ya'll know, and I was class vice president my senior year, AND a National merit scholar. I was at the university on a dual scholarship for academics and..." Here a small laugh bubbles out of her. *"And leadership."*

She pauses, looks at her mentor, eyes wet, not spilling over, tells us that Martha found her in a group therapy session in the state penitentiary, and due largely to her intervention, she's been sober ever since. She gives a breathless nod of her head, and then confronts the possibility that chills her,

"But... if I 'go out' today, if I slip once... if I use again just one time, I will be back on the street in a week."

Direct, no despair she adds, *"It's just the way it is."*

∽ 23 ∾

Justin is waiting in the parking lot for me as I leave the morning session. I don't see him at first, my head pulled down, threads of worry anchoring it to my heart, eyes adjusting to the daylight after the dim interior of the school. His loud call from across the parking lot assures me he sees none of this. He is open and unembarrassed with affection, gives me a big hug, and asks aren't you glad you don't have to listen to those guys every day? He doesn't wait for an answer as he pushes me out of mental conundrum toward the rental car. He is eager for me to see his apartment, meet his adult roommates, whom, he calls *"the docs."*

Driving, I report to him about the morning's presentation, hear my tone tentative and tired. I want to review the information without creating a wedge between us with my fear. He keeps his responses conversational, and I try to pull myself to safety in the aliveness of his voice and wry disinterest. Yeah, family systems is Dr. M's thing, he tells me. He doesn't share my worry, says instead, that he's over-saturated with the facts and changes the subject,

"It's too bad Don wasn't there though... Now that *guy knows some shit... tells it straight."*

He feels seen and heard by the counselor. It is what a mother can't give a son, to be acknowledged by a man he admires and trusts. I mark its importance and vow to seek Don out.

"How about Martha, Dr. M.? She seems pretty awesome."

Justin is quick to answer that she's with the adult group most of the time but agrees she's *"definitely awesome,"* tough, too, and smart. She never talks down to the teens or lectures, *"doesn't put up with any bullshit either."* But, he still thinks the family systems stuff gets old. He's not enthusiastic about the rest of the professionals on the panel; *"Too clinical, standoffish, judgmental or boring."* I ask about the teacher who he interfaces with daily, he tells me he likes her, although she's only adequate as an instructor. But, she cares for her students and takes them seriously.

Interesting that she's the only one who isn't a recovering addict, he observes, the only one that Dr. Morrison didn't help get sober.

And Heather? I ask at last.

"WOW!" He immediately responds, *"She was a real junky wasn't she?"*

She gave you the short version, he says, but he's heard her speak at an AA meeting for over an hour. *"Now she's got a story."* There's innocence in his voice, and I'm glad to hear that for all his street sophistication he can still be shocked.

I listen as he rattles off quick snippets of information about the people, professionals, patients, friends that form his community. He has intact his nose and ear for what's authentic; remains unimpressed by titles. He judges others as he always has; by whom they are today, how they show up.

I search his animated syllables for where he's at, head and heart. I don't hear anger or discouragement. He is spirited, present. I want to match his mood, it is, after all, the first time in years that we are touching our old relationship full of talk and observation. I struggle to dispel the weightiness in my voice and mind. I want but am so afraid to believe that he is better, safer.

Sideways glances as I drive, making turns and stops on his direction, warm me more than words can. I marvel at him, nineteen-years-old, straddling childhood and manhood, alcohol and drug free. Sober he's a package of energy that can become rocket fuel just from the force of natural adrenalin. I hesitate to push the boundaries of our banter, but when he stops, I ask,

"Dr. Morrison was saying this morning that emotional growth, not intellectual or academic but emotional growth retards at the onset of addiction… said it may take years to catch up after someone is clean and sober… what do you think of that?"

He's comfortable with thoughts that unnerve me; accepts challenges that appear to me to be one more daunting hurdle.

He laughs, says he thinks this is true. Martha told them she realized, as a thirty-year-old doctor, with patients to care for, that she was acting the way she thought an adult should act. But really, emotionally and socially, especially with her friends in recovery, she was still thinking and acting like a teenager. She had to teach herself emotional maturity, he says, but with so many addicts around it was hard to find role models. And if you don't believe it, he laughs again, wait until you meet my roommates.

The oldest of the three is in his 60s, a famous anesthesiologist, *"And he is one big ole baby."* Anyway, he says, you'll meet them all soon enough, tell me about home. How's the building of the ranch going?

I catch him up quickly. He knows it's been a lifelong dream of mine, a country property, horses and dogs, away from cities and noise. He doesn't know that I harbor a hope that his childhood love of the same things will bring him there. I hope that my motivations are not just driven by my longings but also by concern or his safety, for the picture I make up when I allow myself to dream, where he will use it to change friends and focus once he's out of here.

He's enthusiastic about the promise of a visit to the ranch if things go well for him at Anchor over the next few months.

He says he spoke to his sister, Lyndsey, a couple of days ago, how good she sounds, how he felt like she understood how it was for him at Anchor, and that she told him she'd be here the next family weekend. Yes, I say, she's immersed herself in Twelve Step literature. She goes to regular Program meetings, doesn't want him to feel like he's here without her love and companionship, even if it is half a continent away.

And Dad? Justin's voice drops, he shifts to look out the window, as if he's not sure he should ask. I want so badly to say the thing that will encourage him but need to tell the truth too. I must have hesitated a moment too long because before I can answer, he turns back to me. *"It's okay, Mom. I understand."* Hell, he's embarrassed I'm here, and pissed too. Right? I protest, no, it's just harder for him, Justin. He's relieved that you're safe, but he's also not sure how to participate, what to expect, and he's started this new business too, and he's overwhelmed.

"You don't have to explain, Mom, you don't have to make excuses for him. Hell, I don't blame him. I'd think my son was a loser if I had one in a place like this."

Loser? My heart breaks. Loser? I ask again, almost yelling, are you kidding? You're here, you're doing the work, and we are all lucky to have you in our lives, to love you. He smiles weakly back, *"Mom, you're so predictable."* It's okay. I get it, let's forget it for now.

We pull in front of an apartment complex that is two stories high with jutting angles and attached corners that allow a series of identical structures to wind together for several blocks in four directions. Dark brown trim is latticed across a beige stucco façade. Not unattractive given its economy, just neutral, unassuming. Justin bounds up the outside stairs two at a time towards the second floor. At the first landing, he points toward an apartment where his new friend BJ lives, also in the company of three older men, all doctors.

"A few nights ago one of BJ's roommates went to a local bar, just got crazy with the Program and flipped out, came home and started busting things up. BJ and his other roommates had to tackle the guy and call for help."

They threw the doctor in jail for a night because, before coming home, he had also run his car into the bar's plate-glass window. Dr. Morrison bailed him out and took him back to the Anchor hospital lockdown where he remains. Justin whistles a *"Jeez!"* Says he wishes he'd been around to see the show. The belligerent is a timid man, short and thin, but all tanked up he'd managed to give someone a black eye. *"BJ said it was a hell of a scene,"* Justin adds, them chasing him, him fighting back.

I realize from the bounce in my son's step, his animation, that he is making the best of a situation that can be desperate and sad. Rehab is meant to break you. Maybe put you together again. Whatever is happening, though, Justin's engaged. *"It's his greatest strength,"* I think. Engagement may mean survival. The will to be alive in his own life and the lives of others may be his ticket to staying sober and conscious. But will itself is difficult to find, harder to maintain. It requires courage, a large dose of self-awareness, and humor, especially the ability to laugh at ourselves. I shake off the tears choking my throat. Glad the challenge of trying to keep up with his long-legged gait breaks the poignancy of thought.

❧ 24 ❧

Justin stops with his hand on the doorknob of his apartment, tells me his favorite roommate, Jim, is home and waiting to meet me. An MD from the Midwest, head surgeon at a university hospital, Jim had his own operating theater and a team of interns and residents who hung on his every word, his teaching, and example. He gives one knock, and before he's finished with his description, a kind, round face appears from behind the door.

"Justin's my greatest supporter, reminds me what I can look forward to when I leave here."

Jim shakes my hand as he continues, *"You must be his mom, although you look more like a sister."* He blushes and blue veins that map his wide nose, marking pathways of too much alcohol for too many years, stream tentacles into the expanse of cheeks. Embarrassed, he shrugs, swallows, adds, *"but probably everyone tells you that…"*

Jim picks up Justin's description, tells me that he is forty-five days sober, twenty days out of Anchor hospital's detox ward. He tried fighting his addictions alone for years. Stayed clean, fell off the wagon, stayed drunk, got clean again. One day his temper, *"always a problem,"* exploded in the operating theater while he was finishing up surgery on a particularly nasty gunshot wound to the chest.

"Another bar fight when everyone went for guns," he recalls.

But this time he couldn't keep the tremors out of his skillful hands. Short of breath from indulging in pharmacy samples of painkillers, he erupted into a full-blown panic attack. Unable to finish his job, he used rage over a supposed nursing error to hide the shakes. He wasn't as clever as he thought, he admits now. The chief resident had closed for him enough times to draw attention. While he was taking off his scrubs, the hospital executives and chief of staff confronted him, threatened loss of license and position. They had already talked to Anchor and Martha Morrison. He arrived in Atlanta five hours later, having drunk eight small bottles of straight Scotch on the four-hour plane ride.

"I don't know now what the hell I was thinking, but Martha met my plane herself with an orderly who had a straight jacket with him in case I was belligerent. Neither was surprised to find me loaded, said it was more common than not."

In the next forty-eight hours of dry-out delirium, he accepted that he had "hit bottom" an addict's hell hole from which they cannot climb out alone. Twenty-eight days later he was ready to commit to sobriety. I am grateful for his candor as well as his protective hand on my son's shoulder.

"I'm Bobbie," I tell him, *"not just Mom,"* but other than that any introductory small talk feels hollow after his self-revelation. Justin interrupts to tell me that this is a big day for Jim too; he's going to see his wife for the first time since he left home over a month ago.

Jim adds that this rehab experience has been a shock to her. *"All this, the extent of my addiction, the fear of losing my career and income. Her life, like mine, revolved around the hospital community, charity events, things like that."*

We are standing in a cramped ten by twelve-foot living area as we talk. Behind us a TV of dubious brand sits on a stand made to serve potted plants. A couch with stiff pillows faces it squarely. Against a wall is a three-legged easy chair propped up with soft covered books in an attempt to give it stability. In front of both is a pressed wood and scratched chrome table, topped with glass, decorated with coffee cup rings.

"Anyone else home?" asks Justin, peeking into the kitchen before heading down the short hallway to two bedrooms separated by the one bathroom.

Jim whispers to me, *"He's got a lot of energy doesn't he?"* But to Justin, who is already heading back to us, having not found anyone else, he replies that Dr. Robert is out back cleaning the mop he used on the kitchen and bathroom floors. *"Watch out—he's in a foul mood."* Jim explains that they are all responsible for rotational clean up duty including toilets and floors. None of them welcome the chores but Dr. Robert finds them particularly degrading.

Their other roommate, Tom, has requested a private session for himself and his family with Martha. *"That's interesting,"* Justin whistles, as he reenters the room.

Jim explains that this is a family weekend for the entire facility, only time of year that the kids' program and theirs overlap, *"Lots of people in and out, lots of commotion."* Tom wanted some face time with Martha and the influence of her experience with his family away from the crowd. Unlike most of the other doctors who come here under duress, Tom signed himself into rehab.

"His wife thinks he was 'weak,' her word, thinks he should have handled his problems alone."

He shrugs at this thought, looks at me for understanding.

"I thought that too once, that I could handle it all alone… just seems a long time ago now."

Jim grins at that, yes, me too, he says. He goes on to explain that their roommate, Robert, is known as *"Dr. Robert."* They all go by first names in recovery but in deference to Robert's age and his former status we all call him " Dr." All of us except Martha, he adds, she thinks, " *We're feeding his overblown ego.*" But, hell, he says quietly so that Robert won't hear, it's not much to give a guy who taught many of us, was a brilliant mentor and is over sixty-years-old and published in the most prestigious journals. Justin picks up the end of his sentence and says now tell her the rest of it. When Jim hesitates a second too long

Justin answers instead, turning to me, says,

"AND he killed a guy, because he was experimenting with anesthetics on himself, probably seeing how much alcohol and drugs he could consume and still go to surgery. He came home loaded, heard a noise in his garage, took out a hunting rifle and killed the fifteen-year-old neighbor kid who had come to borrow the lawnmower. He lost his license and lied to get another one in another state… where was it Jim? Mississippi or Tennessee, I think… As you can imagine Robert doesn't talk about it much! Anyway that was when he was caught and sent here."

Justin is cut off by the arrival of Robert. Old for sixty, silver hair thin and scraggly, walking stooped, he is mouthing garbled disgruntlement. He has not heard Justin through the din of his own agitation, and is unaware for a few moments that a stranger is there. *"Justin, I just mopped every floor and surface, DO NOT leave dirty boot prints anywhere! Do you hear me?"*

He means to say this with the authority of his former self, and even now manages to be imperious. But, his dishevelment makes the scene of mop-as-scepter ludicrous. A big man, probably handsome once, before today's torn T-shirt and baggy Bermuda shorts, he finally sees me and drops his bluster. In one motion he pulls the almost-shoulder length white hair behind his ears, pats down the few stragglers attached to his pink skull, and, squaring his shoulders, looks for a place to dispose of the dripping mop. He thrusts it at Justin who catches it in mid air, while Robert wipes his palms on his shorts before shaking my hand for an extra minute. Justin sees the slight leer in the Dr's eye, hears the sugar in his voice as he says,

"Why you must be Justin's mother. What a lovely boy you have here, rather, I should say, young man. Sorry for the circumstances, but I am sure it will all turn out for the best. We have our eyes on him, you can rest comfortably knowing that... Now! What was your name again, I am sorry, distracted by my 'house cleaning chores.'" Which his tone implies are clearly beneath him.

"Back off, Robert!"

Justin drops the man's preferred title, as he heads into the kitchen, where he props the mop against the sink. He walks back to us, telling Robert my name, that I am his mother not another potential wife. To me Justin says Robert is on wife number four or five. Justin, with a roll of his eyes, admits that he can never keep the count straight. He hugs Robert's shoulders while easing the man's hand out of mine. Jim, who has been smothering a laugh throughout, looks at his watch, says, yes, not only does Robert have a wife but their roomy, Tom, is picking her up from her hotel. They should be here in just a few minutes.

He suggests that Robert get cleaned up, make a good impression after all these weeks away from her. The older man, still smiling at me, takes several seconds to refocus, the shift to alternate activity taking deliberate thought. Suddenly, with yet another mood change, he is jovial, excuses himself with a gracious bow, before whistling a jingle all the way to his room.

"He's out there today!" Justin bursts into laughter, tells Jim this is the most distracted he's seen Robert since he sobered up.

Jim is sympathetic, says the ordeal of being in rehab for over a month has worn Robert out. Asks Justin to try and understand the impact on a man of Robert's age and reputation to find himself at this place after the career he's had. Jim is not lecturing, speaks with affection as he watches his former teacher walk down the hall and turn into the bedroom they share.

But Justin won't have it, emotion rising in his voice he reminds Jim that Robert was addicted to a *"truckload"* of drugs plus alcohol. Feeling sorry for him or making excuses for his behavior isn't going to help.

"Even after everything he's done he's got you guys a little faked out... he's just a nasty old addict with a bad attitude."

I look at Jim worried that Justin has been too familiar, confrontational, and disrespectful. Fearful that the precious bonds of their new friendship will shatter, I warn myself not to step in. My ambition to save and rescue didn't keep my kid get sober, and won't help him now, I say to myself. If truth and healing are to occur, whatever goes on here must be allowed the space to reveal itself without my anxious interruptions. I hold my breath, look back and forth between Jim and Justin.

Jim allays my concern, says, Dr. Robert has been in and out of rehab facilities and AA over a number of years. All addicts have ego issues, but it's exaggerated in Robert, and Justin's right that they may be harming rather than helping by not calling him out on it. The staff, especially Martha, agree with Justin, Jim admits. They remind the other doctors that Robert can't stay sober until he faces the mess he's created.

"It means serious jail time if he can't grasp the fact that humility and courage are absolutely necessary to getting and staying sober, to admitting to his problems and the damage he's caused. I guess he can't surrender to what addiction has done to him, that he even IS an addict, and who he's become because of it."

Our ego's are so human, flimsy and yet, under pressure, resolute. Only here in rehab where the negative effects of ego are glaring, does it seem ephemeral and self-constructed. What are we protecting?

I take a breath, steady myself, and tell Jim I know about the misplacement of ego, too. The thought of not having been a perfect mother kept me out of the recovery Program, Al-Anon, and family counseling that I now believe will help save my life. *"It took me years to surrender."*

Jim is grateful to be understood. Motions to Justin who has moved across the tight space and is tinkering with the TV, trying to get a clear picture. Says, *"Isn't it true, Justin, we've all spent late nights, trying to influence Robert?*

Justin, now frustrated with the orneriness of the knobs and screen, looks up, maintains the slightest patience in his voice, looks directly at the older man and says, you and Tom had big careers too. Yet you manage to be respectful of others including the teens.

"Hell, I've learned respect for this Program, the work and myself by watching and listening to you, Jim. But Robert is still in his shit! Just as arrogant as the day he got here, and now making a move on my mom. Who the hell does he ..."

Jim and I laugh aloud at the hard set of Justin's protective jaw. Interrupting the last of his sentence, Jim says, *"He's just a tired old man who, like the rest of the doctors, has a lot of stagnant ego to deal with including, in his case, liking the ladies, I'm afraid."*

But that they all share a history of terrible mistakes, Jim says, that they have to contend with. Justin stays in motion as he continues to disagree with Jim, in and out of the kitchen, opening and closing the refrigerator, offering soft drinks to the two of us, slugging down some of his. Jim answers him seriously, says Justin needs to remember that AA and Narcotics Anonymous are just that *"anonymous programs."* The names and what people have done, are to be kept in the trust and confines of the rooms where they are shared. His voice remains friendly but is firm, an adult talking to a younger person. And, yes, he appreciates Justin pushing *"to get them all real."*

I pick up this positive cue and tell Jim, that one of my sons' greatest strengths is an absolute need to dig for truth. Hypocrisy of any kind makes his skin crawl. Unfortunately, I add, he also has a need to say it aloud as the mood moves him. I try not to sound like an anxious mama bear.

Jim likes that quality in Justin himself, he tells me, and even has come to count on it. He grins as he remembers an AA meeting they all attended.

He explains that they are required to go to an AA or Narcotic Anonymous meeting outside the facility every day, and never twice in the same location within a seven day period, until they have hit every meeting in College Park and Atlanta at least once.

It takes you some places you wouldn't volunteer to go, including the night they went to one of Atlanta's poorest ghettos, to a rundown church with rats scratching in the attic.

"Hate to admit this now, but we were all afraid of being the only white faces for several square blocks... all of us that is except Justin. He just walked right to the front, led the rest of us in, found a pew we could squeeze into together... had Dr. Robert sit next to him, and believe me, Robert was glad for the protection... then Justin stood, wasn't shy, shook as many hands as he could find, introduced himself and all of the rest of us, as if he was our caretaker... And, well, I guess he was."

Justin smiles at the memory, says,*"It was hard core alright. We weren't just the only white faces, we were the only ones with all our teeth."*

Jim agrees, recalls how people at the meeting were missing body parts too, limbs and parts of hands, lost in Vietnam, gang fights, bar brawls. It was as bad as anything he'd ever seen in an emergency ward. *"It WAS an emergency ward,"* adds Justin, *"But down there it's always an emergency!"*

They recount the rest of the story together, how the meeting went late into the night. They were riveted and moved by the personal stories people shared.

Jim says the docs all went in feeling sorry for themselves and were humbled by the desperation of addicts and alcoholics so like them but so different. They marveled later at the heroics and bravery of those they met, who fought for sobriety despite the long odds and then reached out to help others.

Later, they all agreed it was the best meeting they attended.

"It forced us to think and reevaluate life, ourselves, society… even Robert contributed by the end of the night, allowed himself a hug or two as I recall, isn't that so Justin?"

Justin, able to mimic tone and accent perfectly, contorts his face into the image of a toothless smile.

"Yeah, people were saying, 'who IS that crazy old white guy?" and then he adds that only Jim and BJ ever go back down with him to the church meeting.

"Hell" he says, *"I love the place—no bullshit egos at THAT meeting."*

∾ 25 ∾

A warning knock stops our conversation. Two short raps precede Tom's entry. He pushes the door open and stands aside to allow two women and a teenage girl to pass, then follows them in.

Jim welcomes them warmly and introduces me to the first woman, Robert's wife. She is a vivacious platinum blonde with daring, narrow eyes who looks decades younger than her husband. The diamonds that dangle from her ears, neck and wrists are outshone by the rocks on the fourth fingers of each hand with its red-lacquered nails. She is puzzled why Justin and I are there, asks me twice if I am a doctor too, in spite of Jim's careful introductions. Flustered and nervous, she makes a prolonged jabber of her questioning. Tom saves us, stepping forward to introduce himself.

Like Jim, he is a surgeon, late middle age, and an alcoholic. Neat and tidy, of average height, he seems smaller than that because of his athletic compactness, the tight carriage of his neck, shoulders, and torso. He is controlled and accurate in his clipped diction and social awareness. Smiling, he asks me if I know that Justin doesn't sleep at night, gives my son a playful punch to his shoulder. Justin tilts his chin, with his characteristic, lets-tell-the-inside-story notched smile, eyes cast down in a small squint over the shorter man's head.

"He's trying to tell you I drive him crazy with my insomnia, getting up and down all night… isn't that so, Tom? You can tell my mom the truth… she's heard worse about me."

Tom looks up at him, laughs this off but does not deny the charge. Instead he turns to take the second woman's hand and encourages her forward through the small tight cluster to meet us. The two of them standing together are like bookend replicas of East Coast Brahmins I remember from years of Philadelphia. They exude that prep school, old money comfort and confidence. Her name slips by me in the shifting of bodies. I notice she is handsome and conservative, not fussy in any way, not remarkable either. Loose brown curls twist to shoulder length, framing delicate features. She wears khaki slacks, a button-down shirt with an expensive sheen, loafers with tassels—an outfit almost identical to her husband's. Understated gold jewelry, a plain wide wedding band sparkle against the last of her summer tan.

I ask her name again, apologizing for having missed it. She repeats it in a whisper over her shoulder. *"Becky, or Bunny or Beverly?"* I try to grasp it, realizing her lack of volume may be intentional, as she reaches for her daughter.

"Jennifer!" The mother announces the girl's name loud enough for all to hear, her hands placed on the shoulders of the teenager, now squeezed between us. Dressed similarly to her parents, long hair pulled back on one side with a clip, a sensitive blush to her cheeks and mouth, she looks up from under thick lashes. Jennifer's hands visibly shake in a wave in front of her face as she struggles to extend herself in a hello. Meeting Justin she blinks several times, glances upward to his height for a second before finding the toes of her shoes riveting and glues her eyes to them for the duration of her agony.

The mother, continuing to shield herself with her daughter, informs us with a professorial assuredness about the historical value of Atlanta. They've been on tour since early morning, taking in the monuments and walking the trails of the South's burning and rebuilding during the Civil War and its reconstruction. *"It's been a wonderful outing! Hasn't it darling?"* She is speaking over her daughter's head, does not wait for a response. Like Fred last night, she is demanding some form of family normalcy— just another outing. Her fingers clutch Jennifer's shoulders in an effort to transfer that belief directly into the flesh of the uncertain child.

"I wanted to bring our son because he's a real history buff like his mother, and he'd love to see it too. But this is PSAT weekend for him, and what with lacrosse practice and honors homework… they really pile it on you know. Well we felt it was better he stay home, but we all miss him, don't we, Jen?"

I study the mother's face as she speaks and muse how she strains to stay intact after the confrontation of a private counseling session. She is armored against anything personal that had to be stirred up. But then I notice Tom's thin-lipped smile, and Jennifer as she winces, struggles and fails to escape her mother's white knuckled grip. I try to find appropriate words to respond and am saved by another rap on the door, sharp and demanding. It is Jim's wife. We all squeeze closer together as Jim reaches out with both arms to wrap her into a large hug. She turns her cheek to him so he can deliver only a peck of a kiss, dropping her arms to avoid hugging him back, looks over our heads, and does not respond to any introductions.

Jim tries a second time to give her all our names, shuffling away from her public rebuff by assuming a loud congeniality. I look away from his pained smile, and want to reach over and shake his wife out of her chilly judgment.

Robert breaks the tension, enters the room, showered, shaved, and dressed in slacks and a short-sleeved golf shirt, an almost new man. His wife throws out her arms, curls him into her bountiful chest, and nuzzles his head into the crook where her own head and shoulder meet. She strokes wisps of hair that have fallen across his forehead, croons into him like a mother cat to an oversized kitten. The uncomfortably crowded room oozes with the perspiration of unease and excitement, stickying up the already squalid air.

"Hey, I'm going to be late for my group meeting and lunch!" Justin sounds way too enthusiastic about his schedule and time, but we use it to excuse ourselves as the doctors organize a group lunch.

I stop to give Jim a hug, interrupting his wife's whine about her day of travel. I wish I could say something that will push the pouting woman to recognize his effort and contribution. I hesitate, know I am seeing the complexity of their relationship through the limited lens of today's intensity, the program, my own life and vantage point. In the end I just offer him thanks and a hug.

"Hope we'll see each other before the weekend is out," he says. Justin opens the door and gestures impatiently for me to hurry.

～ 26 ～

On the second story landing Justin stops and gives a loud whoop. *"WOW!"* He gasps between belly laughs, *"What a group!"*

"But, Justin, we're all the same… addiction, codependencies, sadness, grief, blame…" I immediately protest. How about the visible pain of that young girl? I try to keep my voice just above a whisper. And her mother's denial, refusing to admit why they are here? Jim's wife, cold and judging, blaming him alone for the disruption of her well-organized life. It's hard enough for us to be here, to work at our relationship, but these are older men with families in high distress, and it's painful just watching them.

Justin is taking every other down stair in alternate leaps, saying over his shoulder that they each have their plusses, especially Jim who is consistent in his commitments and support. Justin loves some of these guys and *"all of them some of the time,"* but the truth is, you can't let them fool you. They protect, then rat on each other when life in rehab gets too tough for them, or they find someone to blame, often their young roommates, himself included. And then stay up half the night to *"process the 'problem.'"* And that conversation can go in circles with many of them just putting in their time until they can walk out with a thirty-day AA chip saying they're clean and sober.

That's the emotional immaturity and ego that Martha Morrison talks about, Justin shouts over his shoulder. Robert loves to rag on, *'Teens in Trouble'* but geez… is he kidding? *None of us KILLED anyone."*

He stops on the final stair, turns to me, blasts this last point, not for the first time, through the humid air and cloudless sky in one gush. Taking a short breath he steadies his voice, sighs, says, the list of tragedies that can result by professional adults who abuse is far greater than any kids can cause.

"They write prescriptions for every kind of crap there is… for themselves and their patients, and they have lives in their hands, they can do a lot of damage… wreck people including their families, along with themselves… and you know why, they all admit it, because they can hide behind their degrees and titles, white coats and money…"

I'm not making an excuse for myself, Mom, he assures me, or for the other kids here. All I am saying is that it is, and isn't, the same. *"You have to keep your mind and your eyes open."*

He starts to walk again, subdued as he continues, telling me now I should understand why he likes the Sunday night ghetto meeting, how refreshing it is when no one is hiding behind self-images. He adds how he wishes I would be here on Sunday night, could go down there with him, and experience it for myself.

We are at the car by this time and take off, drive back to the Anchor facility, again with his directions but with none of the talk. In the silence it hits me that I am so engrossed by my worry for his survival that I have missed the intricacies of relating, across age differences and subject matters, that confront him each day. I want to blurt this out as it occurs to me; to admit I didn't appreciate the complexity and demands of his fish bowl existence. But when I look over I am silenced by his darkening mood.

I park and wait for him to offer something. He says nothing more, merely watches the other young people walking into the facility. Uncomfortable with the distance between us, I reach over and touch his left arm with my right hand.

He stares directly in front of him, unmoved. I say how proud I am of his efforts, negotiating between school, counselors, staff, adult roommates, AA meetings, and his teen peers and their parents. Many people, I continue, have stopped me to say how much he is participating, and that he has made a real impact on them.

"They all mention that you challenge yourself more than you challenge anyone else."

My voice weakens in the emptiness of his silence. My touch, intended as tender, tightens into a squeeze. I release him, hoping he cannot feel the gripping in my fingertips. His green eyes are hooded and distant. The cut to the bone humor is gone. I do not know why this happened; am afraid to ask.

It is exactly 12:27 P.M. on the dashboard clock. He has to be in the cafeteria at 12:30 or lose hard-won privileges. We stare at the white numbers against the black frame in silence. I feel the conflict of arguing words rise in him. Finally, opening the door and only half turning around to me, he says, voice low and gravelly with an edge of rage, *"I hate this place!"*

He slams the door shut, and I am alone in the vacuum of air that remains.

～ 27 ～

I watch his galloping stride, the toss of his dark head, his unclenching fists, until he disappears into the building. I sit frozen in place, aware that something has drained from me, *"hope?"* I think, *"courage"?* Unable to move from question to response to action, I am leaning so far forward into the steering wheel that my back has stiffened. I unwind, try to release the weight of that good-bye, stare at the inside of the windshield, and, with my mind heavy and blank, trace the teardrop salts left there by College Park's incessant moisture.

Minutes pass before I remember the lunch being held for parents. I try to push up against the sadness that has engulfed me, but I am drained. I reach into my body for a small percentage of the reserve strength I rely on. My fingers don't cooperate to turn the key in the ignition. Instead they freeze, a chill trembling through me on this warm day.

I realize how completely attached I am to Justin's moods and to my desire that he choose recovery every minute of every day. Exactly as the father who started the sharing last night said, by my definitions of what recovery should be. I say to myself that this level of attachment is *"crazy making control and fear and nothing else…there are no perfect solutions, and if there are I don't have them anyway!"* My voice sticks in my throat, and I wish for a torrent of tears to wash over me and clean me out. Instead I gasp for air and try again to force my mind to understanding. I search for words of peace, the calming repetition of mantra or prayer, but it merely dissolves in a leaden sea. Without formations to grasp, I just sit still for almost an hour missing lunch, not caring, my mind played out.

At 1:30, feeling as if I sleepwalked out of a dull nightmare to wakefulness, I notice the time. I have thirty minutes before meeting up with Justin again at our personal counseling session. It is the session I have been preparing for with my private meditation teacher, in therapy and Al-Anon meetings, for weeks. *"Be Here Now!"* The primacy of that familiar command rings through me. I welcome it, decide to loosen up with a walk in the light drizzle. Removing the ignition key, I note the exact pocket I place it in knowing this is the perfect time for an absentminded moment to occur. I walk in straight lines around the outer perimeter of the facility on sidewalks that connect what must be over a mile of squat rectangular buildings. I begin to wake up in the squish of suburban rain under soles on wet pavement. I frown at my blue suede flats, sure they will leave stains on my feet but do not stop.

Recalling I haven't eaten for hours, coddling the gnaw of my stomach, I promise myself *"real food soon."* After a block of walking, my thoughts begin to open in the loosening of movement, in the moisture on my face and hands.

I think idly of the doctors, of all that intelligence, ambition, success, squeezed together in one cramped apartment so far removed from their brilliant careers. I relax and laugh recalling Robert's pathetic come-on and Justin's defense. I review all the faces crowded together, and my own too. It is the hoping for something else, something to end the anxiety of the moment, that stands out in its shared uniformity by old and young. Slowly, I begin to think not of hope but of faith. *"It is a luxurious thought, faith."*

Hope is easier. There is action in hope, a going toward, a certainty that the things I hope for, peace, safety, my son's health, are all good and noble in their own right. I can get very clear and very righteous around hope, I can strive and make a plan and work towards the hoped-for-goal. It is what I've done all my life.

But what of faith? It sounds like surrender, and surrender like weakness. And what if faith doesn't elicit the results I want? In Twelve Step Programs they say, *"Let Go and Let God,"* but what if God is looking the other way? Or if the plan of a higher power doesn't make sense to me? Faith may be a luxury I can't afford. On the other hand, if I am addicted to the action and involvement of hope, the striving, pushing, planning around my hopefulness, then hope is just another form of wanting, of running after a goal that takes me out of my center. Is faith the antidote? If nothing else I have learned faith in the process of the Programs. I have seen and heard powerful changes in people, and yes, in myself too, by having faith in the simple act of coming back to meetings, by meditating and praying and working the process, over and over again. Not so much hoping for specific results, but having faith that the process of opening and allowing may offer redemption. After all, I remind myself, avoiding puddles, stopping to take deep breaths, fill my lungs and laugh at myself; *"I am the child who looks for the pony under the manure."* I do believe that the largest diamonds are found in the darkest cave and that there is light at the end of the tunnel.

I have faith that the hell of addiction brought me the gift of this Program. And that redemption, *"whatever that is,"* may be worth all the suffering. *"It is not how I want it to be,"* but, perhaps, faith will deliver something greater than hope ever has.

Finally tears warm my cheeks cooled by rainwater. They are faint and tender. I laugh again and realize they signal unexpected joy. Strange, after all the heart tearing of the morning, but there it is, coming unbidden—joy. *"Why?"* But I know. It is what I asked for, to be here now, totally immersed, and to feel all the feelings. To not hide, or justify or project them onto someone else or call them by the wrong name. But, instead, to know and experience the whole truth of where we are *"NOW,"* without shrinking away from any of it.

"Be Here Now!! In this moment." I say aloud. All we know for sure is that my son is alive, and I am alive here with him experiencing all of it. *"Afraid? Yes, but not afraid too."* Braver, able to face whatever comes up and *"wherever it leads us."*

It may not be what others would choose, but it is the only way to win back my life, the life of my child. I walk back to the car to gather up my purse and journal, and head over to the Anchor facility, to meet with Justin and the therapist we are assigned for the private counseling session.

Feeling the opposite pulls of anticipation and dread, I command myself to stay balanced between them, to stay realistic, to not give in to either extreme. I have no other choice, after all,

"Escape, in all its seduction, is no longer a viable option."

∾ 28 ∾

Finding the room we're assigned and a folding chair outside it, I sit and reread what I have written, revised with my Teacher, and rewritten for this session.

"Envision a perfect peace. See yourself contained, calm, sure. I will come from a deep well of silence into the truth. I will have no expectations of Justin's response… I will say a truth for its own sake. There is nothing to fear."

I am a woman of resolve. I have faith in today's mission and where it will take me, I promise myself. On these last silent words, as if choreographed, the hallway comes alive. Parents and children are tunneling in and out of offices and classrooms, as the last hour's sessions break up and this hour's assemble. I scan the faces of those leaving, attempt to assess damage and epiphanies, seeking a sign that miracles happen here. But, the faces of parents are sad and hollow eyed, or puffed up in barely controlled rage. A few bear open tears and fewer smile. Counselors bid them well in doorframes of standard size and proportion, a counterbalance of structure set against suffering. I am struck again by how different the teenagers, given their shared status and reasons for being here, seem one from another, by age, size, gender and emblems of cultural significance. Some weep unembarrassed tears of relief or anger, that are easy to differentiate given the smiles or disgust that accompany wet cheeks. Others feign disinterest and don't acknowledge parent or counselor.

The young mother from last night, Sarah, has her arms outstretched around her mother and stepfather. He, with his hands shoved in pants pockets, eyes down, and she crying, her head awkwardly perched between her daughter's shoulder and heart. The young woman is steering them down the hallway, whispering and consoling. Sure-footed, she nods apologies to those who must move against a wall to let the threesome pass by, smiling to each as they make their way.

The hallway empties as fast as it filled. Alone, except for a few stragglers who soon disappear into exits or entrances, I feel five-years-old sitting outside the principal's office in a big urban Catholic school, waiting for a fate unimaginable to the innocent. I check to make sure my feet touch the ground, laugh at myself for the suddenness of that memory. *"I am not a scared child."* I say to the wall opposite me; repeat it to make sure.

Our assigned counselor appears from an open door down the hall. *"Sorry,"* she says cheerily walking toward me as I place my feet firmly on the floor, rise to meet her.

"I'm Ann Brown, good to put a face with the voice on the phone, and so glad you could make the long trip." She explains that our room is still being used for a session that has gone past the hour. *"We try to keep time limits, but it's important to let it flow when it must."*

As she walks, Ann says that we will have to find an alternate location and is afraid our choice is limited to one interior office. She stops several steps ahead of me, opens a door and waits for me to enter first.

I try to relax into her confidence, the honey Georgia roll of her voice, to allay the prickles of expectation beginning at the back of my neck. My returned smile feels forced and frozen. I enter and am squeezed by the Spartan space. I attempt small talk, wanting to discount the tightness and create a bond with her that I can release into. She is cordial, apologizes for the distance between us, caused by the desk that is ridiculously large for the size of the room. But, she notes, if she moves her chair from behind it the three of us will be knee to knee, *"Too tight and just adequate."* She sighs, glances around the room and toward the glass-domed wall clock that records that Justin now officially ten minutes late. Well, it's just after lunch, she notes, and although he complains about the food and the people, he can't break away from either most of the time.

"He's a big bear of a kid," she laughs, *"with all kinds of opinions and an appetite for life. BUT he has to play by the rules anyway."*

Ann heads out to find him, and alone I feel the calm slipping away. I damn the morning's second cup of coffee, and my empty stomach for the rising twitchiness. The monochromatic space should be galvanizing, there is nothing to distract or cling to. But there is nowhere to hide either.

Ann precedes Justin through the door with a look that warns me that he is in a foul mood. I hear him complaining at having to come to a private session. *"Required,"* is her cool answer as she points to his chair and takes her own.

"And what are you complaining about anyway? Most of the kids here are local and have to do this every week. You've had phone sessions, it's not that different... should be glad to have your mom in person."

He humphs a guttural nonresponse, slumps his angular frame into the chair, pushing out stiffened legs, and scowling at no one but himself.

Ann enumerates the reasons we are here, and the purpose and importance of private family sessions. She then summarizes, in one sentence apiece, the four sessions we have had by phone. The first was a month after Justin arrived at Anchor and just left the hospital facility and was entering the halfway house. The second and third were over the next two months. Each session focused on Justin—his health and emotional state, where he was in the process of recovery, the issues he faced or wouldn't, and what was required of him to progress in sobriety. She is without affect as she speaks, keeping judgment and opinion to herself, reporting none of the negatives, steps back or upsets that I recall; reminding us in this way to take it all in stride. Ann stops, looks at me, says she is pleased to meet me at last. Sorry, she adds, that my husband, Justin's father, isn't there. Remarks that she hasn't heard him on the phone either. She stops, waiting for an explanation, looking at us, left and right, when none is offered she goes on without further inquiry.

"Our last session ended as we began to explore what you have discovered about yourself, Bobbie, in the process of your work in Al-Anon, and the other recovery Programs you're involved with."

A groan rises from Justin's sullen frame. Ann continues to smile, nods in a way that lets me know she has heard him and won't respond.

I try to take deep breaths, steadying my pounding pulse, look over at my son, edgy and bunched into himself. Notice my fingers twisted in hooks around each other, and, surprising myself with a sigh I don't intend, force them apart. I am afraid to begin without lifting his downward stare. I jump at a spasm in my heart as I recognize the look of shame on his face. *"He is waiting to be blamed, to have me identify some fault,"* I think to myself. I am sad and embarrassed that Ann's introduction provokes that response. I try to dispel fear of separation by edging my chair closer to him, clear my throat, and say his name. When he doesn't look up, I reach into my mind for the promised courage and intention, instead feel confidence ebb. There is no choice but to press on, refuse defeat by the tremors tickling vocal cords.

Gathering courage the rehearsed words come forward on cue. I listen to my voice, judge it too thin to indicate resolve but can't wait for perfection; I hope the words themselves are strong enough to be heard. I speak a hard-won truth of accountability. I do not confess sins of parental miscon-duct that didn't occur or point a finger at anyone else. I go for something more elusive but true and fundamental.

I talk about how this Program has revealed to me the parts of myself that I could not or would not see and understand. The most difficult thing to face, I tell him, was not shortcomings of which there are plenty, or mis-takes made, but the underlying sadness I didn't call by its right name; the grief I could not abide. I tell him that *"grief unclaimed is not unlived."* I say that I recognize now that it plays itself out in the relationships of the family.

"When a mother's world is her children, they often are the catch-all of what the mother, me, <u>this</u> mother, could not contain or even be aware of within myself—what I was blind and deaf to… what is called a 'shadow projection.'"

I stop myself, know the temptation to hide in psychological jargon and the safety of knowledge over feeling. But, when I start again, attempting to stick to my script, I lose it in my son's silence, in the combination of exhaustion and emotion, contained too well for too long. The measured pace I intend slips and slides away from me as an avalanche of remorse, and worse, guilt, real or imagined, spills over. I try to run after what was mis-spoken, reclaim wrong words but piling more sentences on top of those just uttered confuses it all. Rather than freeing him, I bury Justin under the crush of what he always feared and now hears—responsibility for the grief of his mother. Finally, as I stop to reconsider and take a breath, he tilts up his face reddened with rage. I do not get this immediately, not in the way I can write it now. As he clenches and unclenches his fists, I try a last time to reel back entire sentences.

With everything going very wrong, Ann rises from behind the desk. There isn't room enough for her to squeeze her chair between us so she leans against the desk and forms a triangle connecting Justin to me. She attempts with her presence alone to break my distress, to gather us up with the fallen rocks of words and emotion. Seconds pass before I am able to look away from Justin to Ann, afraid, I know, that if I lose contact with him it will be lost forever.

"He can't hear you," she says, moving so that she is looking at me squarely, saying it a second time. *"He can't hear you."* The repetition releases my mind, unplugs my ears that shut, open, and half shut again from the effort

of holding back tears. I look over at Justin; know she is right. *"It is too much, too out of character. There are too many words for him to take in."*

Ann's voice is even and low. Each syllable is parsed out, meant to push apart thoughts, force me out of my memorized lines. I stare into her dark pupils; allow them to position me. Noticing I am holding my breath, I remember The Teacher says that breath held tightens mind, throat, heart, and voice. So I pause and take slow, deep, inhale, exhale; wait.

"He's felt responsible for your feelings for so long…exactly as you said, not consciously on either of your parts, but, still, so completely, that he can only continue that pattern when he sees your grief now. Because you have never grieved in ways he could see or hear, experience, before."

Her thoughts ricochet through the corridors of my brain, to my heart through my body until they come to rest. I release into the truth of it, am one with it and calm. She has spoken only inches away from Justin but as if he is not there. She says nothing more but her eyes do not leave me, and her body bent forward for emphasis doesn't unbend. I stay silent, unmoving, making sure that I absorb feeling and essence. Turning I take in all of my son, his youth and tenderness, the tension and grip of muscle, his beauty and strength, vulnerability and sinewy rage.

Strengthened by Ann's presence and wisdom, I release duty fed by fear and absorb the fullness of the moment. I realize that for this proud young man my efforts at courage and accountability are "worse than an avalanche." He hears guilt where I mean redemption, and defeat when I want to reclaim what of mine has defined him. Trying to take burden back, to carry it myself, has only burdened him anew. Allowing myself to sink into silence, awareness washes over me and in this windowless room the light of grace slowly opens and spreads, calming my nerves and tight limbs. I shake my hands free and breathe. Justin remains as controlled as the taut pull of a rope clinging to heavy tonnage ready to untether and destroy what lies below. I turn my chair to face him, attempt to pierce his shroud of anger.

Composed, sitting back, my voice quiet and intense, I say,

"It is not the responsibility of a child, a baby really, to bear the sadness of the parent."

My hands quicken in the chill of adrenalin draining. I allow its completion to wrap stillness through me, then go on, lowering my voice again to prevent the slimmest note of emotion to dilute meaning.

"When you were just a toddler, maybe three- or four-years-old, two or three times probably, I remember you saying to me, 'Mommy, why are you so sad? Why are you so sad, Mommy?' It seemed to me to come out of the blue, unconnected to an event... not as if something bad had happened. No, more like in the course of an otherwise sunny day you would suddenly look into my eyes and say that 'why so sad?'"

Tempted to look at Ann for approval, I recognize the temptation as fear, and refuse it. Instead I stare straight into my son's thick-lashed eyes looking partly back at me, hooded in emotion. He remains bent at the waist, elbows on his knees, body alert, guarding against danger. I am in that nexus of tensions, of what insists to be said, and what cannot be said. Knowing I must continue, I command steadiness of myself. Then I tell him that I never understood what he meant by his sweet questioning, what he saw in my face. I say that denial of all of my past and a lot of the present was a powerful force, that just now I am starting, and only starting, to comprehend.

Justin looks up when I remember how the second time he asked me what was wrong, I walked to the bathroom mirror and stared, wanting to see what he saw, trying to understand. I remember fussing with my hair, throwing cold water on my face to get a better look, but I saw only my own image reflected back to me.

He followed me in, not seeking a response but because children follow. I remember crouching down and trying to say something reassuring. But all these years later, when I look with new eyes on that small scene, I recall that even when I shook my head, said I didn't see anything, that he never agreed or changed his mind. *"You never took your words back, either,"* I say to the nearly grown man in front of me.

My thoughts drift to a picture of myself as a young mother, twenty-seven- or twenty-eight-years- old. I notice the slight downturn of my smiling mouth, the watery sadness of my eyes and wonder at what I could not see then.

Looking at the scene on a split screen with today's session, with present consciousness, I try to create a cocoon with warmth of voice and sincerity to gather him in; to have him understand. I go on to tell him that the Twelve Step Programs have given me insight and that other practices, meditation particularly, have helped me realize these things *"about myself"* I try to stress to reassure him,

"That what I had buried within me, couldn't face, wouldn't claim about myself, history, sadness, disappointment, grief, that I somehow cast it off and out. Unconsciously projected it onto you and your sister. Both of you found ways... your own ways, to express it, to carry those parts of your mother's, my stuff, into the world."

I watch him shift slightly, eyes blazing. I think that he hears me accepting all the blame, is afraid I will slip into guilt and shame, so I lift my chest so my heart is openly facing him and say,

"I also have come to see that none of us, including me, is to blame, is completely at fault. Each of us bears individual responsibility, yes, and the family as a whole has to be accountable too... is that what is making you angry? Is that what you want to say?"

When he doesn't respond, and I add that I am not taking away his responsibility for his mistakes or his pride in his own victories, I understand that it isn't all about me. I watch him stretch his fingers, spread them across his knees. Seeing his eyes flash open, his face redden I know he is barely able to keep to the rules of engagement: let a person say the whole thing out, no cross talk, and no interruptions.

Afraid that if I lose this chance another one may not come, I make one last push into his flagging patience. I tell him that I am not sure where on this path of understanding I am, but I know I can reclaim what I projected out. That as I get clearer about my past, and myself, I can also mend the broken parts others may have taken on as their burden. My voice stays controlled, drama and verbosity are out of it. A breath releases that is not a sigh but final punctuation. All that seemed so important to say sits between us heavier then intended, but, I think, clearer and as real as I can make it.

I feel the temptation to ask after his mood again, to fill the space of discomfort, but realize it is anxiety that goads me and so resist and let my breathing lead into silence. The Teacher says to expect nothing and to say the true thing for its own sake. There is nothing left to do but stay embedded in the only truth I own: *"my life, my experience, my responsibility."*

Justin's seething fills the room, squeezes out what little oxygen is left in the corners and ceiling. Without any assistance, but the rising tide of his tightly bound rage, he explodes straight to his feet growls at me looking down from what appears a great height. *"It's not your fault!"* He looks from me to Ann, voice loud and gravelly. *"She just doesn't get it."* None of us moves.

He opens and closes his right fist in frustration, looks at the close wall as if he means to punch a hole through it, thinks better of it but struggles to regain control of his body and emotions. I am stunned and cannot put the pieces together. How did what I say bring him to this point? He stands there a few seconds then asks of Ann, his voice crackling like electricity over frayed wires, *"Do I have to stay here?"*

Ann glances sideways at the clock. No, she says with a cool authority that quells the heat of the room. But he cannot leave mad; he must leave politely.

Justin's face registers incredulity, but he struggles again to regain control, can't, shakes himself, stops, breathes deeply and settles for what calm he can maintain. *"I'm not mad at you."* He finally blurts out. His teeth clenched, shoulders hunched up and tight, staring down at me, not looking away, he rumbles, *"I'm just MAD!"*

In one movement, with only the slightest nod of his head to ask, *"Okay?"* of Ann, who nods back at him, he is out the door saving it at the last minute from slamming behind him. He does not look back.

* * *

Journal Entry, Anchor, 1990: How can it be that a mother, me, this mother, is so in love with a child and at the same time, perhaps at least at times, in ways mysterious and not yet known be the source of his suffering?

Denying the parts of myself that were vulnerable, injured, maybe fragile, I could not *feel* my own distress and confusion. God knows I would NEVER have declared myself depressed, anxious, let alone defeated. I was strong enough to turn away from painful pasts and presents, experience it instead as challenge, a mission, something to conquer or fix out in the world… ALWAYS there was more of that to do!! It seemed so important to DO!!

But now I sit long hours in meditation…what comes up… *feeling,* so much feeling… I squirm, want to duck and hide from all the feeling. The Teacher asks what's there? Sad… sadness. Stay in it she says, but, God, it's excruciating. Sad, sadness, I repeat only the word as instructed, if I push it away, it comes back. Sit in the sadness, she says; keep sitting and feeling. It's only a feeling. Stay in the feeling long enough, and it will change and will transform… look at the pictures that come up, but don't attach to the story, contain it all, be in it but not of it, she tells me.

When I look at the past, at what I did, at who I was when Justin was little, what is it that I see with today's eyes?... that I moved quickly and well into anything that took me out of all that feeling... adventure... being a warrior... goals and purpose... projects, activity. But the unclaimed parts, the shadow within the striving and accomplishment, behind the past that was denied, seeped out like silent vapors into the small bodies, the tender lives of those I loved best... my children. Jung was right—without allowing myself to be awake to dark AND light to all of who I am, the unclaimed parts, the shadow he speaks of, was projected out.

Einstein was right. It's all energy. The energy, bottled up, hidden, eventually leaks out, unseen, no noise. OR it pops out, fizz and champagne like... uncorked, pouring out of its own accord or angry and dynamite like, exploding with ferocious, misplaced intent. Where does it land? Where do you think?

Even here in rehab where we should all know better I hear parents say, " I have no idea how he/she got this way... where did it come from?" Are they kidding?

We would rather believe we were attacked by an outside enemy than stop and look within... that's it isn't it? Addiction is the enemy INSIDE and OUTSIDE smaller and larger systems alike. BUT, The Teacher says that no enemy can exist without our collusion.

I *wish* I believed that there was an enemy outside that bore all the responsibility! It would be so convenient to cast blame outside myself, outside the system, but I know too much now to turn back, I know that in being unconscious to all of who I am, I hand it over, breathe into my beloveds...daughter and son.

The energy of it is drawn in at a cellular level. Children, so organic, at affect of the system, take it in... put it on, wear the castoffs of the generations before them... *my* children wear it in the world for me, yes, like cast off clothes, but measured, stitched up with the threads of their own DNA. Fashioned to suit who they are it becomes theirs, until the garment worn is difficult to recognize as the one given in the first place looks instead as solely their creation. That's how we absolve ourselves, isn't it? Because honestly, we can't recognize their version of that *thing* we never saw, certainly never claimed in the first place...never called by its true name...that shadow is carried into the world not as I might have if I was awake to it but in my son's personal strut and stride. Seeing it I can argue and rationalize, honor and defile it... analyze *him*, justify behavior, condemn, and mourn what is happening to him. BUT it takes a long time, much anguish, and hard work to reclaim the parts of him that are me.

Now here in Atlanta I sweat in that cramped monochrome room, pull off scabs and dig for truth. It all comes to this—I want to excise my darkness from him with a mother surgeon's knife, cut it away in one movement, saying, *"Give me back my grief and anxiety, anything I avoided seeing and knowing about myself. I am stronger... I am awake... I can handle it now... you cannot carry my shield any longer... it is not protecting either of us... it is destroying both of us."*

If I take it all back, feeling and form, memory and substance... call it by its true name, unafraid, will he be free of the projection of his mother, me, and find his true identity? Will *rebel* and *addict* no longer hold glory and be seen for what they are— just too much armor on the thin shoulders of a boy?

Brave as he is, proud as he is, can he hand back to me what is mine and be free forever? Can he, will he, choose a new life? Redefine himself... or are the patterns of the past too powerful for him to turn away from?

❧ 29 ❧

Ann's arm is around my shoulders in a loose embrace to lead me out of the facility. She locks the door behind her, noting that we are the last session to leave. She follows me to my car, says let's stop and talk a minute. I am drained but want any help I can get sorting this out, so I lean against the hood, try not to look up with too much expectation or worry. Her full, brown cheeks spread into a beatific smile. *"What you said and what he hears are two different things. He hears you accepting all the responsibility…yes, I know it's not what you said, but it's what he heard."*

I wonder why she didn't stop him at the door, clear up any misunderstanding between us, but I do not ask. Exhaustion settles into me, my shoulders droop forward, I cannot hold them up, my mouth is too dry to speak.

Ann goes on in kind words, says something about admiring my efforts at *"digging for foundational truth."* Says she recognizes the effort it takes to work this Program, but recreating relationships takes time. I hear acknowledgement, but it stays on the surface of my mind, and I cannot accept it. In a way, I don't want to absorb it. *"What's the use anyway,"* I think to myself, if it didn't help, if he didn't understand. Then I remember and tell her that my Teacher says *to have no expectations.* She smiles back at me, saying nothing.

As minutes tick away I feel satisfaction and no satisfaction quarrelling within me. She waits in silence for all this to transpire, then tells me to go back to my room and *"journal."* She thumps the book I carry. She says to write it out not the story but your feelings about the session. Don't be afraid to say what you hoped for because expectations are often unconscious. *"Write how it went for you, how you feel about his reaction… what maybe you wish had happened instead."* She smiles again, says, sometimes newcomers to Program laugh at all the little AA aphorisms, but, she's found wisdom in their simplicity, so please remember this, you've done all you can do for now.

"As we say, it may be time to 'Let go and Let God.' Give it time, it's in his hands."

I remember to turn right out of the driveway, left at the light, through a quiet intersection. Did I look both ways? Hearing a horn beep doesn't startle me, as the session runs and reruns through my mind.

It appears so intimate, the light of personal revelation, the darkness of fear dancing with each other in the interchange of my son to me, me back to him. Why isn't intimacy enough to change things, to transform our past? I hear what Ann says, I respect her experience and knowledge. And, I wonder what Justin will do with what I've said? Where will it take us?

* * *

Journal Entry, Anchor, 1990:

What did I want to happen? Mind safety, knowledge, information, the rightness of objective analysis of proper steps that yield acceptable results… answers and success… damn me! It is what I wish for! Emotions, the powerful forces of feeling are just too much and are never precise with clear dependable answers. The subjective overwhelms boundaries, a relentless wave crashing on well-made concrete bunkers of "objective" until rock and steel crumble allowing the water of emotion to flood in. And then one cannot see what appeared *so* certain, so clear a moment ago.

She said, "Journal… don't sit in those feelings… let them flow."

I wonder whether she has kids of her own, and whether she knows how deep the well of feeling, how stripped and raw this leaves me. The words roll off her tongue so easily. I cannot blame her for not knowing that any surrender, especially to feeling, has been the enemy for so long that what she asks of me, what I dare to ask myself, takes all the strength and courage of walking into the gates of hell naked and alone. I am used to battling through life, can I now become a warrior of surrender?

Let Go, Let God? Feel all the feelings; let God take care of the rest? Is surrender a paradoxical trick of God or the great mother or spirit translated into this program and presented as "simple"?

❧ **30** ❧

A telephone ring interrupts the outpouring of words in scribbles and scratches. Propped up on a stack of pillows, leaning against the shaky headboard, I reach for the phone in reflexive motion to stop the intrusion. Only at the last moment do I realize I will have to talk to someone. A weak *"Hello?"* peeps out and instantly a familiar, *"Mom?"* answers back. *"Mom? Are you okay? God, it doesn't sound like you!"*

Hearing my daughter's voice, the welling up of love interrupts heavy thought. I tell her I am carrying through with my instructions from Ann, journaling, and trying to make sense of the session. There isn't a doubt, I admit to her, that I had a picture of how this should have gone, even given all the assurances of "no expectations." I recount to her the list of "shoulds" battling in my mind—should *feel* to make progress ...should *know* to move forward, to help Justin, to understand myself ...should *do* to change... should *progress* here and now.

She listens without comment, waits until I exhale a sigh, and, with a soft laugh says I may want to reconsider whether I can be satisfied with progress or if it's perfection that I'm pursuing.

"It is a Program of progress not a Program of perfection, you know that doesn't exist, right, Mom?"

I laugh, relax into her patience and support, and reassure her that I understand intellectually anyway that perfectionism is just another obsessive attachment, that it doesn't exist as an attainable, realistic goal. I'm exasperated with myself, for forgetting that, for denying it. Hell, Lynz, I swear, I don't even know what perfection looks like, but that doesn't stop me from thinking I can create it.

"Like my 'perfect performance' picture in which I say the 'right' things, Justin and I share an epiphany that heals EVERYTHING ...Then when something like the session doesn't go that magical-thinking way...well then I can feel badly all over again and keep reaching for another 'perfection.'"

She is silent for several seconds, clears her voice, and says,

"Yeah, and then we can too... Justin and me... we can feel angry or bad or sad that we weren't perfect enough too... And," she pauses, says deliberately and

slowly, *"then we don't learn what is ours, we look for someone else or something else to take away the ' not perfect enough,' 'not good enough'... something to take us out of our sadness, without asking whether it is even ours."*

This has been our conversation over the last two years of constant Program work; what she and her brother have to claim in order to change and grow and to realize themselves as individuals. Both of us allow silence to center us, perhaps knowing any other talk would be premature and lead us someplace we are not yet prepared to go.

In the pause, I imagine her with her abundant jumble of dark spiral curls, her deliberate almond-shaped eyes. Poised at the knowingness of womanhood, lithe, lean, and nearly as tall as her brother, she shares his sensitivity; his inner compass for true north. But unlike Justin, who attacks anything that makes his skin crawl, she turns her senses into a second sight. And turns that into compassion. She is unlikely to pounce, but rather purrs and embraces resistance into understanding.

She wants me to know that she and Justin cannot be easily separated into convenient parental columns of good or bad child or funny child or sensitive one.   In this way she is telling me they share too much to be anything more than opposite sides of one coin or the reflecting chambers of one red heart. Same energy but different manifestation. She knows I respect that I cannot define her. She will stand in her own truth, in who she is deciding to become.

Lyndsey breaks the silence, says that she got the message I left on her voicemail after last night's session, wishes she had been home to talk, and asks how today went. We talk about the statistics of this morning's staff reports. I don't hide the despair that I believe we all felt listening to it. The enemy can feel so big, so ubiquitous. I admit how challenging it is to keep my head above the invisible water line of fear. *"Drowning in negative numbers,"* that is how it felt. I tell her about Heather, the ride to the apartment, and Justin's roommates. We laugh together about his friendly combatant relationship with them.

"Mom, you don't think he's any different there than any other place do you?"

Anyway, she adds, it's what I love about him, no pretensions. He never acts one way in front of you and another behind your back; never takes anyone else to task without questioning his own motives. We laugh together remembering occasions when his big-hearted sensitivity used jokes and sarcasm to light up a room, poking holes in whatever was being forced into hiding. He has no choice but to expose whatever is there, Lyndsey says. Feeling the discomfort of denial or lies makes him physically ill, nervous, and jumpy. She's wistful, says, *"I wish I was there with you... wish we were sharing this."*

She understands the roller coaster of emotion, says she finds the work of the same recovery Programs often leaves her emotionally drained, intellectually challenged, uncomfortably confronted. But, she assures me,

"We have come too far, know too much to turn back... I get a little more understanding, dig a little deeper, then think, 'well if that is so, then how about this next thing?' and then I know I have to go on until I have unraveled the entire truth of my life... even if it feels bad at times, even if I wish it would all go away."

Yes, I tell her, energized by her understanding and sympathy, I love and hate this work. I get damned tired of it, of repeating the Serenity Prayer and hearing the Twelve Steps. And then in the next minute I cling to every syllable, begging for relief, knowing there is no guarantee. The work itself only satisfies for a moment. Because in the next, another layer of questions bubbles under my skin, tickles my mind challenging me to expose it. The rewards of business are so tangible I tell her, the workplace has concrete payoffs. But in the work of the Program, of the spiritual path, of emotional healing, each small step leaves me exhausted and raw on one hand, and triumphant on the other. But clear, too, that no discernable goal line is in sight. I remind her of a favorite quote, *"Thank you for the tests that have formed me; for the will to go on."*

She interrupts the last of it, oh that was really nice, Mom, she teases, and, *"Just like you to choose 'tests' and 'will' for the standards."*

I begin to protest, stop and reflect, laugh instead, *"Just be glad you weren't raised a long-suffering Catholic girl... you only got it on the second generation bounce."*

But, I question it now myself, the use of suffering as a test to prove that lessons are valuable and learned? I toss it over in my mind. Sounds right but a little crazy too, I admit. Lyndsey is quick to agree. This quote is better, I tell her: *"It was grace that got me here, grace that will see me through."* Better, she tells me, much better. The suffering will find us, won't it? No need to call it in, sometimes only grace can see us through. Maybe it is all grace, the suffering too. Yes, we say to each other, maybe.

We talk on about her Al-Anon sponsor, a recommendation but not a requirement of recovery Programs. Sponsors provide mentoring that comes with the price of exacting attention to the principles and process of the Program. It means reporting progress to another who has walked this way. There's less chance to shirk or weaken at the prospect of painful self-examination when someone whose been there agrees to listen. She tells me her sponsor is her confidante and teacher. That the woman, Jane, has been especially helpful since one of Lyndsey's four roommates decided to get sober. The impact on their social life, two very pretty, popular college juniors who are now not the life of bar binge parties, might have been too dramatic a change without a guide. It's tough not to fit in, she says, after spending so much of her young life trying to do just that. And tougher still to find a new way to present herself to the world. Especially, she says, as that new way is still vague, unformed, foreign.

Yes, I tell her, but the hardest part for me, *"is how to present myself to myself."*

She questions that, says keep talking it out for me, Mom. I don't know, I say, but so much comes up for examination, study and thought. When I call on myself to act, do, perform, familiar responses don't necessarily behave. It's as if old patterns quiver, trying to decide whether to go through rehearsed steps and behaviors and can't quite respond on cue. I can feel glaciers move within me wanting to redefine my interior landscape, but the movement is slow, is like you said, unformed, vague. I stop there, to say more would be premature, would tempt truth and resolve. I liked living in my head all these years, I admit, where I thought I knew all the answers. I could argue and debate with myself. Making up answers that eventually satisfied ego and drive with plans and action. Doesn't work anymore, I tell her. Yes, she says, pauses, thinks a moment, yes, I know. I rest in the quiet of our last thoughts, neither of us speaking. I weigh what I want her to know, decide it is worth the risk of our intimacy, steady my voice, and say,

"Lynz, I want you to know this, too. I was surprised to find that Justin would rather accept all the blame for whatever has happened to him, to all of us, than look at the family as a whole. I'm sure we don't understand all this family system stuff, but it seems clear that both Justin and I would rather take a beating, encourage self-blame and guilt, than understand too much of something larger."

I pause to let her consider that, and then say I hope she knows that although we are all different, no one should be burdened with more responsibility for the system than is rightfully theirs. The system is primarily a creation of her parents, as I understand it, in which she and Justin play significant, influential roles, but it is still a pattern of relating not controlled by any one person, least of all the children.

I hear her voice catch, she retrieves it, and waits. Then she says, thanks, Mom. She's not sure what will come up for her in all this, but that I am right, she can feel the burden too.

"Not of blame or guilt so much as just feeling responsible for other people's happiness. Not that you did it to me, Mom, but just that it is there—that feeling gnawing at me that things won't work if I am not able to make everyone happy"

My resistance to accepting my daughter's interpretation of her life is obvious to me. I feel the temptation to try and change her mind before it's made up, explain away the past, unburden her, and in doing so, relieve myself of guilt. I hear the struggle within between courage and cowardice, and say nothing. She needs only to be heard and respected. So I sit and let her honest and tender phrases settle into me.

Sometimes, I finally remind us both, accepting all the responsibility appears to be the bravest thing to do but is actually far less courageous than continuing to question and challenge the boundaries of the family system. The easy answers don't drive you to fundamental understanding.

"They actually give you an escape route out of the deeper work."

Yes, she says, and worse, they keep in place the family myths and identities *"exactly the ones that make us sick in the first place."*

I agree with her, acknowledge we are coming to understand the same things in our own ways. All that we have shared is a lot. We are at a mutual resting place and do not press for more from each other. We end by saying loving goodnights. I promise to call as soon as I get a chance after the next sessions, she sends her love to her brother.

"Please tell him I miss him, she says. Tell him I'll be there next time."

I turn back to the journal, reread what I have written from Ann's direction, add Lyndsey's insightful words, and note my extreme good fortune at having her in my life.

* * *

Journal Entry, Anchor, 1990:
Here is what people *don't* tell you about the recovery movement, about this Program: they don't say that if you really and fully immerse yourself in it, if you take and explore all of the steps, search out the right questions… accept all the demanding answers… if you are

rigorous (OH IT TAKES RIGOR ALRIGHT!) and brave (that too!) and disciplined, it will tear you limb from limb, the skin off muscle, the ligament off bone. You will feel your heart rip out of your body. It will do this more than you think you can bear. You will imagine your own death. In ways that are mysterious you will die. And then, only then, you may begin to see the person God intended you to be all along.

~ 31 ~

I lapse into a nap until the phone rings at 5:30 P.M. jarring me to semi-consciousness. The glare of red sunset behind thin hotel curtains, my journal still spread across my knees, reminds me where I am. Must be Lyndsey calling back. But I hesitate, fearing an emergency; Kate conveying a business crisis, real or imagined. Dread the stomach-drop possibility of a deal going sideways or coming apart that would interrupt this weekend. On the fourth ring I pick up to hear Justin's voice. *"Hey! About dinner tonight."*

We made plans weeks ago. I am immediately alert; sure he is canceling. Instead he asks, restraint in his voice, whether he can include two more kids who don't have parents here. He explains that Amy's parents came last night, but they went home for a school event for one of her sisters. The other kid, Clyde, well, no one shows up for him, not ever. Justin says he doesn't know the kid well, but he never gets included. *"Everyone else will be out with their families tonight, and I hate to see these two be alone."*

I want to woop for joy, happy he isn't canceling but contain myself, say, yes, of course, glad to have them. Ask about his friend BJ and his folks who suggested dinner away from either the Anchor cafeteria or fast food diners that populate the area. They're all coming, he says, BJ's mom and stepdad are meeting us at the restaurant, proud they were able to find a "suitable" dining room nearby.

"Great," I respond, eager for anything to celebrate, *"I'll add two reservations."* Anxiety encourages me to babble in order to fill the space. I resist and try instead to rest in the relief that I will be seeing my son and that silence, for now, is the better option. Another few seconds goes by before he says, listen, Mom, I'm sorry about the session, about the anger and leaving the way I did. Maybe, he says, I didn't hear you out, maybe I didn't listen. He explains that he went to see Don, his counselor, then stops, laughs, admits well that's not exactly true. *"Don came and found me."* They talked a long time. Justin says Don helped him to see and understand some things. Your words, he tells me, weren't clear, still jumble in my mind. But, Don told him that he doesn't have to understand everything right now, all at once, or even as it's meant. It's okay for him just to acknowledge his mom

found some truth out for herself and is really working the Program, Justin tells me. He stops, considers his words. I know it's not just for you, he says. I know that you're trying to understand for both of us, working for both of us.

A gulp catches in my throat, the strain is out of his voice, his energy is subdued. I drop my head to gather myself and read Ann's words in the journal still spread before me. *"He hears you accepting all the blame, if you do then there is no place for him to be accountable for his life… it keeps him as subject, you as object."* I want to jump in, brave the turbulence between us, make things "right," as if I knew what right was. I hesitate remembering right action takes circuitous paths, and right speech has more meanings than imagined. So, without adding more I say, thanks honey, hear my mind racing to add and distract, but, only repeat, thank you.

We sit silent for a minute, then Justin perks up. Okay, you know how this place is, sarcasm creeping in, I have to give you tonight's *"rules."* Anchor is about protocols, programs, rules, and the straight and narrow. It attempts to constrain and retrain what has gone unchecked and rebelled. We talk about "sign-in" and "out," curfews, and whose signatures are required to take two extra kids along. It's a minimum-security prison, he jokes, but I don't take the bait, contenting myself that the night has promise of good feeling.

Promptly at 7:00 P.M. Don pulls up to the Peach Tree Lodge restaurant in the facility's white minivan. No logo identifies its passengers or purpose. The kids scramble out, laughing together as they join me, Don following them up a cobble path that leads to the restaurant's ornate front door. I ask if Don wants to join us. Before he can answer Justin lets out a staged moan. *"Are you kidding?"* he asks. We have to see him all week. Don is not offended, says, thanks, but I need a night off to attend my "home" meeting, get my weekly fix of strong AA medicine. After all, he adds, mock seriousness lowering his voice, working with the teens tests my sobriety.

"We're so easy. The best group," all four kids chorus in unison. Yeah, how would you like to have the "docs" everyday, Justin suggests with a loud groan. BJ, blurts, *"No wonder you're so tough on us… afraid we'll grow up, be like you."*

Don puts BJ into a playful headlock, says, you weren't the only wrestler around here you know, then agrees, *"Right, he says, wouldn't want that!"*

Don knows Justin introduced me to BJ Friday night in person. So Don says, well you know this character, let me introduce you to Amy and Clyde. Both kids come forward; shake hands as they have been encouraged to do; say thank you ma'am for including them.

Amy delivers an open-mouthed smile as if she anticipates a joke or next move in a secret game. Blue mascara outlines surprised eyes that are innocent and excitable at once. Clyde gives a furtive glance, drops his head as he extends a handshake, his face red.

Don gives me the protocols; BJ's folks drive him "home." I am to take Amy to her apartment first before the boys. Amy lives in a complex west of Justin with three women who are also health care professionals; two nurses and a doctor who will be waiting for her. Clyde is in the same building with BJ, next to Justin's place. He gives me their addresses and phone numbers. And, *"in case of emergency,"* his beeper number. Jeez, whistles BJ, whatcha think we're gonna do? Blow up the place? Steal the wine? Never know, Don answers, smiles, but I'm not taking chances. I can't afford any casualties. After all, "you're my best group."

Invincibility, the doctors told us this morning, it's the kids' greatest enemy and asset. At this age they can't imagine their own demise. I remember, wonder if Don is thinking the same as he says goodnight to each individually, insisting on eye contact, a handshake, or hug. All four kids watch him take off, until the van is swallowed by the night. He has become surrogate parent, guide and father confessor, full of love and devotion, and tough when he has to be but without judgment. He's been where they've been and worse; he exudes inner strength and outer trust. He will tell the truth they can't hear from anyone else, and they'll believe him.

"Grease ala mode," that's what the Anchor cafeteria serves, Justin breaks the silence as we walk a few steps to the entrance. Everyone agrees. Justin says tonight he's having the biggest steak on the menu.

We pass through Baroque doors and into a circular foyer with high ceiling. Amy and Clyde are impressed, *"Wow"* they whistle quietly at the formal dining room. The maitre d' greets us in black tux, bends at the waist with a smile, checks the reservation, and escorts us to a table set for seven. I watch the kids adjust to the high-backed tapestry-upholstered chairs and the generous size of the table. They fuss with their cloth napkins; Clyde watches the others for clues and openly counts forks and knives.

All kids have done their best to dress for the occasion. Ironed shirts are long sleeved; Clyde's is small for him, and he quickly rolls up the cuffs when he realizes they slide up as he reaches for a glass of water. Justin and BJ have pressed pants; Clyde looks fine in washed jeans. The boys are newly shaved, and scrubbed. They look healthy and handsome with no sign that they are anything but upright, happy kids.

Amy is the surprise, I think, remembering her sitting with her parents and two sisters the previous night. The youngest was one of Don's blackboard volunteers. The eldest daughter, appearing haughty, disconsolate, slouched down in her seat refusing to participate, would have been my guess for Anchor resident. Amy sat between her folks, who looked like an average suburban couple, with a small bewildered smile as if she had been plucked from a playground into a circle of people she didn't recognize; Alice in a white-walled, no-frills Wonderland. Her father answered for all of them including his wife when any were called on, and none protested. Actually, I think now, they accepted it as standard procedure and if anything, appeared relieved, nodding their heads to him when he spoke up. Except the eldest, who clung to his shirtsleeve, unresponsive to his communal answers.

The server brings menus, asks after our late guests. Yeah, they'll be here, answers BJ. They're always late, he shrugs. When she leaves, BJ and Justin start teasing Clyde about his mullet haircut, from their tone and canned lines it is evident that this is a performance oft repeated. His hair is shiny clean, cut evenly to his shoulders, straight bangs brushing thin arched brows. As tall as Justin, he is thin-skinned, and rangy. He spreads his hands palms down on the table, and appears to contemplate his elegant fingers like a pianist preparing to play. I imagine he is readying a retort, but he just blushes and stammers, trying to stifle laughter. His shyness is matched only by his evident surprise and joy at being included.

I ask where he is from. He looks up at me briefly still blushing, *"Tennessee, Ma'am."*

Tell her how ya' got here, BJ goads him, why you're *"Miss Martha's pet."*

I try to soften the teasing, ask gently if he wants to share that with me? But BJ responds first, a smile inching its way across his face, looking at Clyde, he whines, *"Oh, Clyde loves talking about Martha, go ahead, tell her why you're teacher's pet, Clyde."*

Clyde basks in the attention, I realize, and doesn't protest. Justin, joining in, takes BJ's side. Yeah, he says, my mom loves these stories, and heck the rest of us have only heard it about a hundred times already.

Clyde shoos the other boys off, says, yes ma'am, they're right, I'm here because of Dr. Morrison; here on scholarship, he explains his voice tentative, tone respectful, eyes more on his plate than me.

Martha found him in a detox ward of a Tennessee hospital. She was visiting there on Anchor business, meaning she was facilitating the intervention of a doctor, outed by a staff afraid to take him on alone. One of the nurses who saw Clyde in the emergency room, motorcycle accident, driving under the influence, asked Martha if he was worth saving. *"She rescued me,"* he says without embarrassment, voice low, eyes shining at the memory.

We are all quiet a moment, but I see BJ's elfin face glisten with anticipation. Ya' know Clyde, he says leaning into the taller boy's side, Dr. Morrison's a little old for you. Don't ya' think, Justin?

Justin is quick to join in. He says he never realized this before, but now thinks BJ is right, that's probably why Clyde keeps this mullet. Isn't Dr. M. from Tennessee or someplace like that, where this "do" is still in style? I don't know, BJ responds, she might make him cut it, *"Ms. Martha"* has gotten pretty hip lately. Come on, the boys egg him on together, you can tell us, *"you have a crush on her, don't ya"?*

Clyde who has been silent for all this, head bobbing back and forth as he listens smiling, still red faced to the teasing, breaks into guffaws, and stifles himself. Doesn't protest. Doesn't disagree. BJ picks up on it, says directly to Justin who's straining to peer around Clyde, *" He's not saying 'no.'"*

"What did you say Beej," asks Justin, *"I can't see you. Actually it's hard to see Amy and my mom too, all you short people barely get your chins above the table. Maybe I can get the waitress to bring some booster chairs,"* he offers with fake innocence, waving toward a server.

Clyde loses any pretense of composure, lets out an uncensored *"hee-haw"* loud and startling. The two other boys burst into spontaneous imitations that send Clyde into another round of clatter. Amy and I laugh along until I try shushing them, concerned for the peace of other diners. As I do BJ's parents are shown to our table.

BJ's mother reaches out to her son, plants a big smack kiss on his cheek, nestles sculpted fingernails in his tight curly hair, hangs over the table, hugs Justin's shoulders with her free arm, and asks what's so funny? Looks at Clyde, says, *"Now son that is quite a delicious sound,"* laughs broadly, eager to join in.

Over Clyde's attempts to gulp down his laughter, she turns to me. You must be Bobbie, how are you? And who is this darling girl? Loosening her grip on the boys, stretching to meet Amy's hands and mine.

I like her immediately. She says her name, Clarice, and gives each of our hands a strong, personal shake. Clarice fits my picture of a certain kind of Texas woman, like Kate, that I love—loaded with big-hearted maternal abundance; whether they have children or not. They are outspoken, quick tongued, impressively turned out. Double-wide trailer living or high society, they are confident, open to the next U-turn on hard traveled roads of life. Of which they have seen many.

Clarice's eyes don't give away any hint of the judgment or anger I've seen in a number of parents this weekend. She loves her boy, is proud of him, whoever he is and wherever he is.

BJ ducks her caresses just enough to ensure the melting sugar of affection still flows to him. His ears are red, but his smile is rambunctious with satisfaction.

Clarice says to me, what a handsome boy you have. Kissing Justin on the top of his head, she says she met him at the last parent's weekend and has *"spoken a few howdies by phone."* BJ interrupts, says, *"and this big goon is Clyde."*

Why he's no goon at all, Clarice croons to the shy Clyde, he just likes a good laugh *"like me."* Still standing she apologizes for their late arrival, says their plane was delayed leaving Houston because of fog.

"Ya'll know Houston? The most Gawd awful weather on thee planet... Swear to the heavens... anyway we missed last night's session and almost overslept this morning, got there just in time to grab the last two seats in the back, heard you speak, Bobbie, thought it was helpful... didn't I say that Major?... Oh my Gawd where are my manners?"

She stops, introduces her husband, Major Jonathon White, says it with unabashed pride, and warmth. Now at home, we call him Major, unless he is *"par-tic-u-lar-ly BAD,"* she raises her eyebrows as if we are all familiar with the trespass. And then BJ and me call him *thee* Major, or just plain Sir, which he likes actually, isn't that right Beej?

The boy laughs but looks at his stepdad as he does, a shy admiration glowing from him. BJ is not embarrassed to stand, formally introduce the Major to the table. The Major shakes each of our hands, gives BJ a hug across his shoulders, tells the kids *"Why you all look very fine tonight,"* surprised but not unkind.

Clarice is rearranging our seating with everyone's blessing, trying to balance the genders, but the numbers don't work. I end up with Clyde to my right, the other three kids across from us, and Amy in the middle.

The Major agrees to take the head of the table after helping Clarice with her chair at the opposite end, but before taking his seat looks around for a proper place for his rich brown, rabbit fur Stetson. A server notices and takes it from him, and I realize he is several inches shorter than Clarice, and the same height as his stepson, whom he resembles in a number of ways. Both, we learn later, were wrestlers and gymnasts. Their build, coloring, small perfect facial features are strikingly alike. Only BJ's engrossing blue eyes refer to his mother.

The Major pulls up his chair adjusts himself to his full height, broadens his chest, squares his straight shoulders. Watching him I am relieved that Justin's booster chair offer is past us. But, I can tell by the upturned crinkling of Justin's smile that he wishes he had saved his short joke for now. The young server returns and, in a general sweep of the table, but focused on the Major, asks if we want to order drinks.

The Major fidgets, clears his throat. *"Dear?"* He asks, hoping his wife will respond first. Clarice is confused, grimaces at him, raises her brows says, well maybe some bubbly water for the table? Doesn't look at anyone but her husband, who clears his throat, shrugs back at her but doesn't speak.

I am smiling to myself, knowing the source of discomfort, but it's Justin who breaks the stalemate, says to the attractive blonde, only a few years older than he,

"See we're all alcoholics, or something like that... can't drink, except for my mom over there,"

He points me out, says she's not an "alchy," but wants to be part of the gang or something so stopped drinking a couple of years ago. I smile, shaking my head at Justin, and take a small bow at the waist, while everyone follows his finger to where I sit. Then he adds that BJ's parents are what are called "normy's," which basically means they can drink and not become addicted. But, he says in one breath, not rushed, or sarcastic, informative, and a little whimsical, they're afraid having a drink in front of us will make us all crazy, send us out on a binge or punish us. He looks from one end of the table to the other before saying, please go ahead, Mr. and Mrs. White, have a drink. We all wish we could.

Amy immediately punches his upper arm, BJ moans, and hangs his head, in mock disgust at Justin. The waitress is thoroughly undone, whispers that she'll be back with bubbly water in a minute and scurries off so fast she has to steady herself on the back of my chair.

The kids let out a collective howl as she disappears, Amy, reticent until now bursts out first,

"Justin!! This is a program of anonymity... remember? It's one thing to tell her your problems, it's another to call me *a drunk."*

She is half laughing, shakes her long curls, points a finger at him.

BJ drawls, *"A-non-y-mous!"* Says, they've beaten it into us, reaches over Amy to strike a second punch for good measure.

And besides, BJ tells him, did you see the way that waitress looked at me? She was obviously staring, trying to make eye contact, thought I was hot, probably wanted me to take her home, and you had to go on and on. He thinks a second, adds, ya' know, I think I'll tell her you're my half-retarded cousin who hallucinates after too many years of glue sniffing. A little whacko and can't be trusted to know anything.

Clyde's eyes dart between Justin and BJ waiting for response and retort, eager. Justin, surprised by the barrage, looks incredulous, says, *"Oh yeah, that anonymity stuff."* Doesn't apologize. The Major says, well Justin I'm glad you broke the ice; a little California Chardonnay is exactly what I need. He reflects on the happy relief in his own voice, stops, clears his throat, collects his smile, and asks more formally of his wife, *"That is, of course, if you approve dear?"*

Clarice's face brightens, she answers giddily, *"I think one itty bitty glass of wine would be okay."*

❧ 32 ❧

Only the phone's red message button is visible as I slip the plastic key card from the lock that guards my darkened hotel room. I pop on the bedside lamp, kick off shoes, train my eyes on the red light hoping it is a reflection and not a flashing call to duty. After twenty seconds, I concede the latter, think it can't hurt to listen. Pray it isn't something that will keep me up all night.

"It's your lee-tle see-ster"

Relief ! It's my sister Nicole, using the accented English of Hispanic friends from high school to announce herself. She hated being the younger one, following me and our brother, the comparisons and hand-me-downs. But in our forties she's happy to remind me that I'll always be three years older. Venerable, wise, I tell her, she smirks; older is older.

"Call me…don't worry, no emergencies."

Hearing the last phrase I think how well she knows me. It's why I asked her to come work with me two years ago. Looking back I must have sensed the fraying of my life before I could name it. Everything was in motion, my company, clients, the family, and me. When the pieces became hard to hold onto, when internal questioning led to more questioning, it was Nicole I reached out to. Not in the way I can say it now. Just with that sense that storm clouds were gathering on horizons, fissures and fragments forming from the push of wind, earth, and fire of life. If you need someone for support and balance, a second ear, an honest, if tough assessment, Nicole is who you call. If you are lucky enough to call her sister, even if you can't name the darkness that whispers, you ask and she's there.

I woke one morning, not consciously planning next steps and phoned her, talked her into leaving Denver and joining me in LA. It came at the right time. My company was growing, and I had to hire new personnel to meet client demands. She had raised her son, Judd, alone since he was three-years-old. Now entering high school he wanted, needed, the dad who had been absent most of his life. His father, Leo, surprised us, invited his athletic son to move in with him in northern California, follow his footsteps as a high school track and football star. The pieces fell into place. Her initial fears of midlife career change from the solitary experience of graphic arts, to the faster pace of national clients in a new industry were overridden by courage earned from her adventurous life.

Ten at night, I note the time in Atlanta, and if I call now I can catch Nicole before she's out to dinner on a Saturday night. I dial her number, keep the phone on speaker, undress, pull on the dependable comfort of pajamas, and nestle into pillow and bed. Nicole answers on the second ring.

That was fast, she says, just left the message a minute ago, and asks where I was, what's going on, all in one breath. Her voice, full of mischief and charisma, cuts through the distance with the intimacy of conspiring siblings.

I tell her about dinner, and Justin's jokes at his and everyone else's expense. Laughing, she repeats Lyndsey's observation: did I really think he would act any different here than at home?

I don't know, maybe, I admit, but it's funny to watch how he can manipulate humor and insight to fit the situation. I report to her the first night's meeting, and the comments from parents on Justin's ability to challenge himself and others to reveal truth, discomfort, causes and effects.

She won't allow me to oversell pride in him, says, you know what that means he's *"rung some bells, busted people on their bullshit."* I remind her it's a trait they share and what I love about both of them. I hear her weigh my words. Yeah, she says, maybe it's a sign of the rebel kid in the family looking for what's hidden before it jumps out from behind some bush and clobbers you.

I laugh and don't ask the begging questions: is rebel a defense to avoid helplessness when the tenderness and idealism she and Justin share gets overwhelmed by the million small cruelties of life? Do they fight back so the mind stops twisting, the heart stops wrenching over what is and cannot be changed? Even if addiction is the price?

But, she adds, distracting my thoughts, that she's not as direct or as funny as Justin. I don't know, I tell her, Justin says you're much better at seeing the "dark side" than he is, that you don't cringe and can nail a lie faster. Practice, she says, just practice.

Also, she says, I don't think I started as early. Remember when you were trying to get him into that great school in Philadelphia, and you had to rehearse for days so he would just walk around viewing the classes and the grounds with the principal, Miriam Brown, and not pipe up with anything? Even Lyndsey who was only eight at the time, practiced with him so he asked appropriate questions, didn't blurt out opinion or observations, I recall. Then, when the day finally came, and just as we finished the tour, wanting to get out of there before he could say anything, Miriam asks if we have any questions.

No, his father, sister, and I answered in unison. Yes, says Justin. The rest of us held our breaths as she bent down to hear him before I could interrupt.

"I really like you, Mrs. Brown," he said, *"but I'm worried. You're really old. Do you think you'll die before we get back here?"*

She was the kindest of people, smiled, looked him in the eye, said, she understood his concern but she didn't have any plans to die soon. Good, he answered, than I can come to your school, unaware that it wasn't his decision. It was one of his milder moments, Nicole observes, but the signs were all there. Now, she says, tell me about the weekend. I run through the sessions, give her a brief overview of parents and staff. She is most impressed with the story of the doctor roommates, having been an intensive care nurse's aide while working herself through college. They were gods, she remembers. The doctors were treated as if mistakes were not possible; their judgment superior in all matters. Has to be hell for them.

I agree, say that each age group, the teens and the adults have similar but different hells. Like BJ's lament at dinner, I tell her, his horror at turning twenty-one in two years, planning to have, as he said *"a big ole Texas BBQ,"* and explaining to his fantasy date why he wouldn't be sharing the champagne. Of course, I tell Nicole, he said it all dramatically, has a wicked sense of humor, exaggerates southern inflections, whined but was sincere.

The daily issues of sobriety for these kids hadn't occurred to me, I acknowledge. My only thought is the immediacy of survival. Long-term challenges just seemed far away.

They are and they aren't, she responds, not one to weigh things out, analyze them as much as I. Nicole is more spontaneous, exposes the tough nugget at the core of an issue without softening the edges.

"You're right," she assures me, *"survival comes first but that's the easy part."*

All the reasons we use and abuse, want to go comatose, avoid life and suffering, well, you get sober, the reasons are still there. *"When I got sober,"* that was the hard part, she says, opening closet doors, having skeletons fall out. There is not a breath of self-pity in her voice. Sad, she tells me, that they, that any of us, get to the point of needing help, but we do. Disease or not, good reasons for bad choices or not, the sooner you decide to take right action, the sooner you face the original pain. She speaks from experience. There is no judgment intended, no punishment meted out. No excuses allowed either. But there is that heavy weight behind her confident words.

"Does the original pain go away," I ask her, knowing she's still in process, but hoping she will say yes. She laughs, says, *"I'll tell you when, or if, I get there."*

I go on to tell her how BJ's birthday vision led us to another subject: powerless. BJ brought up what was really bothering him, the First Step of the Twelve. He tried to keep up his funny repartee but let it go after a few sentences, his frustration and confusion apparent.

"Makes no sense," he complained, we all work so hard trying to learn to be powerful, to be able to protect ourselves, make our own decisions, have a place in the world. But to get sober, maybe stay alive, we have to admit we are powerless against drugs, alcohol, that only a higher power can help us."

A damn shame," he said, made us all smile with his honesty and head shaking.

He never said why he struggled for power, why control, his word, was, as he put it, life and death. And I didn't ask. It's the unsaid rule, people share their stories, and no one disputes their validity or personal importance.

BJ's small for his age, I tell my sister. He became a wrestler, encouraged by his stepdad, who he clearly admires, maybe loves, but has only been in his life a short time. Justin warned me not to ask about B.J's natural father, so I'd guess that's where the story lies. But, one way or another, the boy was erudite in dissecting powerful and powerless, in letting us inside his head. Can't do it justice now I tell Nicole, something you just had to hear, made poignant by his age, and sincerity, his full-of-life masculinity.

"Maybe it touched me because I've wrangled with this myself," I admit. As women, it's true of us, too. We compete in a man's world where we didn't write the rules of engagement, where we are just discovering the muscles of personal, professional power without generations ahead of us. I guess, like BJ, we're trying to rise to our full height. And then this, *"we are powerless to*

save the lives of those we love, even our own babies." In the sweet sadness of the moment of BJ's discourse, I hated that I had no answer.

Nicole, accustomed to my stream of consciousness thinking and talking, is patient, gives me time to unload and piece together disparate thoughts. Even when she gets lost in my swirl of vowels and consonants, when her eyes roll back, her head shakes to calm herself from an outburst, she never interrupts.

She takes a breath, pauses, then reminds me she first did this work when her second husband (*"Let's not say his name out loud, brings his energy too close,"* she whispers) was sent to rehab by his union on threat of unemployment. The only way she could get to powerless, to understanding the concept at all, was to remind herself of all the pain she'd been through with him. I jumped through fire hoops she says, took more than one beating thinking all the time " *'I', the almighty 'I'"* could get him sober.

"Powerless is the only word for the total lack of control any of us has to sober someone else up."

We've never really discussed this, she and I. It was the one time we didn't share our daily lives, didn't talk about all she was going through. It wasn't until years after her short marriage to a binge drinker who turned violent under the influence that she admitted the hell of it; the fear and shame that kept her quiet and struggling alone with her son until she broke away from the marriage and the man. She never asks for sympathy, feels fortunate just to be free.

My guess, she adds, is that BJ probably grasps the larger idea behind the concept, the word, powerless. *"And you do too,"* she assures me.

Maybe, I answer, and add that it is the same in Zen, if we push into it, there it is, powerless means letting go of the small mind, means acceptance and knowing that true power isn't about control but about being in the flow of all life, including its pain and confusion. *"Powerless."* It takes an overriding faith I may not be ready for yet, I admit, I'm not as clear about it as I want to be. Not so I can really, "Let go and Let God."

"And, you know Nic, I'm frustrated by my own lack of progress. There is that pull to control my emotions rather than actually feel them, to make rules and take steps to accomplish something, anything, so I'm so, well, dammit, powerless."

I hear my voice rising, feel tears creeping into my eyes.

"Geez," she says, loudly, *"Here you go again with that not good enough. Shit, don't be so hard on yourself."*

Besides, why would they say, she asks, that this is a lifetime Program, but you think you should get it faster than everyone else? Back off, she warns me, it will come when it comes. You're there and doing the work. Anyway, there isn't a test on the last day, and you don't get punished, she adds. You will be allowed to go home.

I laugh, loving her irreverence, her teasing. But I am not sure she is right. I question myself whether Justin can survive if I fail to understand, on a fast track, each concept, every idea, the disease itself, and my part in it. I want to ask her, my sister, his aunt, can he survive? Can you tell me, please tell me, he will be all right? But the words stick in my throat. Even with Nicole I feel too vulnerable, too scared to voice my fear. Yes, it's paradoxical, I finally say, to gain control you have to admit you have no control? To be empowered, to live a life of calm, of grace, free from fear, you have to give up power? To win the biggest fight of your life, maybe of your child's life, you have to understand you are powerless?

Yes, she sighs in response, paradox, the only word for it. But remember, powerless is not the opposite of empowerment, that's what we want to strive for, that's the positive expression of power.

Powerless is the opposite of obsessive control, which lies at the root of addiction. *"'Powerless to control,' is the key phrase."*

Letting go of obsessive control leads to faith, to a surrender to a higher power, that's what the first step really says. And, she stresses, we are bound to each other, you and I. We'll do this together. Yes, is all I respond. And, Bobbie, she says, wanting my full attention, I called Traci as you asked me to.

How did she take it? I ask, but know the answer. Traci, our baby sister, thirteen years younger my junior, married to a prince of a guy, Michael, and lives in Denver with their five children. She has been out of the loop for the three months that Justin has been in Atlanta. But, even if this caught her off guard, I know she'd be as loving and understanding as possible, neither judging us or never looking away. I hold my breath anyway.

Nicole laughs, what do you think she said? She loves you and Justin, thinks he's a wonderful guy, *"the greatest,"* Traci told her. She said to let you know that he'll be fine, that they will pray for him and you. Nice to know some things are predictable, some people dependable in this world, isn't it Nic? Yes, she says, but we're lucky, anyway, the three of us. We have each other.

❧ 33 ❧

A few seconds pass in silence before Nicole admits she was dying to check in, see how I was doing, but wanted to abide my no-calls policy. Had to look for a good excuse which Kate may have provided via a stack of messages.

I shuffle piles of recovery literature for a pen and spiral notebook, say, *"Okay, give it to me."*

Nicole tears through the messages she thinks can wait, internal requests for assistance with a difficult client or concern over the procedure of a search. Says, I knew you'd want to hear this one right away and reads me a note from Howard addressed to Kate. He knows you're out all weekend, she reads, but he's worried about a possible emergency, says he needs to talk no later than Sunday afternoon. There's an ominous last sentence: "I'm afraid the press may pounce on this one, not sure what Allan and Michael will think! Could blow over but maybe not… best we talk soon."

I feel the practiced shift from personal to professional, the adrenalin pump into mind and muscle. But, with most of me still immersed in the reckoning of Atlanta, I sit and gather myself instead of bolting into action. Nicole works out the logistics with me: scheduled departure from Atlanta, arrival time in LA.

Even allowing for the three-hour time difference, I am likely to miss Howard's Sunday afternoon deadline. No choice here, I say to Nicole, asking her to call Howard herself. Tell him who you are, and he'll feel better taken care of.

I give her the rest of my schedule; notice I have two short windows between events. Don't want to talk to anyone before my private session with Martha Morrison; something tells me I'll need complete attention and all my wits. But I could talk before or right after the last group meeting, before I take Justin to lunch and say good-bye. Try to get Howard to call me here after I have my meeting with Martha, and get his mobile number just in case I need to find him.

Kate has also flagged a fax that came from the Katten Muchin financial team. They are questioning discrepancies in the numbers submitted by Wyman's accountants; the valuation of assets and relevant overhead costs.

"*Damn!*" Frustrated, I bark to Nicole that we have gone over these numbers dozens of times. Of course, I don't have the answers. I tell her that I hope the Katten team has alerted the Wyman group, the financials are their shared responsibility.

Yeah you're right, she says, finding an attached note. It says this is a copy for you, Bobbie, and that they have sent a similar fax to the Wyman management. This must be what Howard is calling about, she adds, maybe he got it first, wants your opinion.

No, I answer, trying to put the pieces together, financials aren't his area, he'd pass it on, and hope someone else could work it out. No, he has something else on his mind. You know he loves the media, doesn't get spooked; if he's worried about the press, it's unusual.

"*And, to tell the truth, Nic, if he's worried, I'm worried*"

I begin thinking out loud, weighing the extremes and possibilities, then give it up, knowing it's fruitless to postulate doomsday scenarios without the facts. I tell Nicole that as important as these deal problems may be, I can't let them make me lose my focus. It's hard to stay in this weekend process as it is. It's so tempting to find an excuse to duck and hide, find something in business, in the world, to make more important. Business problems are easier and can appear controllable. Can give me reason to run away from the commitment needed to be here now. I laugh, "*Can make me feel powerful.*"

Nicole is agreeing with me as I hear shuffling papers. She finds a note attached to the Katten fax, looks like it's from either Michael or Allan, smeared in the machine, hard to make out the signature. She reads,

"*Sorry we didn't catch these things sooner, but now that our guys have questions, we'll have to pursue this. 'The devil's in the details,' you know.*"

Nicole finishes reading, says, "*guess it's more than details or the Devil wouldn't be interested!*" The understated importance of the note is not lost on me, it's potential ramifications ring in my ears. But my mind focuses on one thing. Nic, I ask, have you ever noticed people use those two phrases interchangeably: "God in the details" or "devil in the details"? Isn't that interesting? Details come up for notice, how could God and the devil both be found there?

She laughs, I'm not supposed to have an answer am I? But I hear her mull it over. It sounds like one of those paradoxes, she answers. Actually more like a *"pair-of-ducks,"* one duck, two heads. One head wants God, the other the devil.

Anyway, she adds, *"I wish God and the devil would get together and work out all those damned details!"* We laugh, and make plans for her to pick me up from the airport Sunday night, say a "love you," goodnight.

At the last minute, not sure I want to know the answer; I ask her if she's seen Bill? Heard from him? Nicole lives at our home and I know she should have seen my husband over the days I've been gone.

Yes, she says, had dinner with him Tuesday night, he quizzed me about the Program, rehab stuff, wanted to know what your weekend would be like. Haven't seen or talked to him since, have you?

Yes, a quick conversation from New York is all, but he's busy, has a real estate auction this weekend somewhere out of town.

I can't hide anything from Nicole, but don't want to pursue this line of conversation too far either, not sure why, just know that I feel suddenly hollow and vulnerable.

I don't tell my sister that when we spoke from New York, my husband absently asked how I was. I told the truth rather than the one-syllable response he expected and would require of him a one syllable answer back. Sad, I told him. Excited. Scared. *"All of it at once."* I knew I had broken the unsaid rules between us.

He paused, said, well that's good. He didn't hear me, wasn't listening. I repeated it, adding that I was glad to be going and afraid too. He said, *"Well, good"* again, and I heard rustling papers, turning of pages. And then, *"Gotta go."* I hesitated, wanting to cry out for him but knew that if I did and he said good one more time I would fold into myself, and isolate. I couldn't allow that. So, I said, okay yes, good-bye."

"Bobbie," Nicole wants my attention, I feel myself want to squirm away from whatever she's about to say *"maybe you let him off too easy not insisting he come with you. Are you feeling that way now?"*

No, I say thinking it over, no, in a way it was selfish of me. I knew if he was here, resisting the work, not wanting to be here, I'd fall into my usual patterns, trying to make it okay for him, worrying about Justin, about their relationship, and not be able to be fully present myself.

"Maybe I let him off the hook, but I let myself off too."

She listens silently, then says, yeah, it's about staying in your own center, about not *"taking anyone else's inventory,"* either pushing them forward or holding them back. But you know what, it's lonely work too.

Remember, she says, that we're in this together, no matter who else does or doesn't show up.

Yes, I say, thank you, I love you. We hang up.

Grateful for the few minutes alone, I am slow removing makeup, am quiet and careful washing my face.

Notice the tiny creases down turned at my mouth, smile and watch them disappear.

I stare wondering who I am now, who I am becoming. Feel the tension, the need really, to hold onto something familiar, to someone in the mirror that I know to be me. Watch the lines re-crease with the tremor of fear.

"I am losing something of myself and don't know if it's a self worth losing."

Climbing into bed, yearning for the paralysis of sleep, I am compelled to reread the last journal entry and Ann's analysis. Is she right? Am I accepting too much blame? Can that keep Justin from feeling fully responsible? Or is the opposite true; if I can say my part, will it give him strength and courage to accept what is his? He has never blamed anyone else, none of us, for his choices, or their consequences. I am too inexperienced to understand all the permutations of this dynamic, unable to see and claim what is mine, what is the system.

Patience. Perseverance. Courage. Faith. Old virtues may be the only ones that will sustain me now. I pick up the journal and write, watch my hand move across the page, mind to arm to hand to page. Catching what thought comes, thinking and not thinking at once, pouring out watery words on eggshell paper.

* * *

Journal Entry, Anchor, 1990: hard to stay in a state of 'no expectation' without attachment to results. Thought I had it together but realize now, hours later, how much I wanted a magical breakthrough today that would set the record straight, free us both. The hard won truth may have been lost in that "wanting."

"No expectation" also disappeared with the wanting that poisons original intention, and J. would have heard the silent expectation I didn't intend.

There is this too, when the wanting pulls me out of intention I am far from whatever True Self wants to be revealed…

* * *

Sorrow, insight and fatigue leave me unable to come to resolution. I turn off the light, lay still, and repeat, *"progress not perfection."* I am not afraid of paradox; complexity doesn't scare me.

I won't give up, I say into the pillow and sink into the stillness. The Lord and the devil are bound together in the tiny details of wanting and intention, in redemption and recovery, and I am there with them.

∼ 34 ∼

"They like churches with numbers."

I think as I drive to Martha Morrison's office, close by the Anchor Facility. First Church of Christ the Redeemer, Twelfth Assembly of Jesus, and Seventh Congregation are housed behind glass storefronts, or in antique buildings swathed with fallow roses and tangles of ivy. Another tilts on its pebble foundation but neon signage advertises the unspecified healing that takes place there. A church in a strip mall testifies, in black letters behind glass and framed in chrome, that the time is near, salvation at hand. Presumably the Reverend Sullivan, whose name appears with the service times, is able to deliver on that promise. I read each sign to stay at attention; to not get lost in plans of what to say and ask. Or get distracted by what may be asked of me. *"Stay present,"* I admonish myself to *"be here now."*

The private meeting is Martha's opportunity to focus on Justin, on me, without the generalizations of "you" and "your" required by group meetings. Other parents have told me that she's likely to ask about everything from the circumstances of Justin's birth, to the family's addiction history. She's unlikely to share insights gathered from Justin's time under her care, at least not yet and not unless she thinks there is something vital you can add. But that's rare. I say to myself that I want her to know everything. The more she understands, the more likely it is that Justin will recover. She holds secret knowledge that promises transformation and salvation from the terror of losing him to drugs, to violence. To the fear that outweighs all other fears.

The acid taste in my mouth, my churning gut, warns me that I also fear hearing a message that would be hard to swallow. I know she won't abide fools; can see through vicissitudes of ego and false pride. As I park, turn off the car, walk toward her office, I alternate between excitement of discovery and dizziness of confrontation, confession, exposure. Chastise myself for any clinging to self-preservation. *"Buck up!"* I say it aloud without kindness.

I have less than a minute to cause myself more grief. At exactly 8:00 *a.m.* she opens the door with a polite smile and welcomes me in, gestures for me to sit across from her at a round table as she goes to an open file drawer next to her desk, and pulls out organized papers. I feel a lump form in my throat. Wonder if some steel well of perfect paper trails houses all my faults and my son's categorized, diagnosed, and revealed. I fight off the negative thoughts and search for something to initiate conversation, to create a link to her. I realize that effort would be false seeking, and she would recognize it as such. Instead, I make a quick study of her office and belongings.

Martha's cool professionalism contrasts with the vivid colors, variety of mementoes and copasetic chaos. Several framed pictures with family and friends meander on top of professional materials. She is smiling or laughing with all. Many feature Martha standing by a lake or at dockside holding up large fish.

Who are the men standing with her? Father? Husband? An uncle maybe? Tokens, souvenirs, lean against the photos. I suppose a number are gifts based on the handwritten thank you notes that accompany them. Books are everywhere, stacked one on another and lined on narrow shelves above her desk that faces a window. All attest to a wide reading selection: clinical medicine, poetry, recovery literature, current events. Intrigued, I say nothing and take all this in moving only my eyes, sitting still, contained.

I notice my conflicted feelings. I want her to like me, take me into her confidence, be a friend. Aware of that vulnerability I know I am also well defended. I have to loosen my arms urging to cross over my heart not to give myself away. When she sits down across from me I meet her unwavering eyes with practiced attention.

Martha opens Justin's file, thumbs through pages, without emotion or a pause she reads his psychological profile and educational scores. Learning abilities and disabilities are carefully catalogued. Clinically, professionally, she repeats from what I have been asked to submit earlier, details of his birth, patterns of early walking and talking, milestones, health issues, and asks questions, cool and detached, to fill in missing blanks. We are always researching she says, looking for physical, emotional, family history clues to addiction. Had to put my mother through this too, she admits, finally looking up at me with a tiny smile. It's the punishment for raising a scientist, she says. Data, we love data, *even when it doesn't give us all the answers.*

I meet her attitude, clear, straightforward. I tell her that I think it is significant that I was rushed to emergency hospital twice when he was a baby, that my heart stopped in surgery and again in recovery. Justin and Lyndsey didn't have any consistent care, I tell her. My children were babies, I say wanting her to get the import of what I think was pivotal. For two months they had to be shuttled between friends, relatives, most they barely knew. I was released from the hospital, and they were elated, mommy was home, only to be rushed again in the middle of the night, fever back. There was no way to prepare them. Remembering all this I shudder and hope she doesn't see it.

"I just disappeared, and when I was finally well, they clung to me, distrustful and scared for a long time."

I worried then, worry now, about their feelings of abandonment, left without explanation, without me there to console. They went through hell, I think, but don't say. Can she see it; hear it with as much weight as I think it bears?

She asks, *"Diagnosis?"* I want to say, that's not the point. Instead answer, Toxic Shock Syndrome, feeling my irritation over a question that seems like diversion, *"In the 70s before it had a name."* She looks up from her note taking. I see her assess how that history lays on me. There's so much more to it, I think, but no need to tell her. I want to stay focused on Justin, on what any of it may mean for him, done to him. I run through a litany of the past, the questioning that has haunted me with the onset of his addiction, mothering wrong turns, the obsessive mind games of guilt and blame.

How did I feel the session with Ann had gone, she asks, interrupting, changing the subject.

I want to push back my chair, unhook her eyes from mine, diagnose the question before I answer. There's a temptation to blurt out a confession, say I had a plan, it didn't work, that I screwed up but not sure how.

But I know she's not looking for the weakness of self-blame. It helps nothing, no one. A small voice inside me wants to beg her to fix things, to lean into her assuredness and ask the secrets of healing. I allow the voice its space, then find inner silence again, and speak from there. I say that I know it is only the beginning of understanding *"my part."* Seeing what I couldn't see as a young mother. I slow my speech, control tempo, hear the quaver in my voice, wonder at its source, pull myself up in my chair, so I don't look beaten or unsure.

Martha does not flinch. Her intimate eyes stay riveted on mine, her hands, fingers spread wide, palms down, are steady. She waits for me to go on, but I don't know what else to offer. To avoid a nervous ramble, I straighten my shoulders and stay silent. She waits a moment more then asks me to explain the word *projection* and what it means to me and why I used that particular word in the session with Justin and Ann. I hear the authority in her voice but no demand or judgment. It is important to me that I meet her here on this small field of engagement. I must find comfort and strength in what I have worked hard to be able to say about myself.

So I repeat what I said to Justin, that I was, maybe still am *"not whole."* I detect a blink in her direct gaze, adjust, say *"perhaps no one is."* But what I have come to see is how I projected, sent out from myself, the feelings, worries, even hopefulness, I couldn't contain. I know she understands the term, projection and the psychology supporting it. I decide her questioning is to determine whether I mean to use it in its clinical application, whether I understand it fully. I wait for her to stop me. When she doesn't, I add that Justin never completely accepted the face I showed the world, that I believed about myself. I choose my words carefully and try not to look away into the scenes of the past that slither across my mind's eye. He always knew something else was up, I add, even when I was in denial.

"Hypersensitive," she says, nothing more. Yes, I agree, he could catch nuance, correction of down-turned eyes, forced smiles, but he couldn't contain it, and so acted it out. No, I say, knowing she will object, not just *"my stuff,"* he has his own to account for too. Still, to carry my denial, delusion, well, it's more than he should have to bear. And, now that I understand, I want to take it back, be accountable for all of who I am; unburden him. Strengthen myself. Here at Anchor, he should be free to do *"his work,"* not slog through the issues I didn't claim. I thought it time, I tell her, my voice dry, but resolute, to tell him that.

We sit silently for enough time that I find it hard to be still. I think to explain, to spill out that I was fully engaged with mothering, that my own are the dearest relationships of my life, no sacrifice too great, no task too small, as long as it is for them. Empty mind chatter and defense nibble at my insides, spill out.

"Are you the only one with projections? The only one who lives with Justin?"

Her question startles me out of the revisioning of the past. Of course not, I answer, but hear my indecision. The question seems off-base. I spent so much time twisting on the hook of self- examination, untying every knot, that the teachings on projection provided a closure; the catchall reality.

"There's his father, isn't there," she asks, *"and a sister I believe?"* Yes, but… I begin to answer. She runs over my objection, says, doesn't ask; *"extended family close by and far."*

Stammering I summon arguments. Yes, but I was the closest to him, the responsible parent. I want to end this line of questioning. I don't want to get off on a tangent, do all the talking but then leave without specific answers, without a game plan.

And, I add, the way I understand, it's not my role to *"assign blame."* Don't they say that in all the recovery information *"take only your own moral inventory…if there's one finger pointing out, there's three pointing in"* Isn't that the way it's said? I ask with authority, sure of my position. Again we sit for quiet seconds, she studying me openly, me assessing her calculations

Funny, she says, that you won't assess blame to others but are quick to assign it to yourself. It's not blame we want you to focus on, it's understanding. She tells me that they want everyone to look at core issues, at the entire system, the family as a whole.

"You want to examine the steering wheel without looking at the engine; the role of the tires; how the car is put together. *"Or"* she suggests, *"you would diagnose the cancer, by observing the tumor without seeing where it is attached, what protected the body from it, or contributed to its growth."*

Of course I understand, I am new to systems thinking applied this way, but know it from business, and my interests in the environment. I don't want to appear totally lame, but don't move to agree. Something fundamental to my thinking slows a response, tries to conjure argument.

"Unless a perfect Being, no one who's ever stepped through that door," Martha says with a laugh *"Someone who is aware of all internal dynamics instantaneously, then we all project, cast those dynamics-fear, obsession, prejudice, personal peculiarity out into whatever environment, group, relationship, the world at large, we engage."* "And on each other." That's correct isn't it, Bobbie? In the way you have come to understand *projection*?

The question is a testing of my work, threatens my redemption strategy: take back my part in order to free my son and myself. Maybe it can't be as easy, but it held promise of a breakthrough.

"Yes, of course if you say it that way, it would take a Perfect Being, no, I don't know any either, to be fully aware at all times of their interior landscape, to never project fears, or dreams, injuries or hopes onto others, but...

She cuts me off, says in her flat but consistently determined tone, *"That is what Justin is beginning to understand,"* partly because, as the teens say, we *"shove family systems down their throats."* But also because Justin is keen in his observations; wise in a *"Wiley Coyote kind of way."* He knows there isn't, *"wasn't,"* she emphasizes, only you, his mom, in his world.

He wants to be strong and clear enough to accept his part. He is starting to realize he can't do that until and unless the entire system is understandable, until the patterns of relating are revealed, and he can see how they connect and particularly to him.

Justin argues against the importance of the family as system, shuts down at times, refuses to consider new information. We all do, she assures me.

"We all want to protect our tight little worlds. But, your son has a singular advantage because he can't abide a false reality for long. And so, in his own way, sometimes kicking and screaming and slamming doors behind him, he keeps moving forward.

Martha waits for a minute to see how I will take that all in then asks, *"Understood?"* I nod yes, not sure. She lowers her voice, says that it takes courage to speak to my son as I have done, but that I can't allow myself to stop there. If you do, she warns me, you will miss vital puzzle pieces.

"Incomplete examination will elicit incorrect diagnosis."

To stop now, to decide it's about you, your mothering, your projections, is brave and incomplete. And, she adds, injurious to the person you most want to help. Justin. Stop there, she warns, her strong gaze holding me in place, and you will be blinded, and discount the roles played by everyone else in the system. More importantly, you will lose the patterns that create the system, connect us to each other, and influence everything from the choices we make to our responsibility to the whole. The very heart of the patterns of relating and relationship will never be seen and accounted for. You will stay in self-determined roles: you the responsible parent, Justin the identified patient. The circle never expanded, never understood.

"By looking at only your part, you will condemn your son to continue patterns limited in accountability. When you are the only accountable person, you take away

not only the accountability of the entire system but Justin's responsibility to himself and to the whole."

And, disease won't heal, but, instead become more powerful. *"It's a paradox,"* she concludes.

I feel, more than understand the rightness of her words. I don't respond but sit in the conflict of emotion. It is insane to take responsibility for the entirety, for the projected universe, for generational patterns and the systems created. But to question means loss of safety. Insane as it is, safe is in control of the pieces. Unsafe is not knowing where more examination will take me: into pasts I am happy to forget, into present and future where revelations may bring suffering?

Addiction isn't just a wake-up call for the addict, I realize, it's an intervention of the system itself. All interventions tear apart constructed realities and create choice, but choice of what?

"Change feels like death to the system," I remember her saying; *"Transformation like total devastation."*

Cycles upon cycles of creation, destruction, tornadoes of change, stretch out before my tangled mind.

❧ 35 ❧

I look down at the table to collect myself, not allow monkey mind to take me swinging branch to branch. When I look up, I try to be as direct in gaze and voice as she has been with me.

"Two dots... you are saying I only want to connect two dots."

In a pattern woven from complexity, immense beauty, the music and dance of relating and creating relationship, past, present and future, I want there to be only two dots: *"him to me and me back to him."*

That desire leaves out all the other dots; his father who is my husband, his sister, our daughter, all the interdependent lines and threads to grandparents, relatives and friends, schools, community. Intricate weaving tightens into a static cord when thousands of colorful threads give way to two dots, one line. A straight line connecting two dots, I think but don't say, is not the whole pattern but it is complete in its own way. Connect "bad mother" dot to "injured son" dot and be done with it.

"I can take responsibility for myself and may still be able to influence my son along a straight line. But to consider other actors, include all dimensions of relating, throws all the pieces back up in the air just when I thought answers had begun to fall into place."

There isn't any hope of simplicity, no sense of control or safety among threads that gather all of life into one net. As I think and say these things an invisible hand is at my heart twisting veins, ligaments, tendons, into a fist, constricting breath, and choking my throat.

She reaches for a small box of Kleenex. Discreetly she deposits it at right hand. I steel myself against tears as she says, calm and low, when there are two dots, the world allows the extreme tension of one to the other to dominate and control the drama. Others are happy not to be drawn in, not to have to be accountable. She watches me for reaction, says,

"When no one else is asked to participate, to take responsibility, then no one else has to stand up and tell the truth, or be accountable for what rightly is their part."

I don't know your family, she says, but I know Justin, and he wants to be accountable. Just as you don't want him to carry your projections, he doesn't want you to take responsibility for his actions.

"*He can't get sober any other way,*" she says conclusively. "*He can't grow up.*"

I sit trying to think in straight lines that will bring smart responses. Nothing comes. Martha asks if I have done, "*personal work,*" on family of origin issues, my husband's and mine. I feel a shift inside me from wanting to share and learn everything, to not being sure how much more I want to say. I feel surprisingly protective of myself and tender but don't know why.

I silently admonish myself, "*Don't be foolish… what is there to protect?*" I garble a sentence or two in response, get lost, try again, know she's hearing fumbles.

Martha doesn't prod or get frustrated. Her eyes remain focused on mine and unconvinced. I know I can't avoid answering, but I still delay by telling her about sharing with Lyndsey the journey of the Al-Anon Program, of recovery. I hear the words back inside myself and know it's a feeble response. I don't include anything about my husband because I don't know what to say. I wonder if she notices. She says nothing, but waits for more.

And, yes, I tell her, as a matter of fact I have worked for years, in one way or another, on family of origin issues. Attended workshops, done some group therapy, some private counseling. But, I add,

"*It's a little old…my childhood story… I'm a little old, to be blaming mommy and daddy.*" Aren't we all working to be released from attachment to the past? Isn't the whole point to forgive, forget, accept, and move on? In the last phrases I lose control of my voice, hear the words high-pitched in hurried inflections. I stop and wait for an answer.

Martha lifts her hands from the table and meet them in front of her. Coming from such stillness, it is an obvious movement, and, small as it is, appears to have great importance. She looks down as she stretches tapered fingers, holds them together in deliberate embrace, right over left. She looks up and I know she has discovered something she was looking for, as if it was lost there on her desk the entire time.

She doesn't answer my question. There are three things she wants me to leave with, she says instead. She hasn't looked at the clock but knows the pace and timing of these conversations. She pauses and I take it as a signal for complete attention. I lean into her voice, try not to lose contact with the penetration of her eyes until the silence between us is unbearable.

"*First,*" she says, create enough space in your heart and mind for the entire reality of the family to reveal itself. "*It's made of its own challenges,*" she says, but if you can stay open, while working only, and deeply on personal issues, then the history lessons, the present situation and truth of the larger system will be clear. She tells me that I've come too far to slip either into blaming or self-serving patterns.

"In the end examination of the relationships is still about your personal work, no fingers pointing out and none pointing in."

The essential question is what choices do you make when you see and accept the truth of the relationships, the system as a whole?

"Secondly, forgiveness and avoidance are not the same thing." If you move too quickly to forgiveness of everyone else, of the system itself, you will miss the *"opportunity,"* she chooses the word carefully, emphasizing it, of what is most important. What we are really striving for is *deep understanding*

Without understanding, forgiveness is only a gesture. She adds, *"maybe a gesture of avoidance."*

She stops here without the relief of an eye blink or a throat clearing to give me a chance to grasp her meaning.

"Last," the work you think you've done on your family of origin, on root causes, may have brought you a level of understanding, forgiveness. *"But, it does not show on your son."*

There it is, the gauntlet she dropped on the table lies between us. Neither of us stir. I stare, first shocked then searching for a comeback. No thought rescues me.

A thousand small arguments nestle in clusters at the back of my throat, crease my mind and wish for escape then fall silent. She knows this is the one challenge that will capture my heart. A ragged breath escapes from me. I know it is audible.

She unravels her body and stands, reaches out her hand as conclusion but offers no other solace, no opportunity for further discussion. I wonder at the sledgehammer blow delivered just as time is up. I shake her hand, smile, feel its tightness and abdication. I thank her as best I can, we murmur good-byes, I search a last time for a parting sentiment, but alternatives seem forced and empty, so I walk to the door and hear it close behind me.

The short hallway appears to stretch for miles. My legs rebel against the insistence on movement. As I contemplate standing here on this spot forever, BJ's parents pop out of a doorway to my left, start walking toward me.

Clarice is fussing over the Major's bolo tie, patting down his collar. He is laughing back at her in soft gurgles, nervous for a man used to battle command. They are nearly at the door to the office before they look up and see me, call my name in unison, and wrap me in gracious smiles. I am happy to be swathed in their generosity. The respite is brief as Martha's door reopens and although we don't see her, recognize the signal for their entry.

"Showtime!" Clarice smiles but shrugs her shoulders in resignation, and whispers *"How bad is it?"* She doesn't wait for my response. We blow air kisses, promise to talk later as they enter Martha's office. The hall again falls silent. A wave of despair, depthless, without walls or boundaries or limits of any kind, starts at my feet, rises to engulf me in a vast loneliness.

* * *

Journal Entry, Anchor, 1990:
I want to take this all in as Martha intends it, to easily, no drama, no discontent, no blame, connect all the dots. I sat in the car having howled myself to silence, and I think of calling Nicole and pulling her into this with me. Why? For validation? Asking her, haven't we done enough remembering? But, I don't call, I know I have to think this out myself, that I would be tempted to use a call to her as partial rescue and that I have to sit in this alone until I understand it, allow it to simmer and make its own sense unfettered by too much talk. And, maybe, I'm also not ready to reveal my fear that we passed it on, whatever stained and poisoned us from the past, that we have in our ignorance, in our denial and delusion, passed it on dot to dot, to those we love the most—our own children.

How much of who we are, of who we HAD to be to survive, influences and determines today and the future? How much lives on, is passed on, when we don't know or deny the past? How much of our carefully constructed lives, the choices of mates and careers, friends and relationships that we thought we were making consciously were actually driven from the unconscious, straight out of the fears of childhood?

The children we used to be never allowed fear to show. We were not shy, drawn back, or afraid, at least not that anyone would notice, and in the 1950s, no one ever noticed. We were not children to be dismissed or sympathized with, we were brave, and if not beautiful, certainly attractive, charismatic even, sometimes startling so. We danced and sang and competed, sports, school, stages of all kinds, we were class officers and leaders who won honors and medals at one time or another, for everything they handed out.

Our mother tells us, "never be common," whatever that meant to her, and we weren't, but we were also never consistent. We skid on the edge of chaos, keeping a breath away from total disaster, and we don't know why we can't keep good things going for very long. Privately we say, oh well, consistency is the hobble-gobble of small minds, and we are also never small. Peers remember us as BIG, big deals, big mouths, big personalities, big opinions. Big is good. It is alive, we survive if we are big enough.

We can be outrageous, flamboyant, clever, funny, unprecedented, over-the-top, mischievous, but rarely flat out disobedient.

We NEVER complain, we deride laggards, sissies, and weaklings of all varieties, and we never feel sorry for ourselves. We play hurt, but we play.

We gravitate toward winners, but we also gravitate toward the poor, injured, left out, thrown out, the sick, and needy. We take in dying birds, abandoned cats and dogs, four-legged and two-legged types; we move them in with us and nurse their bodies and spirits, and if they turn against us or don't appreciate us we never blame them. We never turn down the next need that comes along. AND, in this way, we dismiss all of our past. We all four focus on the next challenge. After all, we say, we're lucky, not one of us is deaf, dumb, blind, lame, or victims. Whatever else, we are never, ever, victims.

∽ 36 ∽

"Crap!" Lee Van Leeuwen tilted back his chair in the crowded Century City cafeteria. A friend of neighbors in Pacific Palisades, Lee responded immediately when I called to ask his advice about interviewing at Korn Ferry International. At the time, 1981, K-F was the leading executive search company in the world. Lee was a marathon runner of local fame, a *"real competitor,"* best of the backyard-variety racers that dominated West LA streets. He was said to understand pacing, focus, and strategy, and wasn't afraid of competition or the psychology of never-ending finish lines in road racing and business. He was also a veteran in the field I had chosen to pursue—executive search. As head of all real estate industry searches for K-F International, he had knowledge and clout throughout the business community.

"What the hell else did they say?" Lee found time to see me after I had been interviewed for a half day at K-F, meeting hiring personnel and a few executives, all men, at his level. His wide eyes and the flush that illuminated freckles across cheeks crafted in high shelves, gave away his disgust. Any wariness he may have had regarding his loyalties to his organization had been diluted by our growing friendship, and his propensity for doing the right thing, no matter the consequences.

I told him I thought I'd done well enough, followed his advice and been enthusiastic. But, I was told, K-F was in the midst of a hiring freeze, and since I had no previous business experience the best they could do was to hire me as *"assistant to a research assistant."*

"Crap!" he repeated. *"What the hell else did they say?"*

"That I 'seemed like a smart girl.'"

But, this was the world of big business, running with the big dogs, not across soccer fields or basketball courts like I did as a teacher. Business didn't have anything to do with kids, classrooms, art and clay, report cards and snotty noses. It's an adult world, much tougher, they assured me, looking directly into my eyes, either trying to convince or intimidate me.

"Mental toughness, grit," the men I met told me, that's what it takes to make it in the business where client demands dominate and daily routine

is dictated by stock prices, mergers, international politics, things an individual cannot control. Not like little children. *"Are you up for that?"* Be careful how you answer, they're watching for any girly weakness.

I gave them all the right answers, but, as they spoke, the last thirteen years flashed by reminding me who I was and where I had been. I saw myself as a preschool teacher with a group of inner city three- and four-year-olds discovering the body of a teenage prostitute stuffed into a garbage can on the playground one morning, the air heavy with L.A's sea fog and city exhaust, sun languishing along the edges of rising clouds. *"She's playing hide and seek,"* the oldest child told me as I hurried them back through the chain link gate, locking it behind me.

I thought, too, of sitting next to the bed of a dying ten-year-old at Children's Hospital of Pennsylvania. She was losing her battle with a rare bone cancer; I was supposed to be on floor duty and had sneaked away for my only chance to say good-bye. It took every ounce of courage to go back to the cheery primary colors of the waiting room where I volunteered as play therapist, with a smile, engaged, ready to organize the morning's activities, for patients, parents, and siblings. All needed respite from the wait for spinal taps, chemotherapy, surgeries that could save or extend lives but seemed medieval in their painful demands.

"It was all I could do not to laugh at them, Lee. Here I was having to prove I was tough enough. Give any of them a week trying to 'sell' math and American history to ten-year-old-boys itching for a football game on the last day of fall. See how THEY do."

I told Lee I wasn't confused or scared. More amused, bemused but irritated that the world was so upside down that these guys held my prospects in their hands and they saw my years of teaching and community service, as worthless. *"They should have to try it,"* I repeated.

Lee shook his head, laughed, and said it wouldn't matter. *"They'd just out-source it to an assistant."* Korn-Ferry was his venue, his career and company but not his life. He didn't take it as seriously as some of his peers and, he advised, I shouldn't either. Be grateful to whoever brought those memories back, he told me. Wherever this new venture leads,

"Remember who you are. Don't forget where you came from."

Where you came from." I remind myself of the story as I drive from Martha's office to the motel. "Where am I from?" Reach back for patterns and sources, as Martha suggested. Understand. I tick it off: started my adult years in 1967, as a fifth grade teacher at St. Brendan's elementary in Los Angeles. *"Beautiful kids."* A mix of highly gifted and "average," but if you love kids you know there really aren't any average ones, a few with learning disabilities or differences, unusual challenges, but we didn't have any of the labels in those days or any of the techniques and tools to help them. I learned as I went, blessed by great mentors, the principal in particular.

"What did she teach me?"

I struggled to understand parents who couldn't give their son, my pupil, what he needed—love. I thought in my twenty-one-year-old certainty that the boy needed enough love and support to make him smile, enough that he wouldn't flinch when I patted his cheek. So he could attend a simple lesson without wringing his hands and going silent.

What did the principal teach me? I watched her negotiate the parents into listening. Listened to her tender counseling of them, explaining our concerns for their son. When nothing changed, I stormed into her office sad and discouraged, convinced we needed to talk to them again, angry that her beautiful discourse on *"what kids need"* hadn't cracked the family dynamic open. *"You've learned a very valuable lesson, Bobbie. People can't give what they don't have to give,"*

It took me years to absorb the fullness of her lesson, but the thought has informed me many times, in many contexts.

When I saw her years later she asked if I remembered Roberto. How could I forget him?

"Beaten," she told me. It had taken her three more years to understand. A day came when Roberto refused to change into the jersey he had coveted and worked long hours on the football field to earn. The athletic director finally persuaded him to step out of the crowded boy's locker room and into his office to change. Although the boy turned around and tried to hide it, there they were. Belt marks so deep and long and varied they took your breath away.

You were right, she said, to believe we needed to do more, to understand. It doesn't change the basics though, I had answered, tears forming in my eyes, shock and grief dominating any historic rightness.

"People can't give what they don't have to give."

Where you came from, the patterns and sources. The late 60s, early 70s, was a rambunctious time. I worked for Cesar Chavez and the grape workers of Delano, and represented teachers in the peace movement until it morphed into the hate movement. I registered voters, educated my classes about Vietnam and the poor in our own city, and asked whether we could call ourselves Christians while Watts smoldered and kids, less than ten miles away, didn't have school books or classroom materials. Parents called the Archdiocese to complain, and I got hate mail slipped under my classroom door threatening all kinds of mayhem should I continue my "communist" ways. When Martin Luther King Jr. was killed, we saw the personal and public face of hatred in a new way. It didn't quell our spirits; it just grounded us in an exposed reality, and challenged us not to give in or give up.

My sister Nicole and I had worked for Bobby Kennedy's campaign, and dragged my husband along on June 5, 1968, after California's primary election polls closed. We were together that terrible night at the Ambassador Hotel when Bobby was killed. The next day, John Zaro, a handsome, blonde, smart eleven-year-old, told the class how his surgeon father had been on the hospital team called in to save Bobby. Mrs. McMorrow, he said, people worry about kids seeing too many violent cartoons on TV. But in his lifetime, he'd watched Vietnam casualties every night on the news, Mr. King's death, and now Mr. Kennedy's. *"Are they kidding?"* he asked rhetorically, *"Are they kidding?"* I had no answer.

When my own babies came, two in two years, I stayed home and tutored when I could find time. Partly for the income but mostly to keep me fresh and my hand in the game. *"Where you came from."*

We started a cooperative preschool because the local ones in Pacific Palisades had rules that kept parents out of classrooms. Found the incomparable June Payne, the only woman, I think, in LA at the time who had a degree in parent education, to run it, teach, repair bikes and the minds of young parents all at once. We struggled to keep the school alive, shoe-stringed our way into two generations of kids, and then created babysitting co-ops, food co-ops, community organizations that reflected the age and taste of our children's growth. Eventually I entered elementary school politics and took over a large project to manage the Early Childhood Education Program, organized four hundred volunteers to serve the local public school. That led to being chairwoman of the local school board, where the challenge became integrating the public school system at the most convulsive time. I take a deep breath remembering it all.

What is the pattern? Every challenge met. *"Where am I from?"* Enthusiasm and devotion, love and passion for the game, whatever game is being played. Full court press.

It was a whirlwind life. After years in LA we moved to Philadelphia for my husband's job. I loved my work at Children's Hospital of Pennsylvania and later my fourth- and fifth-grade classrooms in teacher heaven at Haverford Friend's School. Four years later we were back in LA, and I was teaching at a federal housing project where my old mentor, June, had started another co-op for poverty level families, the now nationally renowned, Mar Vista Family Center.

In the rare moments Nicole and I look further back together, and we have less to say. We never rehash the past of our childhood. We don't ask each other how we survived. What little we say gets hazy, confused and lost. Nicole eventually says, *"Just keep fuckin' truckin."* We laugh and change the subject.

Sitting with Lee, a half hour but a thousand miles away from any professional life I have ever known, I accept without qualification his advice, *"Remember, don't forget where you came from."* I nod and smile, but I am, in 1981, despite what I've lived, naïve.

Eight years later, in College Park, worn from Martha's talk, sources and patterns, systems and gauntlets of memory forcing for attention, it's that conversation with Lee that comes back to me, and I wonder at it. *"Remember,"* and as I do, the first chinks of a deeper fissure begin to crack and tiny slices of light push through my soul and into my mind.

∾ 37 ∾

Floppy silk bow ties and gray suits. Alternately, blue suits with white silk blouses. The one certainty, of course, pearls. In the early 1980s, as women emerged in business, the dress code said it all. In teaching, comfort and cost dictated fashion. As I entered business, in 1982, some professional women had begun to leave behind the practice of imitating men for acceptance. But not many. Don't stand out, not too flashy, and hide as much of your sex as possible were the not-so-subliminal messages passed between men and women. We needed to be taken seriously by the boys but not so seriously that we rocked their comfort zone. What better way than to mirror them. They were, after all, still captains of this ship.

I left teaching because I couldn't afford it anymore. I earned $18,000 a year, had one child in private school, one needing tutorial support, and had just encountered the dangerous financial differential of leaving Philadelphia at the bottom of the housing market and reentering southern California at the top.

But, I also was drawn by the *"next challenge"* touted by *Ms.* magazine, flared by ambitious women that the glacier of old and must be was in slow thaw. My family's growing needs dovetailed with a sudden rush to be part of something revolutionary; the move by women to assert themselves professionally on their terms.

For six months I researched and studied all types of businesses, both entrepreneurial and established, in which a woman could make money. I was looking for a business that would pay for individual achievement, preferably in the form of commissions. I thought I was ready for a pay scale that took me off of lock-step pay ladders. I considered everything from leasing commercial space (too boring!) to selling stocks and bonds (too frenetic!) to selling residential real estate (too predictable!). When I read about a career in executive search, I felt it was a perfect fit.

Executive search is a concentrated process that corporations worldwide use to hire key executives. Clients give assignments to recruiters, who conduct a process of research, search for candidates, cold calls, interviews of interested parties, contract negotiations and, finally, the placement of the candidate in the client's business. I love people and networking and creating opportunities and exploring possibilities. I liked the idea that the only product was people, not things, not commodities of any kind, but living, breathing incredibly diverse and interesting people. I assumed, since all the business people I would work with were pros, already established in significant careers, I would be dealing with clear-headed decision makers simply looking for the next best thing. I had a lot to learn.

I entered business with all the enthusiasm of the ambitious but highly uninformed. I tried to get hired by a number of the big eight executive search firms, believing I was a natural for the business of executive search. Unfortunately no one else agreed. In the early 1980s, those firms were all headed by men in white shirts and dark ties who graduated from the right schools and gathered at the right country clubs. Only Lee was different. He enjoyed mentoring me as a personal challenge, asking nothing in return.

Lee insisted on buying lunch, *"I'll let you take me somewhere expensive after you make your first placement"* and gave me a crash course on the search and placement business. He brought me a shelf of books, magazines, and manuals about the industry. He taught me best practices protocols, and caught me up on the current thinking of K-F, from marketing to conquering the fear of cold calling. When I couldn't find an opportunity in any of the executive search firms, he helped me land a job across the street from his offices in a small company that placed executive assistants and office managers for some of LA's most prestigious businesses, among them, Korn Ferry itself. Lee assured me that once I gained a little business experience on my resume, search firms would take a different view of what I had to offer. Besides, he pointed out, at the end of the year the K-F hiring freeze would be over, and he'd find a way to have me come work in his division.

I went to work for the personnel agency, patching together the few real searches that came in the door, convincing the business owner, a young woman who headed the company, that she needn't send them across the street to K-F, which would have been her usual practice.

Drawing on Lee's advice, making up some other rules on my own, I took on two searches. I interviewed potential candidates at coffee shops, where I gladly paid for the pleasure of their company out of my own pocket, figuring it was a small price for an education. I plied the candidates for information, pretending, convincingly, I thought, that I was an old hand at the game. I had no idea what I was doing. But by the end of the process I had two or three candidates for each job. I filled one of the positions, struggling through the paces of search and recruiting, alternately noticing my neophyte's jitters and growing confidence. By the end my appetite was whetted.

At the last minute, I called Lee to confess that I'd bluffed and cajoled and acted my way through a deal. But hell, I said, how do I close it? He took me through the right words, had me rehearse them back to make sure they sounded experienced. He edited anything too humble, amplified the confidence, corrected the digressions, and flattened out overeagerness. His parting advice was, *"Whatever you do, don't let them know it's your first time."*

Victory! With the fee I collected from that search plus the few dollars made placing assistants and executive secretaries I had earned $6,000.00— enough to consider making an investment in my future.

When Thanksgiving came, I realized I would have to work over the holidays and give up the baking and present wrapping that were my beloved traditions with my children. I hesitated for perhaps a second and then handed in my resignation. I couldn't be gone from home to labor at a job that didn't inspire me. My brief exposure to doing real search work, the hunt itself, negotiations, and stretching myself into the business world, convinced me my early instincts had been right. So between all the prep for holiday dinners, enjoying extended family, shopping and singing, decorating and playing, I spent every free minute exploring the businesses of the independent search firms. Women working alone or in small groups ran most of these companies. I asked them all the same question: were they interested in a veteran of one by-the-seat-of-my-pants search?

Everyone I spoke with was honest about the barriers for women. Despite the rumors of a brave new world, little had changed, especially in the established search companies. Still the women who owned these search firms were also encouraging, noting that the rewards of independence outweighed the advantages of working for the boys and climbing their slippery ladder of arbitrary expectations. Two of the agencies offered me jobs, one as a recruiter for marketing and PR executives and the other for industrial positions. The offers were generous, considering I had gotten my feet wet but hadn't proven I could swim.

I seriously considered working for Nancy, whose company handled advertising and marketing executive placement. She was a pro, and someone I could learn from. She told me I *"had what it takes,"* dogged excitement and a willingness to learn. She recognized that teaching, working with parents, and on teacher teams had prepared me for other challenges. *"Screw this 'playing with the big boys' bullshit"* that the tie-and-suit dudes like to preach, she said, there's a place for another way to be, to act, to succeed, and women are discovering it every day. I was flattered, but I didn't take either offer. Something nagged at me that I couldn't explain, not a plan or desire really, but a need for independence. I wanted to walk a tightrope without a net, to create something out of my own imagination.

Before we turned the calendar to 1982, I had decided to start my own business. It was flimsy, foolhardy, and audacious. Had I known more about business, competition, breaking in and being accepted, I would never have mustered the courage to try it. My husband was supportive but guardedly optimistic. His years in the world of finance, sales and business development were a textbook on the pitfalls of the competitive market place.

Once again I turned to Lee, taking him to lunch, this time my treat. At a swank Chinese restaurant in Century City, I shared what I had learned from the independent women I'd met. I didn't fear failure, I confided, so much as I did breaking too many past patterns at once, career and personal, labels and identities. But I couldn't deny the lure of spreading my wings and seeing if I could fly.

The timing seemed right. An executive I met during my stint at the personnel agency had become the managing director, the nonlawyer business chief, of a law firm. He remembered me from calls I had made to try and recruit him for one of the search positions, tracked me down, and asked me to come for a meeting in his office. Law firms had just begun using search and placement companies to recruit experienced lawyers. He explained that he had interviewed a number of the search companies specializing in lawyer placement and found them wanting in many ways. He remembered me, thought I was different and more enthusiastic than the headhunters he'd been seeing and decided to give me a call.

Would I be interested in working with his firm, he wondered. I tried to heed Lee's advice to rein in my impetuousness, but heard myself say,

"Yes, as it happens, I am starting my own business... specializing in executive search for law firms."

It felt like someone else was speaking those words through me. Lee laughed at the surprise of it but not at me. That was all the encouragement I needed.

∾ 38 ∾

I opened my business, McMorrrow Law Search, in January 1983. Guided more by intuition than good sense, I rented half of a windowless interior office, sharing the rent with Rachel, an energetic resume writer who worked mostly from home. Other small businesses, accountants, divorce and personal injury lawyers, occupied the rest of the large floor working next door to messenger services and Hollywood PR pros.

I worked at a rented desk, on a rented phone, answered by a bank of rotating and rented receptionists who served the entire floor. When something needed to be typed, I ran down the hall to the typing service. I was my own "research staff," one and only employee, sole owner, and coffee cup washer. My first address sounded impressive, 2040 Avenue of the Stars, Suite 500, sandwiched between the open air of Century City Shopping Center and the prestigious, Twentieth Century Fox Studios.

"Remember where you came from." I repeat Lee's admonition, as I drive back to the hotel, Martha's challenge tearing at my mind. What is it I remember? Being abysmally alone. I was completely uneducated on the world of corporate law firms, their businesses, governing structures or even the specialty practices that within the firms constitute departments. The fun and challenging parts of starting my own business were the short breaks between daunting and overwhelming. I teetered daily between the joyfulness of discovery and the despair of utter failure. I kept pictures of my son and daughter on my desk, asking myself if I lost nerve could I honestly tell them to keep fighting for their own dreams?

I had to learn the language of the business of law: "partner," and "associate," "corporate law and securities," "litigators" or "trial counsel" and how all those pieces related to each other. I fumbled often and came precipitously close to defeat at least twice weekly. My natural enthusiasm and determination were buffeted, held underwater, beat up, rescued, only to be submerged again. Some days drowning seemed like the best option.

"Potential candidates" never were truly that. They were more like the imaginary friends of childhood, figments of my own yearning for signs that I was connected to the cast of characters in this world of business. I got the phone slammed in my ear so many times a day that I often went home with a buzzing sound in my head. That first client, Cox, Castle, and Nicholson, a one-hundred-lawyer firm specializing in real estate, had left me with the impression that search professionals were needed and respected by lawyers. We were not. In fact, disdain and dismissal were better words to describe the typical lawyers' opinion of us. I had dreamed of walking a tightrope without nets, never realizing there were alligators below!

On the long list of things I did not know about law firms, was their members' deeply held institutional view that they were superior in every way to ordinary business people. In their eyes, they were the highest in the descending order of "professionals." My chosen field, headhunters, was on the other end of that scale. Headhunting for lawyers was only a few years old when I started my business. In 1983 you could count on two hands minus a few fingers the number of companies in LA's legal search field. And there was a reason for that. Until the 1980s the notion that a partner would leave his law firm for another and take clients with him, was not only rare, it was dismissed as aberrant, even crazy behavior.

Traditionally, lawyers joined a firm straight out of law school as entry-level associates and those lucky enough to rise to become partners of the firm stayed for life. Truly only a few of the hardiest actually survived the entire marathon. Most associates were "let go" over the years before survivors were admitted to the partnership. *We take care of our own* was the motto—more fantasy then reality, but still a way to propagate the comforting, no-change-necessary cocoon.

The 80s aggressive era of mergers and acquisitions on Wall Street, fueled by junk bonds and inflamed by hostile takeovers ended all that. The business environment turned predatory, as corporate raiders brought up the stock of target companies and forced them to submit through fear or force to their acquisitive will. New York law firms scurried to hire armies of lawyers needed for the battles that became nationwide. Law firms from Pittsburg to Portland, afraid of losing clients to New York dominance, followed suit. Suddenly, search, recruiting, or plain old headhunting for lawyers and law firms became not only acceptable but also necessary to feed expansion. I opened my business just before the tide turned in favor of executive search for law firms.

The following years brought the single most dramatic change in the history of law as a business: national expansion, in which lateral hires became the rule rather than the exception. In the 1980s my largest clients were law firms of two hundred fifty professionals. Today they are almost all closing in on a thousand lawyers per firm globally, with the largest numbering three thousand.

That first six months on my own was hell. I made futile efforts to convince law firm managers to follow the executive search model of corporations worldwide. I urged them to adopt the policy of hiring one search firm to represent them exclusively and to allow that firm, me really, to conduct a professional search, reviewing the entire market for the best possible talent, fulfilling virtually all their lawyer hiring needs.

The idea was too new for managing partners, the CEOs of law firms, who had only just begun to accept that they had to hire lateral partners and associates at all. They were suspicious of anyone in my business. It didn't take me long to tip the funnel and represent individual lawyers seeking new posts, becoming essentially their "agent," which was the more familiar way of hiring. That gave me a different in-road into the offices of the managing partners where I could continue to preach my new model.

I scraped together contacts to help me open doors to potential clients while I stayed up half the night, after doing homework with kids, making dinners, doing wash, going to Little League practices, and driving carpools, to read about business, law firms, the current events that drove business strategies.

The academic research and motivational strategies of success and failure, the power of intention, and the law of attraction also fascinated me. I studied all of it in Eastern philosophy and Western psychology, and wove these lessons into my personal drive and ambition and then used my knowledge to convince others of their potential. Why would any of us stay stuck in jobs and careers where our full potential wasn't realized?

Like crystal prisms caught in sunlight human beings sparkle with endless chambers of possibility. Of course it was time to explore all of who we could be!

Fortunately I loved research and reading and was good at both. Breaking into an entire world that was as foreign to me as setting up housekeeping on the dark side of the moon required self-education, but I had indomitable faith in a future I couldn't see but could sense and dogged determination. Fear of failure didn't hurt either.

The hardest part was being alone. I came from a professional world of sharing, the buzz of activity of classrooms and the constant engagement of children. Without feedback or positive reinforcement, teamwork, or shared goals, the rock in the road was a boulder; the few victory dances moved to silent symphonies. I felt suffocated by the windowless walls of my office each time the phone got slammed in my ear by angry lawyers unwilling to believe the future was happening now. With no one to commiserate or cheer at appropriate cues, I had no choice but to dig in deep and keep working, to buoy myself with the language of change, opportunity, possibility, and choice.

~ 39 ~

By the end of that first year I had learned, failed, recommitted, found allies, and convinced more law firms of the benefit of exclusive, retainer-based search engagements. My first New York firm client was desperate to hire. The young LA managing partner had tried and failed with the conventional approach of running ads or using headhunters who gave him and his firm no special attention. By the time I met with him, he was under direct orders from headquarters to fill an important position immediately. When I proved myself, hiring for him that needle-in-the-haystack lawyer, he was happy to give me additional assignments.

I marketed those successes with other reluctant firms, relentless in my efforts to break into the business. A series of opportunities opened that I parlayed into valuable relationships. Before long a small onslaught of new business poured my way, providing the impetus to hire people to join me in a real company, McMorrow Associates, Inc. In quick succession I hired Kate McNamee and five other women that I trained to be such personnel. I figured if I could do it from scratch, I could pass on skills, art, and what had become technique. None of them had an executive search background, but together we had guts and flair and a belief in our own espirit' de corps. We opened new offices at 1925 Century Park East, first with borrowed furniture and rented desks that we later replaced with fully designed common areas. Each of our individual offices had a window from which light filtered through the geometric spheres provided by the tall, angular office buildings of Century City.

Together we celebrated each and every victory, personal milestone, and holiday. Regularly, I bought flowers for everyone in the office, and presents to celebrate whatever moved me. We hired our children and the children of friends to research, and answer phones during the summer school breaks and were generous with stay-at-home policies to ensure that carpools ran on time. When some of our young workers needed help with college tuition, we created scholarship funds, tied them to community service and sent the girls on their way. It was the most democratic of companies. No recruiter was left out of the searches at the highest level. Where our competitors locked employees into working only with law firm associates or having no client contact, I opened the opportunity for everyone I hired to work with the CEOs and their staffs. A new recruiter was given responsibility for a client almost immediately upon joining us. We valued enthusiasm, street smarts, and work ethic equal to a track record in the profession.

In the autumn of the second year, business was brisk, and our dance card full. But the realization that a growing business had to stay ahead of competitors or die nagged at me. I wrestled with that thorny issue until an idea woke me in the middle of the night. In the morning I rushed to tell Dassie Kallenberg my inspiration. Dassie, nicknamed from Hadassah, was the first Jewish baby born in Rotterdam at the end of World War II. Her parents, both highly decorated Freedom fighters and resistance leaders, were teenagers who lived and fought from the sewers of Rotterdam. When the conflict was over, they moved to New York with their baby girl. Dassie was the queen of knock-you-to-your-knees one liners, finding joy in irreverence toward the high and mighty. She was also a successful businessperson when she agreed to join us, and a savvy confidant whom I turned to when I needed advice and support from someone bold.

When I told her that I thought the entrance of New York law firms into the LA market was going to be a land rush and not stop at the few we were currently representing, she agreed immediately. Within days we made a dozen cold calls to the managing partners of the leading New York firms, introducing ourselves as "experts" in the legal and business scenes of LA. We assembled marketing brochures that touted the opportunities of California, access to the potential business of the Pacific Rim, and recent developments in the LA law firms, and, of course, McMorrow Associates. Almost all the executives we spoke to agreed to meet with us when we were "next in New York." We made sure that would be soon.

One of the recruiters called her brother, who lived near Gracey Mansion. He offered a futon on his apartment floor for three nights. I took my small savings and bought a hot new dress, two couture quality suits, shoes and accessories from samples I weeded through at the downtown LA clothes mart. Dassie gave me the gift of a fabulous designer scarf that I have to this day, and we were on our way.

A week later, I stood at the entrance of One Wall Street. The whirlwind two years since I left teaching preschool near the projects of Mar Vista, California, enveloped me as I looked up at the auspicious skyscraper. The tumult that marks and defines the great city swirled around and through me. I laughed out loud at fortune and incredulity, bucked up my confidence to the strains of Frank Sinatra singing "New York, New York" in my head, and thanked the gods of impossible circumstance for the fun of it all. The trip was a home run. Eight of the firms we saw that week became our clients, and the ninth never opened in LA

We established our national reputation in the next five years, building on the growth of California and the Pacific Rim and the examples of the successful New York firms. Law firms from Chicago, Washington, and even smaller cities, established California offices during those years. They, too, turned to our company. We made sure of that. We learned to leverage our reputation into national search assignments and began representing firms establishing offices outside Los Angeles, first in San Francisco, then Washington, and then soon in the Big Apple itself.

Early on I created processes and protocols, search reports, and how-to manuals on everything from making cold calls to closing deals. Lee Van Leeuwen's advice guided my first attempts, but law firms were different from corporations in all matters, from the way they governed themselves to the way they chose partners. I tailored search business practices to suit this unusual group of clients, then revised and re-created until the line between technique and art blurred. We helped instigate a wave that transformed the law business.

In a matter of a few years, the growth of law firms through national offices and lateral hiring became an established practice. The once-controversial business of hiring a partner away from a competitor gave way to the more aggressive strategies of luring entire departments from a rival. Some aimed even bigger, acquiring a smaller firm to gain instant credibility and size in a new market, making law firm mergers acceptable. This became the new challenge in which we made our mark.

∾ 40 ∾

At the height of more success than I dreamed of, my personal life began first to unravel and then to twist and dive and tear at every stitch of what I believed defined happiness, shredding everything that I knew as "me" and "mine." Everything that I had created in the world began to look and smell and feel different. The thrill of the marketplace, of creating a vibrant company, of doing the big deals still called me to ride that powerful outer edge of the wind wave of success. Public acknowledgement, professional status still beckoned, but after years of denying my personal history and with the growing chaos of my present and very personal life, the immediacy of my son's addiction and my collusion in it disassembled the careful mooring to which I had tethered myself.

Unknowingly I put everything at risk, often with painful results, and followed the opposite pull into an inner truth, a deeper way that might save my son, might help me understand what and how so much good could have gone wrong. I questioned everything and everyone I held dear. Within and without, from the public edge of the tornado that was my life, to the inner vortex that consumed all light, serrated and turned and pulled me so far inward I was unknown even to myself. I felt I had no choice but to plunge ahead.

I agonized over every detail of Justin's life, how he was raised, where I had failed him, what I hadn't seen or understood. I taught in the schools he attended, handpicked his teachers and coaches and every activity. I was his closest companion and playmate. What did I miss, where did I let him down? I asked: was it the family, bad genes, a working mother, over or under indulgence? Can one love a child too much and have him feel it as not enough? Is it some dark secret, a hidden thing? Or is it none of these things? I berated myself for every slight I had caused him, for any misunderstanding. I reviewed every detail of old school reports and psychological testing, consulted experts, and former mentors. I damned both my family tree and his father's for the long list of alcoholics who had been tolerated, and for exposing him to his young aunts and uncles who were still college partiers when he was a child. I turned over and cursed every rock of societal and neighborhood influence. But mostly and all of the time, I blamed myself. I was the responsible parent, the one at Justin's side. If he had problems they were my doing. It was all I knew to do, take responsibility, own up, and show up.

In the winter of 1986, a client wanted me to fly to Chicago to interview intellectual property attorneys being considered for an important search. I considered sending someone else but the client insisted that I give the assignment personal attention. I knew I was burned out from conflicting demands of family and career, and a gnawing ache that had developed overnight in my tight stomach, but I downed a handful of over-the-counter medication and went anyway. By the time I got there, the ache had turned acute and I asked the hotel's concierge to call the house doctor. *"Probably an ulcer"* he told me over the phone, ordered something stronger, told me, *"no coffee and get home soon."* I struggled through two days of interviews, smiling, talking, worried, sick, and not showing it, until I could catch a plane home Friday night.

My personal doctor, Roberta Smith, met me at the emergency room, hooked me to an IV of Tegument, and gave me a sedative. The next morning she was at my bedside as I regaled the attending nurse with my story of being stuck at O'Hare airport in last night's snow storm, every lounge and bar crowded with hundreds of football fans, all seemingly wearing crushed beer can hats on their way to the Super Bowl. Roberta dismissed the attendant, closed the door and pulled up a chair.

"Bobbie, I've seen you go through more shit, Justin's back surgeries and infections, your husband's health issues, all the stress of starting your business, your own lingering issues from the Toxic Shock Syndrome, but when I walk in here this morning not only are you laughing, but you're entertaining my staff. After all of these years together, I realize there's only one thing I've never seen you do... I've never seen you cry. Why don't you cry?"

Before I could think of a clever response, I answered, *"Because if I start I don't know where the bottom is."* I heard my words as Roberta did, dropped my head, tried to take them back, amend them, but instead quelled by the meds, I reached for courage, the kind that came the hardest for me, heard myself say, *"I need help."*

Roberta suggested I see Cara Shenk, who had started a support group for families of alcoholics. Cara let me do what I couldn't give myself permission to do; she let me cry, stop questioning and analyzing and tearing at myself. She let me cry because I couldn't and because I had to. She listened and advised and nudged me to Al-Anon. I found a sponsor, and did the Twelve Steps religiously.

I took my personal search further, into meditation, Buddhism, Hinduism, ancient Daoist practices, Native American cosmology, the Christian Desert Fathers, and the study of the Kabbalah, and Sufism. All led to the search within oneself, the demands of rigor and practice, the refusal to blame anyone else. And, the letting go into a space where all things are one. I invented my own convergence of philosophy, spirituality, of ancient rituals with psychology and the tenets of the recovery movement. My daughter Lyndsey, and my sister, Nicole, shared much of my journey, but most of the time I walked the path within myself, quiet and alone.

Often I stumbled, eager to hold onto all I had that looked solid and important in the world. Some of the time I raged against loss, scrambled to control the people and context that used to be my life. Other times I pushed up against the tornado of deconstruction and smashed any convention, any old pattern that felt like it would limit finding an ultimate truth or some elusive greater good. As I moved like the Mariah wind through my interior landscape, pulling apart the structure of familiar, leaving no prisoners among my old belief systems, my skill at the art of the deal actually became more profound.

Crazy as it seems now, paradoxical and incomprehensible as it was then, my sensitivities to the nuances of people, their issues, challenges, motivations, became more finely tuned. It was as if I could touch the actual elements that made them who they were. I could see bull-headed egoism and pretension for what it was: fear and the source of self-protection. Where once I may have aimed at the frailties of decision makers, allowed judgments to blur a deeper understanding, I now found myself attuned to the core of discomfort, the humanity that lies right below the surface of even the most powerful.

Law firms are really just about the intellectual property, talent and brains of human capital, weak and brave. The peculiarities of the personal, and its nexus with the professional determine the outcomes of the deals that firms do for themselves, merging and acquiring, expanding geographically or by practice. Economics, market dynamics, financial analysis is essential, and often drive those deals, especially the mergers. But no deal gets put to bed without a weaving of the personal, prejudice and opinion, shortcomings and fears, brilliant ideas and lame excuses, all that human element, crass and profound, having its sway.

The more excruciating the decomposition of my inner life, the greater my sensitivity became to the tenuous, tough and tender filaments of people and their deals.

With my eyes open I also saw how my overindulgent sense of responsibility bred insanity in my home and also in my company. There seemed to be dysfunction everywhere, and the common denominator was me. All the "yes's": "yes, I'll take care of that," "yes, I'll fix that problem you have with that client, co-worker, money made on the last deal," "yes, I'll find you another answer," I now saw as stalling and avoidance techniques designed to ignore underlying and deeper issues.

"Remember where you came from."

I want to come from truth and action, from compassion and understanding, but clarity and right-effort had to evolve out of a deeper conversation, and so for that period, "no" was the antidote to too many years of "yes." The Teacher says that *"overgenerosity breeds contempt."*

I didn't know how to amend and change "yes." I hadn't dug deep enough to come up with the right conclusions. As things at home and within the company unraveled, I just started to say no. Not no, followed by a brilliant explanation or solution, just "no." And when I did, people left. They left the company, my life, and my family. My core group, Kate, Nicole, and Dassie, all applauded truth telling and departures. But that did little to alleviate the long, lonely, depressing path of deconstruction of all my relationships and myself. A tornado of change ripped through my life tearing up the sacred and profane, one and the same at once and together.

A day came when Cara Shenk said she found an Al-Anon meeting she thought I'd relate to, where the attendees were serious about their commitments to change and rigorous about the demands to accept responsibility without blame. The meeting at St. Timothy's Church, only blocks away from my Century City office, provided that and more. There were plenty of "old-timers," Twelve Step talk for people with many years of Program commitment, who refused finger pointing, feel-sorry-for-me stories and breathed compassion, understanding, and courage to change. I began going every Tuesday, too confused to share much but buoyed and comforted in the safety of community.

One day at St. Timothy's, in the school auditorium where the meetings were held, sitting in the shit from another round of worry about Justin, torn by my inner turmoil, of wanting solutions when none appeared, of feeling impotent, and afraid, I stopped fighting myself.

The Teacher says that *when you are sick of your sickness, you will heal. So sit in your sickness, do not push it away, do not antidote it, just sit in it, wallow in it, taste it, and know it until you are sick of it."*

That day I killed my inner critic, its large and loud voice, with its excuses and grinding self-judgment, the race to the next thought, which never was a solution, and sat. Nowhere to go, nothing to do. Surrender.

For an hour nothing penetrated. Words and people floated by. I stood when they stood, sat when they sat. Silence within, silence without. And then there it was. Unsummoned. Grace. Amazing grace flooded over me, coursed within me, released me into the void. Resonant warmth filled me, light poured in of its own volition. Everything changed forever, and everything was the same.

But, years later, as I leave Martha Morrison's, the success and failure, skill and lessons are of no interest to me. I sense grace on the outskirts of what she offered and demanded, and know when I open to grace it will present itself as it had that day at St. Timothy's. But some old anxiety dominated, and I couldn't reach out of it to grasp the light. Standing in the Anchor hallway outside Martha's office, minutes go by before I forced my feet forward, before my tired mind emerged from its lonely cramped space. Slowly, small repetitive thoughts nag at me, *"I have done that 'family of origin' work."* Sounds innocuous; it is not. I should have told her, hell, screamed at her been there, done that, and got the scars to prove it. Therapy, group work, Cara Shenk, done the painful processes, completed the course, uncovered the past, all designed to end in forgiveness. My mind-voice blares full volume until I hear the words within my heart. Fear. But, fear of what? Of what? *"Anxiety fear always hides always covers fear, pain and trauma, real and imagined,"* I remind myself.

Name the fear and you can uncover the pain, claim the pain, soothe and heal it, and it cannot scare you. I calm, driving on automatic pilot and try to find my center, reach, breathe and open to grace. I ask myself: "What do I feel when I see Martha's look so steady and so without affect? I feel seen by one who will tell the truth with a righteousness that has no regard for fear.

Slowly, surrender forms and when expressed melts a glacier of feeling. A long jagged scream rips my chest, explodes, and careens loud and fumbling out of me as I pull into the hotel parking lot done and spent from the howl of it all.

* * *

Journal Entry, Anchor, 1990: What did she say? The results of your efforts, of my efforts, "in looking back, in understanding your past, do not show on your son." Is it true? And what if she is right? What if there is more to do? Will I see patterns and dots and lines I did not see before, will it bring me peace and understanding and healing, or will it only increase the rate and depth of my life's destruction? Does it matter? Am I compelled to go forward under all conditions? If this backward looking helps me, helps my son, then do I have a choice? Am I too long on this path to refuse one more turn? Refusal and acceptance. One more gauntlet, one more challenge, the onion has endless peels, the road, endless circuitous paths. Am I up for it? Can I say no?

∾ 41 ∾

Shaking off emotional outcry, attempting to quell the conflict of personal demands and face the call to Howard with some level of professional concentration and demeanor, I rush to my room one last time. I throw books and rehab study aids into my overstuffed bag and reread the notes I took from Nicole. *"Devil in the details,"* I mutter aloud dialing Howard's number, hoping it's not too early in California on a Sunday morning. I remind myself that he expressed uncharacteristic concern, and like me, he'll be awake and ready to work.

Business discussions and plans can provide a counterpoint to emotion, and worse, a way not to face the confrontation of Martha's last words to me. I remember saying to myself early in the week that I can't live like this any longer and wonder again at all that might mean. I know I cannot let her challenge die on the table we shared but dread facing it too. It would be so easy to make the latest business crisis an excuse to compartmentalize, and choose avoidance.

"Don't make it an escape," I insist to myself aloud, *"Control is an illusion."*

Before I pursue these thoughts Howard answers, says he's glad to hear my voice, apologizes for the interruption. He assures me he wouldn't have called if he didn't think it was important, and then asks how it's going.

"'Best of times, worst of times.'" I quote and laugh.

Don't worry, I'm glad for the distraction. Anyway, being here is not too different from this deal, *"very tough, and oddly wonderful."* Howard laughs, yeah, I get it, he pauses a moment then launches into the problem that has him stymied. Been in plenty of battles before, he tells me, but this one has its weird twists. His anger and exasperation leak out. Checked with a forced laugh.

When he continues, his voice is subdued. He tells me that a number of the young partners have decided to leave Wyman Bautzer rather than wait to see if a merger gets done. They decided instead to join another law firm downtown.

"I'm embarrassed, blindsided," Howard's agitation is obvious, his voice heated. *"Hell, Bobbie,* he swears, *"these are the exact guys we were fighting for*

in the Chicago negotiations." Hearing him I feel my loneliness ebb. Eager to rise to match the demand, I am concerned, disgusted, angry, alive and engaged. He went to bat for them against his own best interests, and so did Craig and Alan. I say, *"It was the right thing to stick by them, and it's still the right thing."*

And, we were all blindsided, he's not alone in this. These same partners talked to Craig from Los Angeles halfway through the day Tuesday, I tell him, remembering how agitated Craig was when he returned to the boardroom after taking that call. They had asked for his support, inferring, if not guaranteeing their loyalty.

I pause, try to figure out the myriad pieces that will have to be addressed, sort through the variables of response and fallout while keeping my own emotions in check.

Are they committed to leave, I ask? He assures me that they are, that they're ready to announce and so is the firm they plan to join. They want to go to press with this tomorrow, he says, not hiding his exasperation. *"It's just the kind of story, the ongoing demise of a famous law firm, that sells papers."*

He's right, but we can't wallow in this latest crisis. Okay, I say, let's lay out the pieces. First of all, we all have friends in the press, so let's put out some calls and see if we can stall a full-blown story and front page attention. I ask Howard for the names of those leaving, note with him that Katten was not enthusiastic about allowing these same folks to join the combined new firm.

"Damn," I think to myself, *"always surprises,"* remembering Craig's impassioned speeches for a number of them, the hours, now wasted, spent defending their careers. I feel my concentration sharpen; strategy dominate my thoughts. Howard says he's afraid we, *"managed to piss off Michael in the process,"* and with this glitch may have to give up other treasured deal points.

I remind Howard that Katten Muchin is my client, that I have gotten to know Allan and Michael well. These are deal guys I tell him, nothing slips by them. They might worry that your team doesn't know their constituents as well as they should, and they don't like surprises either, but they are realists. Remember, they debated the inclusion of these exact partners not because of skills or competence issues but because they thought they were too costly for what their contributions were to the bottom line. Michael may complain about press exposure at this juncture of the deal, but he and Allan will both be pleased to have fewer expensive lawyers in the a final count.

Saying it, I know I am right; that Michael and Allan will see this as lessening the debt. They never wanted to put their firm in the jeopardy by striking too rich a deal with an oversupply of equity partners.

They'll be pleased, I assure Howard, thinking it out again myself. He pushes back, says Michael was pretty tired of the arguments for and against these characters by the end of the day, how can I be sure they will see the positive in these departures?

I weigh my response. I have an overriding obligation to my client and don't want to give away any more of what may be their future negotiating positions by being too optimistic. But I also must maintain my position as confidante to Howard, which personally and professionally is the right space to hold.

What I've already said is true and compelling; Michael and Allan will feel they got what they wanted in the first place without giving anything else up. It's a win for them, they'll see that immediately. Finally I just repeat my position, adding that there are plenty of talented young partners in Chicago to take over for the ones who might leave in LA That is the beauty of a national firm, I tell Howard. The very reason to do this kind of merger is to get access to the best talent across the country.

Howard doesn't respond, and in his silence I remember how personal this negotiation can be for him, so different from the performances he has mastered in the courtroom. *"Must feel like you went out on a limb for these guys only to find out they were sawing it off behind you."*

Howard laughs spontaneously, no victim this time or any other. Hell, he responds, I guess everyone has a right to make their own decisions when things fall apart, but still he can't help asking himself why he signed up for this in the first place. He hesitates, says, *"Well, I couldn't let Craig, Alan, or any of the rest of my team down now, could I?* It's a rhetorical question.

"You could, but you won't," I answer, not knowing why really, just knowing he has made commitments he won't betray. Anyway, you're right Bobbie, he says, his natural positivism returning, Allan, Michael, and their firm's client base, can provide great opportunities for me. I saw a lot of synergy with the Chicago practice.

He tells me a quick story about a professional ball player they all know, talks about the opportunity he will have to represent the star if this merger should go through, something he wouldn't be able to do at a regional firms such as Wyman.

I don't want Howard to discount the negative impact of today's situation with his humor and quick-draw repartee. I agree with his assessment, say it will have its benefits, but remind him that he did put his self-interests aside to support these partners. *"It still has to feel like hell right now."*

He issues an audible sigh. It would have been nice to get a warning, and here's the part you don't know, Bobbie. I got on the phone with Michael on Friday, just three days after the Chicago meeting, reassured him about partners he questioned including some in this group readying to leave. Howard laughs at his own vulnerability, a place he doesn't usually find himself, wonders aloud how this will affect his ability to negotiate, whether it will dilute his assertions on issues still undecided.

Let's handle these issues one at a time, I answer. That's what Michael and Allan will do, not allow one surprise to color the entire negotiation. But I am mindful of the deal's twists and turns: objectivity of some details, subjectivity of others and the threading together of both in one minute, the collision of both the next.

I caution Howard, this new circumstance may cause Michael and Allan to dig deeper into your collective opinions and want more objective analysis; they've already sent for additional financial information. But, in the end, their scrutiny suits everyone's long-term goals and relationships. *"Right analysis, better results."*

I suggest he call Michael and Allan immediately, tell them about the departing partners and media coverage before they hear it from anyone else. Michael and Allan are definitely in charge of their firm, I say, but they still have to collect votes to move the merger forward. We don't want to put them into an embarrassing situation with their partners, have them face additional pressure because we blindsided them.

Howard mulls this over, practices a line or two, and makes his mind up in a split second. *"If anyone else tells them it will appear as if I'm avoiding responsibility."*

Let's go over a press plan, he says. He hates to see this as front-page splash just as he and his partners are returning from Chicago. Hell, he swears, we're just gathering votes among our partners too, a story now could be devastating to the best situation, a completed merger, that would help the most people.

We talk through plans and how to execute them, timing and allies are discussed, who to include and who won't be helpful. We agree it would be great if we could get the papers to hold the story a day or two. Maybe by then we can reveal more about the merger; have the potential bigger deal steal the headline. *"Balance bad news with good and make our own splash."* I like the idea, I tell Howard, would be great if he and Michael could both be quoted too.

"Will Michael do that, Howard asks, you know him better than I do." I laugh, Michael and Allan aren't always easy to predict, but they will discuss it for sure, they'll see all the benefits and downsides. One thing that's assured, I tell Howard, they aren't easily scared. They'll take this challenge straight on as they do the rest. However, they will have a more serious concern that we have to be ready to address; Will the partners leaving disengage others who have been loyal and whom you need for a credible merger. Michael and Allan will see this whole affair the right way, but they may ask themselves whether this defection will shake up the people we want to hold.

I know Howard's got to be worried about this too. None of this is easy. As I recall, I tell Howard, you are a reluctant and embattled leader not of your own choosing. Rather than complain or seek sympathy, let along revenge, he laughs at the reminder. *"Irony; it keeps popping up, doesn't it?"*

He tells me the story I am now familiar with, how he joined Wyman after a number of high-profile trial victories convinced him that he needed more support and a bigger firm than he could build on his own. The very guys who caused the firm's near dissolution were the ones who talked him into joining Wyman, promising stable management, reliable leadership. *"Now they're suing the firm they led, and I'm here trying to save what's left."* He laughs, but I can hear the unease and stress, behind his words.

"The world is full of paradox and irony, Howard, I agree. I wish it were so easy as black and white, good and evil. But it's complexity that reigns, beautiful and terrible, and we get an opportunity to show up and play our best game. Maybe that has to be enough."

I do not say more. We sit a minute in silence and I know he hears all that goes unsaid. *"Okay, let's go over this again,"* Howard says. We divide up the calls; agree on the facts we are able to discuss without giving away too much to the press. I make quick notes on the small pad of paper bolted down on the table next to the phone. I ask Howard to call me after he's talked to Michael and Allan, so I can call them, knowing they'll want to talk this through. I tell him again to call as late as he needs, that I'll be home tonight in LA, give him my home phone number again and my flight schedule from Atlanta. We end on encouraging comments to each other, promising to speak soon.

I sit on the edge of my bed tensed between the pull of the world to perform; by the opposite pull within myself to let go of all form and all need to perform. Neither tension persuades me, not that day, to completely give up the other.

Martha Morrison, the private talk of only an hour ago is still liquid in my mind, oozing around my brain's list of things to get done before I fall asleep in LA tonight. I have to separate these two conversations to stay present in both realities, but I sense them moving together in me, recognize that the neat compartments are dissolving.

I think of the quality of Howard's voice, its bristle and mercurial energy. Realize I can hear nuance and suggestion even when he tries to temper or guard it. Sensitivity is growing as my personal journey weaves and extends into my professional life. I can hear motivations and fears, the hidden threads of what people say and don't say in a new way. I know it's because of this program because of a spiritual path and the testing of vulnerability, but I don't know how or why it affects me this way. Thoughts of power and powerless, who I am, who and what I am becoming, stream through me too. The professional life provides escape I know, gives me a place to put thought and dynamism, thrust and striving while the inner life feels vague, uncharted, frightening. Uncontrollable. I love the relief of specific goals. Worldly challenges are not daunting; they fire me up to accomplish, to go forward. But I am pulled, too, to surrender and seek that which is unknown within me. I want to tear apart the fabric of my life even while I cling to it.

"Balance. Wholeness." I demand of myself aloud, I can no longer live split and torn. Parallel paths, inner and outer, construct and deconstruct, must live together in me at once, somehow and sometime soon. The prospect is mind wrenching, body and brain exhausting. I shake as if a tremor of electricity has sent volts through bones and joints disconnected by anything resembling tissue, ligament, muscle, blood.

Slowly I get up, cram last minute items into my overstuffed bags, and call for a bellman. Disparate appearances, role and costume changes have caused way too much baggage. Nearing the end of this trip I know I can't carry three bags down myself.

～ 42 ～

"I can't live like this any longer."

Who says this? Is it the objective Seer behind all thought? Is it the unseen eye that in meditation we associate with the universal within, the Divine Consciousness, unattached to personality, to subjective whims and inclinations and ego? Is it the Great Knower? Or is it, after all, the True Self that is behind this thought? Or is it a subjective thought, I, the person who moves through the world, has a name and place and ego attached to all outcomes, determined by small notions of have to, and right and wrong, and must, be, do, have for happiness to be certain and attainable and concretized?

Which *I* cannot live like this anymore? The personal *I*, wanting the world to look, feel, and respond in a way I have come to know and feel protected in, safe and identified? Ego bound? Or the objective *I* who is in the world but not of it, is separate and yet one with all things, fearless and authentic? Howard's sentiments, worries and opinions, directions and tasks intermix with mine. It is this way in all deals, we are driven by vision, strategy, execution. Think, move, plan, create something new, something unique and yet necessary too, something of value to pin the future on, to stabilize, to point to and be proud of.

We try to stay objective. Objectivity, after all, is proof. Cold linear metrics make us feel safe. Objective is cool, precise, and unemotional. Subjective is messy and invites chaos; it unsettles careful plans. Subjective won't stay in neat columns. Objective appears solid as earth. Subjective, like water, knows no boundaries.

The iciest dealmakers admit to the persuasion and power of the subjective. Personality, ambition, charisma—all can sway the outcome of a deal. We look around the negotiating table for peculiarities, prejudices, and selfish goals that give us access to the subjective whims and cravings of others. Few accept, however, that subjective is as powerful a deal force, as consistent in predicting the likelihood of success or failure, as the objective.

Objective numbers, carefully drafted, based on fact and data, spring from the minds and hearts of people with subjective dreams, hopes, and fears. Our love of everything in a deal, market analysis to strategic advantage, is influenced through the lens of personal history, both our own and those of experts we trust to advise us. We give away the capriciousness of our tastes, the surety of our dislikes, what we deem important and valuable, in how we negotiate a deal. We comfort ourselves that we are on the right course if we can prove a subjective point with objective data.

A chance for market dominance drives deals. The numbers get worked out to prove or disprove that strategy but ideas dominate numbers, and ideas are subjective. Potential success may be based on analyzed and educated opinion, but it is still opinion. Dealmakers are known to manipulate opinions, to influence facts and figures, and leverage greed through the language of numbers.

Anyone good at doing deals knows how to sell and spin, how to evaluate competitors, find soft underbellies to tickle or kick. Yet even the most sophisticated among us cannot fathom the cleverness of subjectivity, the complexity as its layers show themselves in others or ourselves. Can we ever be sure we have stripped away the hint and taint of the twenty-eight dimensions of DNA and RNA that selfishly course through all our veins? Can we separate ourselves from past-present-future that inevitably informs us in each new situation?

We want to believe, inside the cool detachment of boardrooms, that subjectivity is checked, that objectivity reigns, but that is never the case. It is the subjective and objective push-pull that guides a deal along its path. They collide in the face-off of "deal points," across the chasm between the past, and the vision of the future. In the moments in which deals get negotiated, torn apart or restructured, subjective and objective perceptions and proclivities duel to determine outcomes.

Think of it as a double-edged razor. If you are uncomfortable with ambiguity, you may cling to objective data as the determining reality. So when personalities or power plays collide, or honest motives move the negotiation away from reliable "fact," you will get nicked by clinging to the sharp edge of objectivity if is not informed by its opposite, subjective, tension. If you can't see the importance of the often hidden and oblique subjective, you can bleed all over your safe numbers.

On the other hand, enslaved by subjectivity can get one equally slashed and bloodied. To be ignorant of the importance of objectivity, to refuse the analysis of the numbers, statistics, data, is to sink into personal delusion, and become enmeshed in fuzzy thinking.

Balance and a refusal to be owned by either far tension, objective or subjective, is key. Astute dealmakers know best decisions do not lie in attaching to either extreme. Rather, they come from traversing the bridge at which the dueling opposites meet.

Eventually, if we are aware of all that is human, if we stay conscious, we come to understand that subjective and objective are best understood as dependents of one another.

When we attach to dogged extremes, instead of being informed by the other tension, we become zealots. Entrenched in rigid thinking we lose the beauty and value of the other, and the wider perspective that spells success.

As deal makers we have to look for where edges, dark and light, objective and subjective either blind or give sight. Where they melt and fall away. It is in that void, in the deep chasm where they become one another that the deal finally gets done.

As I learned to do deals, I felt the seduction of being in the play and power defined by external markers. I learned to love the masculine, muscled world of deal making, of being in the rush of get-it-done adrenalin. I exhale with the wind at my back as I rush into the far horizon of possibility. The intoxicant adrenalin makes me hypervigilant on the edge of that ride, picking up clues and not-so-hidden agendas.

Bold moves and stake-in-the-ground positivity empowered me through the temerity and lack of vision of others. I learned to stay in a controlled skid on the powerful outer edge of the tornado of change that a deal creates: to be alive in the whirl of forward energy.

There were big problems to be solved in the world at large. There were plans and solutions, rewards and bragging rights and even a fan or two to cheer along the path.

The deep work within came with none of those bright signposts. Objectivity is rare, subjectivity spills over everything, blurring well-paced markers. I always stoked a rich interior life as balance to the seductive pull of the exterior. Prayer and contemplation, psychological awareness, and philosophical searching were bedrock of my life from childhood. But I avoided a more dangerous stripping away, anything that I couldn't analyze with my overactive mind, anything that threatened to take me back to deep memory, to times and place I did not want to remember.

The Teacher says that *"the closer we get to the truth the greater the fear."* I know now, the greater the fear the more I proved myself in the world, where the demons who came to battle had names and faces and could be identified. But interior demons have their own time schedule, and when they came to be faced, I couldn't lie to myself anymore. I did not go easily into the dark night. I tried incremental transformation and fooled myself with book reading, workshop taking, and other diversionary tactics. I talked a good game on a conscious level, convinced it was enough to maintain sanity, to stay safe without being completely asleep. It took me years to see that I was brilliant at constructing a remarkable life by being objective, and emotionally distant from the past.

"The work you've done does not show on your son," Martha said.

I came to see that only subjective deconstruction, taking down each brick, peeling away all the mortar sometimes with fingertips bleeding from the effort, would bring me the truth of my life. Running as fast as I could, smile on my face and determination as my wind, did not destroy the past or heal the present. Only when I thought I would lose my son, after all the steps I knew to save him didn't work, did I fall to my knees and surrender to the rock-strewn journey within.

By the time I am in Atlanta four years of struggling, falling, picking myself up, latching again to the interior cyclone, have passed and all I know is that I cannot let myself quit. I do not know where the bottom is, but I do know I'm not there yet.

I love and hate the work simultaneously. Bitterness and hope rankle my stomach and mind. Fear and salvation are my constant companions. I search for clear and precise advice, for the objective strategies, goals, and rewards I have come to expect and receive in the competition of business. But the road within is opposite from the very public road of business success.

Epiphanies come to be my rare joy. I long for the occasional "ah ha" when grace brings the light of self-discovery, some opening into higher mind. It is as close to a deal rush as I can get. When epiphanies do come, they bring the courage to ask the next question, to plunge into deeper interiors. It is not the drive for objective success that leads me forward but silence and the breath and the struggle to keep my heart open in hell.

In Atlanta I am only beginning to think about objective and subjective, to see where they meet and fall into each other. I begin to outline an inquiry: what is driven from within and demands to be addressed and what is better suppressed? What marketplace objectives are real? And, what is "real" anyway? Is real objective and can it be separated from subjective? I repeat again and again the sentence that froze and motivated me at the beginning of the week, *"I can't live like this any longer."* I try to see myself with new awareness brought by interior questioning but I have trouble keeping things in neat columns. I write this question for myself: *Am I split between an inner and outer life, between objective and subjective, or are they both me? Does each mark me in a different but equally important way? If I give up either do I relinquish something too precious to understand now?*

Somewhere in this time, I begin to see objective and subjective fall and rise together. Like shadow playing with light, like light birthing shadow, there is a dance being danced. The Knower and that which needs to be known pull for attention. To not be drawn to either extreme occurs to me to be my only strategy in the face of no clear answer.

* * *

Journal Entry, Anchor, 1990: I am afraid to ask these questions of myself: turn right or left, go deeper within, or further out toward success in the world? Question the patterns and sources, or leave them there between Martha and me, unanswered? I am afraid of the loss inherent in choice. My skin cools and heats, stretches to cover the tensions in my body, and to still the drumming and swelling threatening another headache in my temples. I fear that if I am taken by this interior quest I will lose the sharp focus demanded outside. I don't want to lose the safety of the objective world and its reliable measurements and success. And I fear that to reach into the family system will threaten ALL of it, objective and subjective together. But, then again, can I continue to live like this? There isn't any way to deny the spirituality that calls me, the emotions that drive me. But I question whether the internal will destroy its opposite. I fear that if I give up either, inner/outer, or objective/subjective I lose the slim hope of deep healing; I think in some undiscovered way they are linked to all the great mysteries. And then I feel my own split again and sense the voice of no safe and sure answer. Only more work, only more discovery will get me there. I tell myself anyone split is by definition not whole. Only wholeness, The Teacher says, brings peace. I think he is right.

❧ 43 ❧

In just three days so much has changed that the black asphalt parking lot fronting the Anchor Facility looks welcoming as I pull into a space bordered by painted white lines and the chipped and dented bumper guard. What appeared foreign and confrontational on Friday night, I now accept and find solace in.

A few other families have arrived for the final community session. They sit in their cars idling conversations along with their engines, the steam on windows shut tight giving them away. I wonder whether this talking has a beginning or end, feel a wave of longing for someone to share this with. I remind myself how fortunate I am to have my son and that we are here together.

The door to the facility is open, and I decide to go in with the hope of getting a few moments alone with Don. He steps out of the building just as I step to the sidewalk. The corners of his eyes crinkle into a smile. He offers me an unexpected and very welcome hug, then holds my shoulders, and pushes me back to arms distance.

"*I hear you had quite a session with Ann?*" He asks this looking at me, assessing the damage. I relax into a smile, embarrassed yet happy to be seen and understood.

Well, hell Don, I tell him, standing stock still not wanting to fidget out of his grasp, surprising myself with the emphasis of my exhale. I know there are worse stories this weekend, but yeah, I thought I'd gotten somewhere important, a breakthrough in my work, for me life transforming. But now, I don't know maybe, "*The wrong timing, the wrong words,*" I half state, half ask.

"*I was so, AM SO, over eager for change, for healing, that I may have asked too much, too soon, of myself, expected too much from Justin in return.*"

Gone from my voice is the crisp direction and clarity I showed to Howard, devising strategies on a multi-million dollar deal. This careening of realities of knowing and not knowing, of sureness and dismay, of precise plans and no plan at all is confusing but altogether true too.

Don pulls me gently, still holding my shoulders, away from the open door to allow people to file in, giving us a tiny private space. He says that my expression of what I've learned, the responsibility I am willing to accept, is brave. *"Profound,"* he adds on second thought.

"You have given your son the example of an adult who is willing to be fully accountable."

He lets his comment rest in me a minute. Then he says he understands that it may not seem enough today, but the session will simmer in Justin. *"He will revisit the words, your honesty, and commitment. It will make a big difference at some point."*

I hear him but am not convinced. I don't know Don, I say, fearing I sound ungrateful; it just doesn't seem enough somehow. My voice catches then trails off. We both know I want a quantifiable, objective result to count on for safety. We know that doesn't exist: not here, not now. Don drops his hands from my shoulders, smiles again and says,

"Do you know what they call cocaine? It's the 'drug of choice' of overachievers. It was my drug of choice because enough was never enough—'good' could be better, 'better' could be 'excellent,' should be 'perfection.' It wasn't until the cocaine was gone, sitting in isolation in a jail cell with DTs, that I could start, just start, to sweat out all that was 'not enough.'"

He says it took him years in program just to start to feel worthy of being alive, accepting that 'enough' was okay. He moves closer to me, makes sure my mind is not wandering into private argument. Even in attempting to save the life of our child, he says, sometimes good effort has to be enough for right now. In this moment, today, it is all we can aim for.

I long for the comfort of his steadiness and experience but cannot let this go. My voice, dead calm, I say, *"Yes, but, there is this new wrinkle, this tough folded-over piece."* The life of my child, of my only son hangs in the balance. Is just *"progress,"* whatever that means, *"good enough"* to keep him alive? I look at him as directly as he has me and remember that he has lost a child. I wonder if my insisting voice pains him, if I have gone from not enough to too much. But I am obliged to finish, hoping that there is a secret that he is ready to bestow.

"There is no place I will not go, no purpose, no striving, no blame or guilt I will not accept, or work I will not do in the hopes of an answer."

I stop my trembling voice then because my throat clenches back a sob, my chest tightens, no air lifts and collapses my diaphragm. I bite my lip, squeeze my fists against tears.

My mind screams at me that I have said this before, why again and again? Because for all of everyone's brave and tough and empathetic words, the power of those thoughts, "son … grieving … loss… fear of his hands losing grip of my fingers, of watching his body hurtle though a dark void where I cannot follow him," pounds my mind, rips through my heart. I am desperate to make this real for someone, to have him then, to have you now, know the fearful force of grief and loss within me. I never feel as if anyone can hear, or see or taste the way it is for me, swamped and drowned in that fear.

Don takes in my burning mind, narrows and widens his dark eyes. He does not look around at the parents and children quietly entering the room. He says finally, *"I know where you are, what this is like. I lost a child who, to this day, many years later, I grieve and ask of her as I do myself, what was my part?"*

He says he doesn't have all the answers for either of us. But he's sure of one thing: *"Peace"* comes with progress in this Program, in pursuing a spiritual path, with the focus demanded by hard work. Peace and serenity become the process. At some point, "enough" comes from doing courageous work.

"You cannot, we cannot, control outcomes."

Working a rigorous program, getting more honest, refusing to slip back into denial and delusion, those are our personal commitments. We only have control over the decisions and the choices we make, *"The outcomes are up to God."*

He looks me over again, tilts my head up with a gentle flick of his hand, says commandingly, *"Do not get trapped in the aloneness of this work."*

"And, Bobbie," he smiles as he says my name, *"Give yourself a break and Justin some credit. He is one hell of a guy. You have to trust as I do that God has a purpose for him, maybe including this trial by fire, doing battle with this disease."*

Hearing him against the backdrop of unexpressed feeling, his words calm me but I fear believing in them will give me too much hope that can't be counted on for permanent results. My natural buoyancy reined in by retentive fear twists my mind, leaves me holding my breath, tightening my fingers. I realize he sees this and I want to say something to show my appreciation and that I get it, but when I open my mouth nothing comes but a sigh. Don smiles at the shakiness of the exhale, says, *"Yeah, I know, I was there too, wanting to believe and afraid of blind faith."*

Out of the corner of my eye I see the assembly gathering, and know I have to let Don go. He smiles and greets someone who passes, then he pulls me in with his sincere eyes and says, you're right too, it's never smart to think we can predict the future of a person, especially a young person under the influence, but, as positive as I can allow myself to be of anything in this crazy world, I do see Justin as someone who will emerge from this.

"Yes," he continues, *"he will do it his own way, and on his and God's time-table, not ours, but I do believe he will eventually be all he was meant to be."*

I want to know where his faith in Justin comes from, what informs it, but the crowd is all around now waiting for their private moment with Don. I know I can't hold him here any longer. He gives me a quick hug and disappears into the small swarm of people who all want just one more word with him

I hear The Teacher's admonition in my head: words alone will not bring healing, only by consistent deep looking, refusing easy answers, refusing extremes, staying centered, expecting nothing, grasping nothing, will truth be revealed.

I realize that even more than Don's words, what I want to cling to is his understanding and compassion, the kind you can only get from someone in the belly of the beast. I force myself out of my frozen spot near the front door, look around as if my whereabouts are unknown. I feel dizzy in the light rushing in, and the swirl of people greeting and finding each other.

I am not contained enough to find a seat and join the group. So I go to the ladies' room, splash cold water on my face, try not to smear my mascara and allow inky black lines to tear down my cheeks. I hold both sides of the porcelain sink for balance, then take the brown scratchy paper towel and dab at the last of the streaming water. I look at the dark circles that have formed under my eyes, at the hollow indents of my cheeks and think about fixing my makeup. *"Who am I trying to impress?"* I bark at my reflection, *"and for what?"* As agitated as I am with myself I do not wait for an answer or rearrange my face.

∽ 44 ∾

One of the last to find a seat in the completed circle, I look around and see Justin bounce into the room just as Don begins the Lord's Prayer. Balancing a basketball under one arm, he stifles a teasing half smile, takes in the entire room with a sweeping glance until he finds me with the widening of his eyes, and points for me to save the seat to my right.

"I hate to see this end," this temporary community of strangers, I think. Odd and different as we are from each other, in our struggle and strength we bear witness to a certain kind of human suffering, to small victories and even triumphs. It's a "community of necessity." Only in this hour of our need would we choose to be joined. Still, it is community, and if illness is its genesis then maybe, ironically, healing can be its apocalypse.

We have embraced the last three days. Volunteers are now eager to read the Twelve Steps and the traditions of AA and Al-Anon. When we finish, Ann says this may be the last time this particular group is together and, since she is also missing her favorite Baptist gospel choir to be here today, would we mind if she read Paul's letter to the Corinthians? In her deep tenor the words rush back from my years of assemblies while teaching at Haverford Friends in Pennsylvania. I whisper the phrases, feeling their galvanizing strength;

"Faith, hope and love, but the greatest of these is love."

The words rain good intention, better days, communion, transcendence. The added ritual provides a breathing space. Weary minds stretch, feelings and nerves untangle.

As Ann finishes, Justin eases in next to me. He shoves his Wilson basketball under my chair, since there isn't enough space under his old and battered desk, then leans over, gives me a quick kiss on the cheek. I can feel the heat of play on his flushed face still moist under the short stubble of beard. It is difficult to imagine that only a few moments ago Don and I contemplated his very survival. I take a mental snapshot of him pulsing with life and mischief, tucking the quicksilver image into my heart and mind.

Don asks for volunteers to share their weekend experience, remember, he says, use the *"what worked," "what didn't,"* protocol, it keeps us all honest. *"No one expects perfection,"* he says, reminding us of AA's bottom line:

"Take what you want, leave the rest behind."

No one volunteers. Not because of the embarrassment or shyness of Friday's assembly. Rather, we are contemplating thoughtful response, one that will reflect in truer ways who we are now, how we have changed. Anxiety lingers, fear has not taken a holiday, but wisdom and positive resolution have ripened. Don indulges the silence then breaks our stalemate, calls on Fred whose son, Jason, is going home with them today.

Fred starts slowly, shifting hefty buns on the small chair, unable to find any comfortable spot. He doesn't look at his family, keeps his eyes on Heather who stands across the circle from him. He says he doesn't know where to start, that it was an important weekend but not what he expected. His look is tentative but honest. Heather was our family counselor, he says after a pause. *"And I have to say she did a great job!"*

His conventioneer's voice suddenly booms out in that gotta-gush-gotta-please blast of empty air. Instead of invigorating him, the effort deflates him. He takes out a crumpled handkerchief, wipes his eyes under his glasses, soaks up his sweaty face, and the dribble on the corners of his mouth. But, well, he says, *"I dunno, things were different than I thought they would be, Heather."*

Heather moves around the circle so that she stands next to the last child in Fred's family lineup, visually forcing him to address them as a group. When he notices what she has done, his face assumes a childlike innocence, but he is still unable to include them. Instead he says to Heather that she was right, that he had a picture of what this final weekend was *"supposed to be."* He pictured them going home, *"ah, kinda, 'happily-ever-after.'"* He yields an unintentional sigh, having wanted to say the cliché jokingly but delivering instead chilling irony. He says that what he found was just how much more work there was to be done, *"how much more I need to understand, about all of us."*

Fred dissolves in a wash of noisy tears amidst the silence we allow for reflection.

After shaking his head back and forth several times, shifting in his folding chair, breathing a rattling sigh he settles himself. His voice tempered, looking around the circle, he addresses the room,

"Now, I thought I got this family system stuff, but over sessions this weekend, listening to my kids, well now I am not so sure. I want to understand, I do, but it seems to be an idea that just keeps tearing things down!"

He pauses, unable to keep up any charade of inquiry, or to prevent rage from entering his voice,

"And HELL, I just want for all this to go away! I just want my son home! I don't mind sayin' it, well, hell, here's the truth, I want it all to STOP!"

His heavy body trembles so that no inch of him avoids the quaking. He takes out his handkerchief again, examines it for a dry corner, pats at his face, finally gives up pretense, and blows his nose loudly. His children openly gawk at him. His unnoticed wife looks down and away.

We all measure their drama against our private thoughts. We examine love, diagnosing its capacity for test and strain, commenting in our hearts at the loss and gain of it. Is digging for truth worth the possibility of rejection, abandonment, loss?

The multiple small bondages of family, the latticework values of society, culture, and heritage are unthreaded, and let loose in this room. We stare at the rendered parts fearful of looking into the face of God, awed by loyalty's ability to blind us to the things that could save us. Understanding. Truth. Compassion. Surrender. Courage.

"Son," Fred addresses Jason, his cause for being here at Anchor. The boy startles, reddens slightly, regains composure, looks up guarded, to hear his father say that he realizes that he, Fred, wanted to believe, *"YOU had the problem but I could solve it."*

He pauses, looks around the room, picks out two men, Charley and John, whom he has gotten to know during the weeks that their children have been patients at Anchor. Reminding both men that he had been out of work for over a year, but feels that now, with the start of a part time job, he won't be so distracted by his own failings, that he'll be more able to meet his son's needs and, *"solve this thing!"*

He reconsiders his last words, clears his throat, turning his attention back to his son, says,

"I mean WE could son. WE could solve it, and go on, but now, after all the talk of this weekend, well, it just doesn't look that simple."

Charley, the chain smoker from Friday night, leaves his seat and comes to stand behind Fred, lays a hand on his shoulder. John, stays seated between the two red heads of his wife and eldest son, and says to Fred,

"Maybe things have to get very complex, twist and turn a lot of ways before simple solutions are seen. You know in engineering we have a saying, 'If you can't find the solution you may be looking too hard.'"

He looks around to see if he is understood, when he goes on his voice is strong,

"Whatever this takes, recovery, healing, it seems to me that understanding has to come first. And to understand, well, there is just more we have to know, about ourselves, about each other. We have all lived in families we thought we knew well. But maybe only under the intense pressure of examination can we come to really understand."

Although shorter than both his wife and his son, he appears suddenly to overshadow them, no longer lost to the heated dominance of their relationship. He reaches a protective arm around his wife, which causes her to move into his chest, drop both her head and belligerent attitude. His son stares at him, then smiles, John responds by resting his right hand on the boy's knee.

"'You don't know what you don't know.'" Charley, says, loudly, to the group, and then repeats it, winking at John, and saying it's another good ole engineering dictum. He tells us that he had a professor who would push his students to uncover possible problems before some sewer line exploded on someone's Thanksgiving dinner. *"Guess Anchor is just another time and place to dig for the source of the busted pipe."*

He glances over at Don who smiles, waves his hand encouraging Charley to go on. Charley addresses us all as he says,

"I have to admit Fred, for most of my kid's time here I thought if there was a problem it was someone else's and if something needed fixing, it should be done preferably by them. I'd rather be home enjoying Thanksgiving. Hell, I don't want to dig for no blown pipe either, but, now, well, as best I can, dig I must."

Charley's square-from-the-shoulder words give rise to nods of agreement, to murmurs of tangible warmth. There is a drawing together, as if, for the first time all weekend, we are responding as a group of fellow seekers and questioners. No longer isolated in our personal hells, silently we acquiesce to our place in this community. The generosity, honesty and humility of these three men coalesces our energy. We accept their words and our pain without turning away. Reservation of judgment spreads through the circle, warms its center, pushes separateness to the far boundary of the room.

Don takes advantage of the pull into the silent tide of union, says he thinks most people assume the identified patient is the problem. Most, think, maybe hope, that the solution is to fix the patient, and change the situation that started the problem. There are many enemies to point to, wrong friends, wrong neighborhood, wrong job or marriage, bad schools, get rid of the enemy and all will be well, *"as if it was before."*

Don looks right at me without drawing anyone else's attention, says that a few parents or spouses think they are the problem, or their relating to the addict is the problem, and if they can change, everyone will heal. But, he says, no two dots drawn with a straight line between them create the whole picture, not of a family system, or a societal system. *"Sorry, wish it were that easy."* The whole truth is held in the whole system. No part, no relationship is exempt.

I smile to Don, acknowledge his point. Yes, I get it, I may not like it but I get it.

Don asks Fred if he would like to continue. Fred throws his hands up, palms open to the group, says, *"I don't know where to go from here."*

Don looks inquiringly to Fred's family, all of whom look away, stare back blankly as if nothing was asked or shake their heads no, they don't want to respond. Don allows the silence to speak to us. No one coughs or gets anxious or interrupts.

Confused and without perfect answers, the genuine outpouring of collective understanding that we are all in this together, cools and comforts the room. "Grace," I think, "genuine and authentic. It is a subtle form of grace."

Don turns back to the group with a beatific smile that belies the grasp on reality that is his strength. He asks who would like to be next. None of us wants this to go away, the drawing together. Fred's problem is our shared problem, we have come to see and own it with him. The dominant theme has become community. We are thinking, how can I share and still feed this positive energy.

The voice of the young mother, Sarah, sweet and light draws all of our attention. Her baby girl is sleeping between she and her mother in the complete abandon of infant exhaustion. The grandmother rhythmically rocks the stroller back and forth, as her daughter begins. *"It worked for me to have my ma and step-daddy here. I know I started out a shit."*

She says it to all of us but turns to make sure her parents get that she is talking to them. *"But, Heather nailed me on it right away Friday night."*

Sarah flashes a broad smile in Heather's direction as she reaches behind the stroller and grasps her mother's hand. And, while her mother covers the extended hand with both of hers, Sarah adds with a laugh, *"I argued at first, couldn't let Heather win without a fight."* But, Sarah adds, she called her parents at their motel and made amends, and that set things right. The rest of the weekend, although *"loaded with plenty of hard work,"* has gone well. She leans over her mom to pat her stepfather's shoulder, thanks them for forgiving her.

"What doesn't work for me is saying good-bye." Her voice chokes, eyes blinking back tears she says that she hates when her mother and stepfather leave; hates to say goodbye to her baby girl. *"I wonder, does she think I don't love her, that I'm sending her away?"*

She's scared the baby will remember her at Anchor and have nightmares about it, about the leaving and her mother not being home for her. Sarah shudders for a second, stares over our heads at a future she cannot see, cannot control. She blinks back tears to continue, says what she wants to share is that, like Fred, she thought she could solve all the problems herself. She looks across the circle to him, says she knows it's not exactly the same but that after all, she's a parent too, and she thinks she gets where he's coming from.

With the intention of her direct eyes, the resolve of her voice, she closes the circumference of the circle that separates her from Fred, who stares intently at the teenager addressing him.

"I thought if I had this baby I could run away from all the past ... that I didn't have to belong to anyone's 'system,' although I didn't even know the word then."

She thought she could be on her own, that Emmy and she could *"just not have a past,"* only a tomorrow, a future. *"Y'all remember that* Annie *song when we were kids,"* she asks of the rest of the teens. She sings the first line, on key, *"the sun will come out tomorrow."* I look at Justin, smile, remembering that when I taught at the elementary school he and his sister attended we played it over and over, singing it on our drive every day.

Sarah continues, saying that was her song, but here at Anchor she's come to see that she can't be in denial of the past, abandon the present, cling to an undefined future. Or at least, she admits, she can't deny and run like she tried to do. *"The system, the family, is always with me."*

When I tried to escape, she says, *"it chased me down."* Her delicate body tenses and moves forward in her chair as she speaks. Loose curls unclench from her ponytail, stray from behind her ears. She appears to notice her damp cheeks for the first time, takes a swift swipe at them with a sleeve cuff, thanks the anonymous hand that offers her a tissue, shudders again and quiets. We watch as she pulls at the bright blue scrunchy holding her thick hair, and unwinds one layer of the band, rebinds it, pulls again to tighten it, tucking in the disobeying shorter strands. Her lips are pursed, her eyes looking down in self-absorbed concentration. When her hands resettle in her lap, she addresses us again, without eye contact, staring into the empty center of the circle.

"My real daddy, not my step daddy here, well, all these guys know," she waves taking in the other Anchor kids. *"Well, he was a bad man, I didn't want to be a part of any family he was part of ... nothin' he could see nor touch, nor none of his kin either."*

Her voice is sharp and raised, resolute. She tells us she drank and drugged, and ran as far away as she knew to go. When she found out she was pregnant, she was glad because she thought she could go somewhere no one knew her. *"And me and the baby would be brand new, with nobody's finger-prints on us, a brand new family, with a new name in a new place."*

She pauses, touches the baby's filigree of curls, then smiles faintly at her mother's tears, and squeezes her hand. She turns to face us.

"I've learned I don't have to be them, my daddy and his family, that there is a way to escape but it isn't by denial or running away, it's first by understanding them, and myself, then by making different choices."

In the long pause before she speaks again, there is relaxing of faces in the room, relief flows, and smiles appear. A few heads bow as tears, quiet and unchecked, fall.

Sarah begins again in a series of stammers, *"I, uh, um, I've been very rebel-lious here, well most of the time, I guess, and I'm sorry for that now."* But, she tells us, choking back tears, now that she only has one week before she leaves Anchor she's afraid to go home. *"That's what doesn't work too."*

How does she know, she questions herself and all of us, that she won't create just another dysfunctional family when she's away from here without constant reminders and support? How does she know, her voice pleading, if she can create a new family without repeating the patterns of the old one?

"I know it sounds crazy but y'all have become a family to me, and I feel safer here than I ever have anywhere else."

She acknowledges her mother, and stepfather, says she knows they'll be there for her, but still, will it be enough to ensure her that she won't hurt her own baby the way she knows she's done in the past; the way she was hurt? She waves her arm to include all of us, says again, *"this is the family I'm afraid to lose now."*

The trust and acknowledgement of this gentle, wild young woman honors our grief and worry, encourages us to believe our suffering is worth the experience; that understanding is ample reward. Spontaneously, we lean into the center of the circle towards each other and the plaintive voice that gathers us in. Cast-down eyes and turned-down lips shape shift into tentative expressions of hope. Some of our thoughts go to Emmy remembering the fresh-start newness of the children who sit next to us, three-quarters grown. Others empathize with Sarah's parents, proud of who she is becoming, confused by who they must become to meet her needs and their own. We resonate, and we agree. The unity in the room is tentative and tender. And it is tangible and uplifting.

"Can I respond?" One of the older teenage girls asks Don. He nods to her looking surprised that she was the one to come forward. She clears her throat, flushes red under pale cheeks, says her name is Kari, she's a recovering addict, sits up, and then collapses into a hunch. Her broad, thick shoulders tremble as she begins.

"I didn't like you much when I met you, Sarah," laughs a guttural rasp, says, *"Well hell you know that!"*

She thought Sarah was the pretty, screwed-up, cheerleader type, driven into drugs by a breakup with the captain of the football team, *"Or some other such gets-all-the-boys bullshit."* Kari hears her own infraction, apologizes straight to Don, *"Oops, sorry."* Gets his nod, goes on to say that she's come to see that Sarah is the bravest girl she knows, that she does the most honest work in their group. Kari says she *"is sure"* that her friend will raise her daughter well, and *"teach the old system some new tricks"* on how to be a parent.

Sarah blows a kiss to her across the center of our circle. Kari, embarrassed, pulls at the ends of the stiff spikes of her short hair where the receding purple dye blends into the natural dull brown in disorganized angles. Her boyish wide face melts into a puckered smile.

Dissonance mends once again throughout this morning. Both parents and teens ask to speak, echoing Kari's words to Sarah. Some acknowledge Kari also and are quick and sincere to honor her. *"The pretense is gone,"* someone volunteers, *"that nasty attitude has changed,"* another parent adds. Kari grumbles a protest, *"don't be so sure,"* she hesitates, then says, *"But, you could say, I understand now that yesterday's bitch can be tomorrow's good mother."*

As the laughter subsides, Doris raises her hand to speak, says to Sarah that if she only knew, when she was a young mother, what Sarah does now, *"I think, no, I know, things would be different, for me, for mine."* She is not showboating, not looking for attention or forgiveness. Her right hand is twisting a forlorn white tissue, while with her left she reaches across her husband John to touch her son's knee. She moves to bring her hand back to herself, thinks again, and gives her son a second squeeze and a broad smile. Startled and unable to respond, Tim studies her, but can only stare at her face so like his own.

Faith can be dangerous where life is this real. Fred's family, in their head hanging nonresponse, remind us not to be naïve. Yet, in Fred's awkward questioning and even despair, in Sarah's confession, in Kari's bluster, and in the outpouring response of the group, oneness sweeps over us.

Sarah has another week, and after that the odds for sobriety are long. Good intentions and roads to hell are well-known in the rooms of recovery. Fred may be more truthful today then three days earlier, but he still weighs 300 lbs. and his children still don't look him in the eye.

The Teacher says not to rely on good cheer for miracles; remember this is a Program of progress not perfection. My daughter is right; *"Perfection Programs don't exist."* But, still, the power of unity, of gathering, of sharing and suspending judgment pulls us toward the healing center and one another.

∾ **45** ∾

Don allows our communion to guide the silence, mellow the room. But it's not his job to leave unsaid what must be put into words. Without looking around for who's next, he turns to other newcomers, sitting in the sparsely populated second row of our circle. He asks them by name, Dexter and Ali, to share their experience.

I recognize them as the couple huddled together, grim and unresponsive, at yesterday's parent education session. Their understated elegance of correct labels and perfect tans, now drained and tired. The crisp, identical, white polo shirts, are wilted and crinkled from the creeping heat and humidity, and, maybe, from their present circumstances. The only child with them is their son, who was recently admitted to Anchor. He is young, maybe only fourteen, the slightest peach fuzz rebelling against his unlined skin. His designer clothes reflect the taste of his parents but hold their starch and crease. I try to place the look in his eyes, the slight hitch of his lips. Sardonic? Is he old enough to be blasé? He seems cocky but not wholly arrogant. It's more a look of confidence that he can run whatever game he chooses with his parents; maybe with us too. He hasn't been here long enough to be stripped down by his peers and counselors in group therapy and probably can't imagine what lies ahead if he tries to cop an attitude. Today, I guess, he is deciding which camp to choose: his parent's delusion or our wakefulness. Sitting tall for his average height, I sense he wants to be here, and that he has parents right where he wants them too.

"Private plane," Justin leans over to whisper to me. I arch an eyebrow. *" They came here in their private plane, and their kid let everyone know."*

Dexter stands, positions himself between his seated wife and son. Says to Don, that he hopes they'll be forgiven but that they don't have *"anything to share."* He says "share" as if it is a four letter-dirt-and-gutter-beneath him word. He looks at Ali, for agreement. Eyes and smile only on him, she nods an immediate yes.

A collective in-breath from the circle draws my attention. Some of us pull back, like a group of turtles seeking refuge in their shells. Other faces register alarm with a slight shake of heads or down cast eyes. Dangerous strangers are suddenly in our midst.

Don allows Dexter's derision to create its own kind of demand.

"Look you all seem like nice people, I am sure you are, after all. But, to be honest with you, my wife and I are here for our son, Peter, who we do not believe has any of the problems of your children."

Dexter goes on to say that they don't see Peter as the *"'identified patient,' certainly not as an addict."* Dexter can't mask his disdain. *"We believe Peter screwed up some, that's for sure,"* he pauses with a laugh expecting us to join his private joke. We don't. He coughs, gathers himself, says that after the twenty-eight days it takes to please the courts, the boy will be back with them in Dallas *"where he belongs."*

He says *"courts and twenty-eight days,"* as if they are hiccups in the child's otherwise perfect resume. He thanks Don, says he knows the entire staff *"means well,"* and that he and his wife can see that the work of the counselors has helped people. He adds *"But, honestly, we are just, well, different from everyone here."*

He stops, absently runs a manicured hand through thick hair. No one moves to object or correct. Faces tighten.

Ali speaks up. Her accent, melodic, sounding like English gentry greased by oil money.

"We do believe you are all doing a great deal of good for your children by being here."

Large perfect diamonds at her earlobes and on her fingers catch the sun as she speaks, sending rainbow shafts above our heads. She looks up at her husband but not at us. He returns her gaze, smiles.

She says she appreciates especially the staff for their contributions to her son. But, she says on full exhale, that she, Dexter, and Peter are not *"a family, with, uh… problems."* They have always *"been there for our son."* After all, she adds, where they are from, folks know how to *"take care of their own."* She looks over our heads as if at a reassuring Country Club image of her son years from now, perfect and polite. She says that she and Dexter do not believe that they as parents or that their son are delinquent in anyway.

In fact, she says, as she lays a hand on the boy's arm, leans over and tries to engage his cold eyes, which he averts, *"in fact,"* she repeats at his rebuff, that her paramount concern is that Peter not identify himself as an addict or alcoholic. I just don't see, she continues, how it is helpful for him to think he has a disease or is impaired or defined by any *"demeaning term."* She does not say, "like the rest of you," but we hear it anyway.

As years go on he will grow out of this *"period of his development,"* and, when he is *"back with his own,"* she is confident, he will be *"just fine."*

Her dark blonde hair, highlighted with gold and rusts, stays sprayed and coifed and stationary. We all watch as she folds one lean leg carefully over the other and reaches absently for her husband's hand. She looks up at Dexter for the agreement he gives with a white-toothed smile.

Just a few moments ago the rest of us longed to discover something beautiful in each other, to share, finally, what we could not do with relatives, in our hometowns, or with old friends. We saw ourselves holding one hand over our own beating heart, stretching the other to hold the hand next to ours, no matter whose hand that was, until a continual circle formed, hand to hand, heart to heart. The discordant voices of pressed khaki people have frayed our tenuous reverie and we risk now seeing ourselves as small, distant and apart. Lesser. I look around, expecting to see on the faces of others what seemed to me obvious. Money or not, their superiority is silly, stereotypical, and devoid of meaning. But instead I see how their remarks harm the circle. I want to holler *"Hey, get a grip, these people are arrogant and spoiled, screw 'em, someone tell them off!"* But, I hesitate, still new to the rooms of recovery, still looking for the 'right' timing, unsure of protocols and the appropriate cue. No one moves. I feel my anger rise, recognize it as fear and judgment, and remember The Teacher says *not to just look but see, and not to just hear but listen. Calm. Breathe."* I try to center myself and look again.

What do I see? A twitch, imperceptible, forms on the right corner of Ali's mouth, where upper and lower lip form a perfect lined wedge. There is a furrowing between her eyes, a long crack of skin that will become a deep line in old age. The poised hands open and swipe at the air in front of her face, although there is nothing there to disturb her, then move from her husband to son, and back again, never resting until her arms twist right over left ribs, left over right so tightly I imagine they form a knot behind her back.

"Where have I seen this before?" On my own face: in the unrest and anxiety, forced calm and resolve of my own heart. Am I so different? Don't I cling to status at times, to right labels, to something that will bring me safety and peace? False realities are not unknown to me.

All of this happens in far less time than I can write these words. The community created over three days is separated in a few ragged heartbeats, in the reflection of my own thoughts, I sigh and wait.

❧ 46 ❧

Without a pause or defensive inflection, Don asks," *Would anyone like to respond to Dexter and Ali?"* The teens, not easily dismissed or captured by failures, disappointments, or the embarrassments of their parents, raise hands, and strain to be noticed. They know a lie when they hear one.

Justin is poised to jump to his feet. He shoots Don a look that says "Are you going to let them get away with this?" Don catches Justin's eye gives him a half smile that's half "back down" warning without even a nod of his head or gesture of his hand. But, Don is acutely aware of the deflation in the room, the cracking of good feeling. A powerful polarizing force has risen on the vapors of our discontent causing us to tear and be torn and grind against the precious, hard earned threads of union. He glances around then smiles as he calls on a young man with exotic mixed race skin, jet-black hair swept back and gelled, who appears from near the door almost out of the circle. Age-wise he fits somewhere between the teens, and the adults. Confidence illuminates him, glistens off his perfect skin. There's a professional sophistication to his comportment, the erectness of his shoulders and head. Cuban or maybe Brazilian, I think, noticing that the teens shrug to each other, seem not to know him.

I look at Justin questioningly, but he shakes his head, doesn't know him either. We are all curious. He asks Don for permission to speak.

"*Go ahead,"* Don nods. The young man carefully lifts his chair out of our circle and places it directly in front of Dexter, Ali, and Peter, close enough to have their full attention yet still not invade a certain physical boundary. He faces them relaxed, eyes wide and clear. He speaks with a deep baritone softly, measured.

"*Hi, I'm Mike, Miguel to my family. I'm an alcoholic and drug abuser. My drug of choice was cocaine."*

When he came here three years ago, he also knew that he was different. "*Maybe, arrogant, conceited are better words to describe me then."* At any rate, he says, he felt and acted, "*superior."* After all, he tells them, not looking at any of the rest of us, that he was just a kid having a good time.

"*No way was I an addict, whatever that was."*

And, no way either was he staying longer than the minimum required. *"Getting clean,"* or changing his life were not in his game plan. *"Why would I want to change my life? It worked for me."*

He laughs softly, doesn't expect an answer, explains that his parents sent him to Anchor after he flunked out of the University of Miami his freshman year with a GPA so low there weren't enough zeros before or after the decimal point to calculate it. His college counselor kept warning his parents that their son's apartment was party central. A sly smile creeps across his handsome face, the other kids laugh at the description, familiar with the pleasures of party 'til you drop. He waits a moment for the picture to sink in then adds that his parents took away his car, apartment and allowance and wouldn't send him back to school until he did twenty-eight days in rehab.

"I was supposed to graduate college … be a good son … take over my father's business. In an immigrant Cuban family, success in America is not an expectation, it's a requirement."

So he put in his time at Anchor, marking the calendar. He says he was so cool he could *"barely be in the same room with myself."* He must have been more sophisticated and older than Peter, but with family wealth and good looks to insulate him, not so different either. He goes on to explain how in his group session one day with only five days to go before he was *"set free,"* everything changed. He stops, looks sideways at Don to see if he remembers, they exchange subtle smiles. Mike continues, *"It was late one Friday night. There had been a lot of talk, we were all tired, perhaps my 'screw this place' machismo wasn't completely locked and loaded."*

He pauses, looks down at his hands hanging over the front of his knees, laughs again. *"Well at least not as much as usual."* And, more importantly he was now almost a month sober for the first time since he was thirteen-years-old, so some of the *"drug bullshit"* was out of him. He could hear what he'd blocked before. His voice steady, without drama, he tells us of a young woman, Mary Catherine, who that night broke down under relentless questioning of her behavior. The other girls challenged her, said she stuck out her boobs for attention, flirted with *"anyone in pants."* He recalls the therapy group as street raw and edgy, influenced by a contingent of inner city kids who weren't raised on middle class *"bullshit manners."*

He stops, seems to savor and roll the rock of memory around his mind. We hear his long inhale, then he says that Mary Catherine broke down in big convulsive sobs and stopped fighting back. That surprised him. She was good at defending herself and great at getting sympathy, but this time she just fell apart.

The group didn't buy it. They said tears weren't going to cut it. They wanted her to *"cop to something,"* to get off her *"high-horse-pretty-face and sexy body bullshit" and "be real."* He raises his baritone, mimics the high-pitch city whine of inner city girls. They were out of their chairs and in her face. Don had to physically pull everyone off for them to realize Mary Catherine's breakdown was not an act.

Mike could hear Heather whispering to the girl to *"let it all go."* I look over at Heather who has moved a foot or two behind Mike, she shifts from her left foot to her right, does not nod or comment. Her eyes are moist and soft.

Don stood sentry to give the group time to quell, Mike recalls, forcing everyone back into their seats. Heather sat next to Mary Catherine giving her space and support to cry it out. *"It took her a long time to tell us her story,"* how her rich uncles kept yachts in Miami, Mexico, even the South of France. Their sister, Mary Catherine's mother, without a husband and generally drunk herself, would take off with some guy on a binge for days or weeks leaving the girl, in their "care." He enunciates the last word so that there is no one unsure of his sarcasm. The caring uncles molested her until she was twelve, developed breasts, and started her periods. After that they must have decided she was a woman because they began raping her, passing her between them, and offering her as a gift to drugged-up friends. Mike doesn't change pace or inflection, but we all squirm.

At the same time, he says, they spoiled her with clothes, money, maids, and soon, drugs. One day she took off in one of their sports cars. She was fifteen-years-old, high on cocaine, and suicidal. She planned on driving the car off the Miami Causeway and drowning. Instead she crashed along a road in a town she had never heard of, slammed into the side of a police car that was stopped to give someone else a ticket.

"A police car." Mike shakes his head, looks down then back up at the family in front of him. *"Ever heard of a louder cry for help?"*

We wait in the silence that follows; many of the teens have moved to the edge of their seats. Mike, too, sits forward. Memory twitches the sculpted angles of his cheekbones, quivers on his thick lips. His eyes and hands remain quiet and steady.

Mary Catherine's story, *"broke something, or, maybe, fixed something in me."* His sigh audible, Mike slouches under the weight of what more needs saying. He notices it himself, straightens his back, raises and squares his shoulders.

"Hours later, in the middle of the night, two or three o'clock, I woke up in a panic, remembered my uncle, the beloved, Padre," he says with a flourish of perfect Castilian Spanish. His uncle was the favorite priest of the family *"whose vocation blessed us all, as my father would say."* The priest came to visit the family compound once or twice a year. Mike says he was *"honored,"* to assist his uncle at mass, in the private chapel of a famous Miami church. The whole family would be there, he tells us. His mother made him wash his hands twice and use his dad's pomade to slick back his cowlicks. The priest told Mike to be there early to rehearse his prayers, make sure he was prepared for his performance.

True to his reputation as a religious taskmaster, the priest put Mike through the paces in Spanish and Latin. Then the uncle told the nephew that he had done so well he deserved a treat.

"He gave me wine in the sacristy, the same wine they use at communion, unblessed as yet, by his prayers and authority. I'd had sips of wine at family celebrations, but I wasn't prepared for the long drink my uncle encouraged. He waited until I complained I was so dizzy I was afraid I'd puke, and then he molested me. It was a week before my twelfth birthday."

His voice drops but is strong. His uncle told him if he ever said anything the priest would have to protect himself from what would be heard as lies anyway. After all, he reminded the boy, a priest is the *"special envoy of God."* He ordered Mike to kneel and pray with him that, *"God would forgive the boy for leading the man into sin."*

From my position in the circle I can only see his aquiline profile. There is no self-pity or blame in his wry smile.

Shortly after his visit, the uncle became a monsignor and the émigré community held a celebration. Mike says he snuck half-drunk wine glasses off tables until the buzz and puking returned. *"I count that time as the beginning of my addition, not that it was his fault, my uncle's, just that is when it started."*

There's a story that follows: how Don intervened and supported Mike in the middle of that long dark night of remembering. Then helped Mike get up the courage to tell his parents at the next family weekend, *"one just like this,"* their understandable shock and denial, then rage and finally the outing of the uncle just as he was being considered for a bishopric.

At some point early on in his sobriety Mike decided to leave Miami, the family, and come to Atlanta to study psychology *"maybe grow up and harass kids for a living like Don does."*

Mike turns away to give Don a thumb up, and Dexter relaxes. He watches Ali squirm in her seat, then composes himself, says, *"Well, son, I am sorry for your story and your friend's story too."* He says it's all a *"pitiable, damn shame."* But, he's unsure what this has to do with him, his family. *"We're not ..."* Dexter's voice rises, anger seeps in, he clips it short, pauses trying to recover, but is interrupted by Mike, whose voice, clear, decisive, fills the space of Dexter's hesitancy.

"Not like anyone else.'"

"'Not like y'all,'" Mike's exaggerated Texas accent draws the point. We all say that, he adds, *"It's what I said too,"* Mike points out. Prestige, money and name-in-community, being a *"someone"* kept him in denial. They had it all, his family and himself. Their identity bought them safety, but also kept them from being present and honest, *"separate from our own suffering."*

The last thing that any of them would have wanted was to *"'Scratch a scab, make it bleed in public.'"* This afternoon, when he heard Dexter and Ali say, *"not me, not us,"* he realized he'd heard it a thousand times, and he just couldn't let it sit.

"I just wanted you to know it's not unusual. You're not, we're not, no one is, 'special'."

Mike speaks in a steady stream of words. Dexter's face pales, then flushes again, the left side of his wide mouth is tucked up and under as he bites the inside of his lip. Ali looks from Mike to her husband, squints as if she's trying to bring him into focus, loosens her hand from Dexter's, stretches her fingers then returns to the comfort of his tensed grip. Before Dexter can respond, Mike tells him that he doesn't know Peter, has never seen him before, but, in a way he knows all he needs to about their son.

"Anchor is a serious place, and he wouldn't be here unless they thought he needed to be ... and one more thing, Sir, he can't get well unless he's here. Bringing him home won't make things go away, believe it or not he's with his 'own' right now."

I look around me; stretch my tensed shoulders and neck that threaten a headache from the intensity of silent engagement. The community is still fragmented, but Mike has melted some of the icy distrust set in motion by

Dexter and Ali. Once again a movement toward wholeness, to heal, is led by a patient, a recovering addict. "The ones we think we came to 'help,'" I say to myself.

I know that this is not about Dexter and Ali, who are confused, stuck-up, scared, and delusional. It's about us and our willingness to align with fear and judgment, finding fault in ourselves and casting it out on others.

The Teacher says that if you make a stand, call disturbing influences by name, pull them out of you, and face them as yours, then you rob the *"old division"* of its power to restrict and influence and hinder your progress. He *invites his old friend lust, rage, fear, greed, gluttony, to join him in the party of life, but tells them that they can no longer control him.*

Our children, faces flushed and eager for engagement have grown brave with Mike's story and his elegant telling of it. They brim with enthusiasm, ready to support him; prepared to speak their own truths. In the faces of their parents, I notice the opposite: trained acceptance, exhausted confusion.

"As within so without, as above, so below." The scripture quote comes to me, speaks to the moment. Whatever is not healed within will be cast out and will draw discontent. But, the opposite force holds a greater promise: *"whatever is healed, draws healing to it, assists and brings peace."* We forget that our permission is required to go into agreement with disease, discord, and fear. And that the opposite agreement can bring us the things we pray for: *"serenity, courage, wisdom."*

It is easier to cast out what we cannot understand or tolerate within ourselves: "those," "these," "mine," "yours," "foreign enemies," "good" "evil," than it is to face down our own demons.

I know this by then, Anchor, Atlanta, 1990, "The effort within must stay constant. We must drive for wholeness, at any cost." What I don't know, not yet, is the cost.

I slip my journal out of my purse and write these few words to focus my intention, and commit to it before I, too, split and fragment, wanting peace but tempted to believe that the Dexter's and Ali's of the world have the power to change and influence my best intentions.

I write these words easily. But the task itself, to refuse fragmentation and fear, to find a personal truth in the midst of dissension, to refuse polarization, is, again, a great and mighty task. The extremes of the journey through addiction, confronting loss and grief and accepting recovery, surrendering ego, embracing faith are its own sort of divine intervention.

I question the paradox, writing in my journal, open in my lap.

* * *

Journal Entry, Anchor, 1990: If life is too easy, do we miss the signposts that lead to roads of transformation and redemption? Do we 'hit bottom' as a catalyst to search for the light at the end of the tunnel? Sitting here in this strange place in Atlanta, it is more painful to have faith that we are okay in the midst of the storm, in the vortex of the tornado of discontent and confrontation, than it is to align with the hard edges of self-righteousness and judgment.

* * *

The temptation to polarize, split and fragment, oozes from the plasticized floor up our legs, until we wobble in place and our brave thoughts turn angry and lash outward against others. That polarizing, splitting force plunges into the middle of our circle, seeking its collapse.

Opposites give balance, meaning, and definition to "other." They are not at war as opposing energies. But polarization is something else. It is a force that attempts to destroy equilibrium and equanimity and has consequences that ripple out into the future, poisoning the present and the past. What follows? Discord. Anger. Hatred. Disease.

Each successive generation bound by duty, tradition and conscious or unconscious belief systems maintains the wars, large and small, exterior and interior, that give rise to that which destroys the only things that bring life and healing: understanding, unity, compassion, courage, truth, and love.

As carefully as possible, Mike pushes his chair back into an open curve in the circle of chairs. Only then, watching him apologize to others who need to move to accommodate him, do I realize how young he is. And I understand his performance, strong and clear, was an effort. A self-conscious shyness overtakes him as Don thanks him for sharing, noting his personal growth and *"the tenaciousness of his commitments."*

As Don speaks the shifting tides of emotion and choice move through the room and look for an opportunity to determine outcome. Mike has asked all of us to choose our own center, and from there, to search for balance.

Native Americans call balance, seeking the "Good Red Road." Not the black, the road to war, not the white, the road of passivity, of "no fight," but the center where justice and truth find common ground. Where, "my friend, the enemy," is understood. Buddhism and Daoism, call that balance the "Middle Way," the path of mindfulness. Awake and aware, fully present to all alternatives, to all opposing energies, unmoved to attach to anything that would destroy the other, that would blind us to possibility. This middle and centered path takes greater courage than either opposite tension. It demands pure compassion. It requires all possible forces to be considered. It doesn't mean having no point of view. It does mean no attachment to any polarizing extreme. It does not prevent us from taking a bold and decisive stand, but it does take enormous courage, and intention to walk this difficult road.

I look to my right and see Justin. He is bent forward in the desk that barely contains his size. Leaning on his elbows, hands on either side of his face before he flattens them on the desk top, he looks up at me, sees me staring, asks, "What?" with the up lift of his chin and inquisitive eyes.

"Nothing, nothing," I nod, but I feel my tears and reach with my right hand to hold his left forearm a brief moment, overwhelmed to understand and express all that is between us, wondering how far the Red Road will take us and how brave we can be.

∾ 47 ∾

Lost in reflection, I am vaguely aware of parents speaking, assessing their progress, of quiet, respectful voices speaking back to them. A determination has retaken the room that is more cautious re-alignment than true unity. The underlying tension of it rubs my skin like sandpaper; I shiver as Don calls on me to speak.

Like Justin, I want to jump to my feet in defense of truth. But where he would confront, I would crusade, in my old cheerleading, all-for-one-one-for-all practiced and familiar way. To rally the fallen, inspire the faithful; push back disdain with enthusiasm. And, yes, probably make Dexter and Ali dead wrong along the way. "But I've learned haven't I? Didn't I just tell this to my son?" That for the sake of my own work, for me, I must stand and speak without judgment, feeling all my own discomfort, accepting the fullness of my fragile humanity, awake to this moment. It is the only way to heal my fragments, the ones itching to make me right, that want to split me from feelings of discord, within and without.

Don reminds me of the essential questions: *"What worked, what didn't, and what are your 'take aways?'"*

My mouth and mind fill with sudden interruptions, "fix-it" ideas, and a desire to create happiness. I look down, remind myself to say only what is true for me, at this moment, to "stay present, stay mindful." Be honest.

I start by acknowledging my son. Justin looks up at me wide eyed. Wanting to reassure him he won't be embarrassed or betrayed, I reach for his arm, hear him sigh as he covers my hand with his in as much of an embrace as is possible across the restriction of desk and chair.

"Justin is here, and he is working as brave and honest a program as I could have hoped and prayed for, and believe me, I've been praying!"

I exaggerate the humor, hear the laughter, but keep my attention on Justin. I tell him that he is open, participating, present, which is inspiring to me and that he makes me brave by his example. I tell him I know he didn't choose to be here, that the work is demanding, often discouraging, that there are no *"guarantees of outcomes,"* but that to see him healthier, and especially to see him reaching out to others, well, *"it was the best part of the weekend for me."*

Looking up from Justin, turning to Don, I say that what didn't work was, *"my own wanting."* I admit I want to be perfect, to be able to understand, put into practice all the knowledge and experience of the recovery Program, *"right now,"* transformation on the spot. I laugh and say, *"I have even taken workshops that promise that,"* after all I'm from LA, the land of instant gratification.

But, the truth is the *"real goods"* cannot be delivered like a breakfast drink, *"add water and stir."* Rather, it takes all of this, coming to meetings, meditation and prayer, outward action, and inner work, acknowledging fear instead of denying it or casting it out in judgment and efforts to control. To make progress will take a commitment to be consistent over a lifetime and maybe more. *"I don't like it,"* I tell them, this *"one-day at a time stuff."* I want it all now, and I want quantifiable, dependable results.

"Vision, strategy, execution," is so much more controllable than what transformation demands. *"Let Go, Let God,"* is often nerve wracking, and makes me feel impotent. But, at the same time, I have come to understand that *"analyzing, fixing, problem solving,"* constant motion, and even hyper-responsibility are double-edged swords when wielded without an inner awareness and have brought more anxiety than peace.

I hear my thoughts as I say them, reflect on the truth of the spontaneity, feel my face flush, wonder for a second about what more my heart wants to say. I am beginning to see, I start again, that any *"wanting for,"* even for healing, that takes me out of the sacred center within, brings a type of fear, and leads to an endless, circuitous path away from a True Self. Wanting leads to grasping and to attachment, to the hope that something outside myself will deliver an ultimate peace and happiness; wanting leads to fear and delusion.

I hear in all that wanting an endless list of *"if onlys."* If only Justin was sober, if only all the bad guys weren't dealing drugs, starting wars, if only the world would turn away from violence, if only someone could explain all the *"if onlys,"* then finally the conflicts of my own mind and constant worry would disappear. It is confusing, I confess, it is ironic *and "feels upside down"* that after a life of setting goals, of solving problems, and seeking achievement, that the way to serenity, courage and wisdom, is to go deeper within, to be one with an inner mindfulness, *"to be still and silent and find God there."*

I repeat aloud the words I have spoken to myself all day.

"In the gospel of Thomas, *Jesus says, 'As within so without, as above so below. If you bring forth what is within you what you bring forth will heal you. If you do not bring forth what is within you, what you do not bring forth will destroy you.'"*

The current reality that I argue and worry about, that I damn and suffer from, is my own. The wanting and *"if onlys"* are within me and I must bring them forth for healing to occur.

I stop, afraid I've gone on too long, that my internal debate pushes and pulls me in directions too personal and unformed to be expressed. Don, moves around the circle so that he is directly across from me.

"What didn't work for you, Bobbie, was your desire to be perfect and what you've come to find is that grasping for perfectionism causes you to attach to it as if it is a real thing."

Yes, I answer, glad to be clarified, and then *"perfect mother, perfect Al-Anon Program, weekend participant,"* takes me away from the inner turmoil that I must address, and I move out toward elusive if not impossible goals. Outside myself enemies will always present themselves for battle, and if I engage, I lose the opportunity to win the war within myself, the only one that counts.

"And, in a way, I have to settle for minor victories."

We live in a world of violence: separation, addiction, fragmented, isolated, judging, being judged, controlled and controlling, polarizing. True Self refuses violence, including the violence toward oneself that is a drive for perfectionism.

"The cure, if there is one, must be found within myself."

I couldn't name it then as I can say it now, but the personal war is not between an inner life and one in the world. The inner manifests the outer. The outer life expresses, influences, whispers but does not deny the inner: in True Self the two become one.

This is the ultimate reality, if peace doesn't exist within me, within us, it cannot exist in the world. When unhappiness rankles and unnerves me, I create enemies in the world to battle. When peace exits within me, I find no one to call enemy. Real peace is being one with all the victories and vicissitudes the world offers.

Great, Don says, in a way that sounds as if he agrees. Then he asks, *"and your take aways?"*

I feel the rattle of exhaustion, release the restriction in my throat and look down at Justin. I want him to know I am saying this as directly to him as possible.

"It was all so immediate, your survival, the worry of whether there would be an accident, another school calling, another crisis, everything spinning out of control, that my focus was on cures and fixes, on fear and chaos."

I have to work to keep the terror out of my voice, to avoid a slip into the melodrama of anxious days and sleepless nights as the past four years fly through my memory, strike my heart and mind. But now, I tell him, with you here and sober just the need to feel safe is not enough to bring me change, or the transformation I now believe is possible. *"And so I am,"* I hesitate unsure of the right word, *"committed."* To the next layer of work, to finding and understanding sources of suffering, addiction, the patterns and sources that keep dysfunction, delusion, denial, illusion, and fear in place. And, I realize as I say it that I have made a decision to meet Martha's challenge. "As within," I think, but don't say, "so without."

I lift my head and say to the circle that it won't be easy. There will be more surprises, painful and joyful, that will change me, change my life, that I cannot control the process or results. But, I know, in a perverse way, I have no choice but to follow this to the end curious but unwavering.

"I am afraid of unpredictable outcomes, but I am more afraid of delusion and denial"

I don't want to finish this way, thoughtful but heavy. I want to push back at any hint of negativity or at any conclusion of loss that might feed the polarizing energy that lingers at the edge of the conversation. I say that my other big takeaway is the bravery and kindness of strangers.

"This disease, addiction, is a lonely companion."

Friends and family turn away; rejection is commonplace. We are often judged and ignored in our most difficult hour by those we thought loved us the most. So, for me, to come across the country, to gather with people I have never met before, may never see again, and to feel hands, hearts, and minds open as these amazing kids reveal themselves, without self-blame and without blaming others has been moving and enlightening. I am immensely grateful for the experience.

"Thank you for being willing to be here for me and my son."

I look the entire group over, face by face, to steady myself and to be reminded of the stories that were told here and the courage it took to tell them. I try to keep my hands from trembling uncontrollably. I steady myself so that my knees won't weaken. Justin, smiling at me, reaches a hand to grasp my shoulder as if to balance me as I sit down.

* * *

Journal Entry, Anchor, 1990: I look at Ann across the room and I remember she said to me, "Be careful not to idealize Justin." I recoiled from that thought, angry, but now I actually realize she is right. I choose to remember the baby boy or the young child before the insanity reached the boiling point, and I couldn't ignore it, call it by the wrong name, or deny it any longer.

After the session with her, Ann said to me, "If you forget the past, you risk slipping into denial, and if you cling to the past you squeeze out the possibility of change."

The Teacher has said this too——that we must hold onto all the pieces, past, present, and future as one reality. Each informing the others, and NONE to be denied, ignored, or overrated. We must live HERE in present, one minute, one hour, and one day at a time.

Ann said, "To do less is to marginalize Justin and not see and experience him as a whole person. It makes it impossible to see yourself if you deny him any of his parts."

I try to clear away the denial/delusion cobwebs and think of everything that brought us here.

What do I see? I am the anxious, burned-out, screaming, overwrought, angry, and scared mother. I am the loving, compassionate, accepting, cheerful-to-a-fault, striving shoulder-to-grindstone, and protective mama bear. I was at the worst of times, and I am at the best of times.

I look around at my son, at the faces of the assembly that supports us here, and at humanity that stretches past this one small spot on the planet and ask myself again, "What are we all so afraid of?" Why do we not know that absorbing ALL the chaos and disaster is the only way to absorb ALL the joy and enlightenment?

"Wanting and finding solutions is what makes America great. It's what makes for success."

Heather steps forward, her voice warm with southern inflections, she acknowledges my sharing, and, she says, Bobbie's right. If we are looking for fixes *"we could be striving for the wrong goals."* She has come to see this, too. She understands that wanting can be just another addiction, a veer off the road of recovery.

"I am still learning," she adds, *"to stay open to possibility, to work the process, and to wait for truth to be revealed."*

Instant gratification is a sign and by-product of every addict, so process and patience are part of the antidote.

"Mike was right. No one is so special that these rules don't apply."

The Program has endured because the community is based in sharing simple truths that are spoken honestly. She allows her last statement, said in her signature way, with the flip of her hair and a sunburst smile, to find its mark in the room, cascade into tired minds, and rest there in silence.

With each sharing, a mellowing enters the room, and trust tenderly reasserts itself. Maybe we realize that the strength of our individual integrity is louder than any disparaging voice, or maybe not. I look around the circle, try to gauge the depth of our unity and decide that one way or another, people are present again.

Heather is watching too, making an assessment as she walks halfway round the group to where Ann sits next to the only mother from whom we have not heard. Both counselors ask the woman to stand, Heather at her elbow with a lift, and Ann whispering encouragement and giving her support on her other side. The woman stands briefly, then sits again, and perched on the edge of her chair, shakes herself in an attempt to throw off shyness and gather strength. She grimaces, nods to each counselor, takes a resolute breath, and stands.

"Hi, I am Alice," fingers gripping the steel-framed chair in front of her and tears unchecked as she weaves her statements with mine. *"For me, too,*

'what worked' this weekend was y'all." She straightens herself, as if indeed we have given her courage. Her voice rolls out in soft rushes that remind me of sweet tangles of night blooming jasmine. She looks down at her hands, loosens them from the chair, stuffs them into her jean pockets, and then thinks better of it and lets them hang loose at her side, until they move, seemingly of their own volition, and come to rest under her chin in a prayerful triangle.

She tells us she didn't want to come to Atlanta from Tennessee, had never been this far from home, that she doesn't have a child here, *"well, not yet."* But, that her pastor *"pretty much insisted I come."* The cheeks of her face are paper thin, and I am reminded of old *Life* magazine photographs of Appalachia, of people so broken and forlorn that the hollowness in their eyes matches that of concentration camp victims. Alice takes another long pause. Then she tells us about her small town, once prosperous in its way of hard work and rich community. *"Tradition, family ties, and church. Folks caring for each other."*

In her *"daddy's generation the unions meant something."* Hospital bills got paid and groceries got bought whether someone was sick and out of work, had a death or accident, or new baby. The union took *"care of its own."* But the factories slowed and then closed. Union meetings were replaced by drinking. Families fell apart, and some moved away; for those who stayed, unemployment became a way of life. Welfare was a shame they bore to keep their kids going, but it led to more drinking. When the last of the money ran out, the small health clinic closed. The high school kids had to be bussed out of town, and there wasn't any Saturday night football or off-tune music recitals or local sock hops. When things couldn't get worse, the crystal meth came. *"And it came hard and with a viciousness,"* her voice, shaky and keening, finally finds its timber. *"It's taken our babies..."* Her voice cracks, and she silently steadies herself on the chair again until Heather stands shoulder to shoulder with her.

"I had to turn my brother, my own baby brother, the sweet boy who I helped raise, over to the state police."

She looks us over, moving deep-set eyes around the circle, taking us all in. She says the police were the last resort. Her brother was making meth in their garage, in the house their daddy left them. By the time she got honest with herself, he was giving it to her thirteen-year-old son, *"his own nephew."* She pauses, Heather's arm goes round her shoulder, and Alice gives a thin-lipped smile and pats Heather's hand as she says so faintly we strain to hear, *"Can you believe that? Is it possible to believe?"* Then she straightens again and speaks to all of us, *"that it's so bad a thing that families poison each other."*

She doesn't let tears stop her, hangs her head for a second, and looks up with renewed resolve. Alice tells us that *"In a town like ours,"* they know how people look at them from the outside. *"We know they think, 'poor, stupid, and uneducated.'"* But, she tells us, they were three and four generations proud: proud of their work, schools, the local football team, the mills, and being Americans.

"Lot of veterans lived in our town—veterans of all wars. The sayin' goes there's never been a resister among 'em. But first the drinkin', then the meth, and now we pretty much are becomin' what people thought we were all along."

Families that once gathered at the union hall to solve problems or at the church when they couldn't find solutions are isolated. Even among themselves, they're shamed and damned by the drugs. Most are beaten down by the loss of jobs and the fear of poverty. When the drugs got bad, she tells us, there weren't enough people to fight back. Only the pastor and the principal of the one remaining school rallied and made a stand. *"I have often felt cold stone alone—cemetery cold and alone."*

She rests there a moment, looks from person to person, leaving no one out. People here at Anchor, she says, have been helpful, and caring, especially the counselors. *"But y'all too."* Apologetically she adds that she and hers have been forgotten for so long that nothing in her would have believed that strangers in a big city would reach out. Reflecting private thoughts aloud, she has become firm within her desperate clothes and thin frame. Her humility touches us in delicate ways. She tells us how there are days when she thinks she can't go on, working two shifts, waitressing by day and being a janitor for a gas station at night.

"TAKING long rides to and from bad payin' jobs and no sleep but plenty of bills. But you do it because if you quit you think your child will die, and you will do anything to keep him alive. Then the drugs come, and you think he'll die any-way..."

She pauses seeing, I think, all those times, all the years of hard work floating by her. But now, she says, coming here, she's glad for the first time that she's kept going. This weekend has left her *"feeling unfrozen."* Anchor gives her hope, she says, that they can change things at home.

"Guess this is why the pastor sent me—to get faith and hope back."

She has exhausted herself with the effort of speaking all those words and wants to sit. But before she does, she finds Mike, addresses him, and thanks him for his story. Says it's easy for her, and all of them in her town to be feeling sorry for themselves; none of us believe she ever has.

"I was thinkin' it's just us that are friends to misery and bad luck. But I see now, this kind of sorrow don't choose one kind, and one kind don't choose it. And I thank you for bein' brave enough to say it, and givin' me hope for my son, too."

She shudders from the adrenaline rushing away and reaches back to steady herself as she sinks into her seat. At the last moment she stops, looks back up, and smiles at us. That smile coming from the blank palette of gray, is Technicolor. I believe that everyone, even the toughest among us, smiled back.

The last half hour has unplugged the seduction of separation. We have rejoined the heart of things where private thought melts and shared truths gather.

Don asks for someone to recite concluding prayers. Then he reminds us to participate in weekly counseling sessions with our kids and to go to meetings. There is physical awkwardness as we stretch legs and hips, bend and yawn, and look around for special good-byes.

We are drained and filled by our departure. Happy to have shared, to have gotten it said, and sad that it is over. We all face the unknown; going home to the familiar that no longer understands us and without the community of strangers who do.

A few parents, in the effort to honor nonjudgment, work their way over to Dexter and Ali, whose son has disappeared into the crowd of kids. The couple stands and receives them, no one completely comfortable, but no one willing to reject them either. There is a sheepishness in smiles and nods, a southern gentility in the *"Good-bye, glad you could join us,"* it is the old-fashioned kind that refuses rudeness in any situation. As the last of us drift out from the comfort of those we have gathered with and have gathered with us, Dexter and Ali are still standing unable to leave.

* * *

Journal Entry, Anchor, 1990: To be here now and not split or run away in heart or mind, to sit and not judge, and to be one with the suffering and the grace, I have to open again and again and push even those boundaries until space is created where no barrier can exist, and where there is no need for understanding or compassion because the space itself is all that...all that.

❦ 49 ❦

"Slow down!" I plead to Justin who is cutting a determined path through the crowd and using me as battering ram. I half turn and dust at his hand on my left shoulder, which he ignores, asking, *"Got all your bags?"* He wants to stop at Aunt Polly's diner for a milkshake and cheeseburger before he *"goes back to the crap they serve at the cafeteria."* As we find a clearing on the sidewalk, I see his roommates waiting in front of the facility. Two of them stand by their shared car, faces turned to each other as they talk and laugh. The third, Dr. Robert is hunched down in the backseat alone, grim, and ashen with hair askew. Justin tells me they just finished their last family session. *"Musta been something,"* he whistles, points at Dr. Robert, *"probably thought his wife was going to bust him outta here."*

Caught by the contagion of his light spirit, I find myself laughing along, feeling released and relieved, and a little triumphant too. "We've made it," I think but don't say. We are together, changed and still the same. Both are okay.

Justin gives his roommates a thumbs up and tells me they are joining us at the diner and will follow us to the airport, so he'll have a ride back to their apartment. *"Can't go anywhere without supervision,"* he reminds me, a tremor of resentment darkens his mood, but he lets it slip away.

During the ten-minute drive I ask if he knows Peter. A little, he says, distracted, then, *"God, I wish Don had let me say something."* A whoosh of a sigh lifts his spirits again. Dexter and Ali were *"asking"* for a fight, he insists, inferring he was the one who could give it to them. Hell, he says, he saw that kid, Peter, just after he was committed to lockdown. Justin had taken BJ to the hospital to get stitches in his hand after BJ had hit a concrete wall playing basketball.

"BJ's short, but he plays hard to keep up…came down from a jump shot and landed sideways against a wall… says I tackled him—didn't! Anyway, who told him to put his hand out at the last minute?"

They were in the dispensary when Peter goes *"berserk."* The younger boy had been in the hospital less than twenty-four hours, coming off *"some pretty hard shit—pcp and crack."* He was running down the hall screaming about spiders in his hair. His feet were bleeding because he broke some glass, *"God knows how he got that in the first place,"* and he stepped in it barefoot. He had vomit all over his hospital gown, *"smelled like crap, literally."*

Justin tells me there is a *"HUGE"* black male counselor that works in lockdown, *"Joe… a great guy, ex-con, ex-heroin addict, ex-everything kind-a-guy. You don't mess with him,"* and he's chasing Peter, who backs himself into a corner, from which he attacks Joe and two orderlies with a shard of glass he still has in his hand. Joe is three times the boy's size, Justin claims, but *"the kid is so fucked up, so full of fury,"* that he is jabbing at Joe and the others with the glass, going for their faces and eyes, and trying to kick at the same time. *"I mean he is nuts and, skinny as he is, he could do damage."* Joe finally yelled, startled Peter, then went for the boy's knees, tackled him, and the two orderlies threw on a straight jacket. *"Shit, a straight jacket … it was a scene."* I say something inane like, *"Wow!"* I find it difficult to place the boy from this morning in the drama Justin paints so well for me.

"What's that called?" Justin asks, as we pull up to the diner lit in neon at midday. Oh yeah, he remembers, as I turn off the engine, *"Self-righteous. And here are his parents today, with all that self-righteous bull!"*

You know, mom, he continues, unbuckling, opening his door, there's a lot of crazy people here. *"Shit, I may have my issues, I'm no angel, and I have no trouble admitting that,"* but, he insists, none of us in our family is *"THAT crazy."* And that's what he was thinking about that day at the hospital, how really nuts this kid Peter was and his family must be too and then to see them today so self-righteous, *"like their shit doesn't stink … like their kid is 'just being naughty,'"* he says this in a sing-song high pitch. *"Who are they kidding?"*

"Mom!" Demanding full attention, he stops and spreads his hands on top of the car hood, looks at me more determined than inquiring, *You gotta admit that we're not as nuts as most of them."*

Is he really asking? Does he expect my agreement?

"'Not like me and not like us,'" I say back to him.

Isn't that what Mike was saying to Dexter and Ali? Maybe we aren't as blind, I say, or acting out our chaos in the same way, but if we separate from each other, if we go into our egos and false pride, then we are no different than they, we are just as self-righteous.

"And we lose the chance of understanding all of the links of a shared humanity."

I say it knowing it's a risk, afraid it may take him over some impending cliff he wants to avoid, I wonder if he is testing me? Still making up his own mind about who he is, who we all are? "Truth," I hear in my mind's voice. I say to him that we're all crazy in our own way, that there are no mistakes, *"we're here because we also need to be here, different but the same as the others."* Maybe there are degrees and variations, and maybe there are levels of guilt and insanity, but do degrees really matter? Isn't it wiser and more fruitful to learn from everyone here, from the commonality and the differences, instead of looking for escape?

"Do we really want to escape into not me, not us, or into the denial that helped us get here in the first place?"

He shrugs, not ready to go there. I shiver at the thought of the alternatives of denial, of jail time and the threat of the streets, losing the slim thread of sobriety he's gained. I watch myself attach to the fear inherent in it all. I shake it off the best I can, and say to myself, "Okay. It's okay. He can only be where he is, and at least he's here."

"So today with that uptight Texas bullshit going on," Justin says, he hoped Don would bring up Peter's first day, and his condition when he got to the hospital.

"That's what he would have done in group where no one gets away with any of the crap they allow the parents."

And, besides, he says, Peter's parents have been told about it, and they have all the drug test

results, so their attitude is even more insane. I try my point again, *"We all slip into denial."*

"Hell, there are slips, and then there's a cannonball into a black-bottom pool!" He insists, adding, *"then there's Fred,"* who has been in his *"ain't rehab grand,"* grandstanding for weeks, and how it's all about his son, Darren, and *"HIS disease."* Justin stops me before I can interrupt. Yeah, I know. He says, Fred admitted today that maybe it's a family problem. *"Big of him."* Actually, everything is *"BIG of him,"* he laughs, but the truth is Fred blames Darren in this pious way, and the family takes it. But, Darren has been opening up in group, broke down one night that his dad doesn't drink or drug, but he eats, *"as you can see,"* Justin indicates Fred's astounding girth with the bulge of his eyes, the motion of his hands into an enormous bulge in front of his own thin body.

It would be funny, Justin says turning serious, except that sometimes he eats literally for days without stopping. It's just like a drug binge. Fred sits alone in a dark room, downing gallons of ice cream, whole twelve packs of raw hotdogs; he eats until there is nothing left in the house, *"I mean nothing!"* Darren came back from delivering newspapers at 6:00 A.M. before school one day and found Fred eating raw pasta, with a lineup of empty ketchup and mustard bottles he had just drained into his mouth.

"You know how Darren got in trouble with the cops and put here at Anchor?" Justin asks, as we begin to move toward the diner. Darren started dealing drugs to buy food for his mom and younger sister and brother. He said he went crazy watching the little kids go to bed hungry, watching them do their homework with flashlights because the electricity was turned off. Fred never tried to get another job after he was laid off. His wife took on two jobs so they could pay the mortgage, but she got sick and had to drop one. Their food money came from Darren's newspaper route and college savings, which Fred ate away.

"Hell," Justin moved and astounded, says, Fred broke open the kids' piggy banks one night in a rage and bought bags of candy bars, locked himself in the bathroom, eating them until they were gone. He emerged hours later, and the bathroom floor was ankle deep in wrappers. When Darren makes money to feed the kids, he has to hide the food at a friend's house and sneak lunches to them at school. *"That's some pretty crazy shit."*

Justin pushes the door of the diner open over my shoulder, telling the hostess we want a table for five, the others are right behind us. We slide into a booth on the same side.

"So Darren turns to selling drugs, but the funny thing is, he doesn't really use drugs much because he's too busy trying to keep his customers happy and the kids fed."

I think of Fred in a food coma, alone, and with the lights out. I say to Justin that it's more than the food itself, it must feel to the kids as if their dad is sucking the life out of the house, literally vacuuming their life force with his gorging.

Yeah, he says, that's pretty much how Darren said it in group therapy. Justin adds that he hates that good family bull that Fred hides behind with no adult calling him on it. Maybe Fred has made a little progress this weekend, at least he's admitted, *"Oops, this is a family problem."* So, yeah, maybe you're right, Mom. We do need to stay out of denial to accept that all dysfunctional families are similar, but, you know, we're not all alike, not exactly, either.

I nod but know that to push on the finer points is beyond both our endurance and energy. We have so little time left, do I want to spend it this way? And if I don't push, am I leaving too much unsaid between us?

∾ **50** ∾

"Do you two want some time alone?" Jim asks, as he and Tom reach the table.

Justin says, *"Aw she's tired of my bullshit, besides I gotta know why Doc is still in the car?"* We all glance out the large-paned window on my right, see Dr. Robert huddled, still angry and shaggy, looking more like an old punished sheep dog than a famous scientist. The men slide into the booth opposite Justin and me, and begin telling us the highlights of the morning session. Martha Morrison turned the doctors' general session into a deep examination of ego and not just the patients' but also the wives'. There was a lot of resistance, they say, by everyone, especially those who had come to cast blame, or be absolved in some way.

"I hate to say good-bye to my son." I think. I keep a smile on my face but feel the warmth leave my body, and a shiver run through me. I have no appetite and don't remember ordering the greasy food that arrives in plate-fuls and gets passed around the table by the three men laughing about the overgenerous quantities. "I fear losing him again." I know the thought is true but chide myself for slipping into negativity, and for allowing fear a place at the table. After all, he is safe; these men, the community, care about him, and look at them, wrestling with the personal face of a common demon. They speak in intimate and self-revealing ways, they reach for strength, and they are not hiding any longer. It's more than Justin could get anywhere else, even at home. He tells it straight at Anchor, and they listen, without the behavior of social patterns, expectations, and systems that work against truth. Crazy as it seems, I am more relaxed and trusting here than I have been almost anywhere else. And, I think, "How odd, how weird this all is" to be in the jaws of the tiger, addiction, and be comforted by the honesty and acceptance, "and, yes, the love," of people I may never see again.

Dr. Robert appears suddenly, pulls up a chair and sits at the end of the booth, ignoring the congestion he's added to the crowded passage between tables. He misses the glower of a passing waitress, hot coffee in one hand balancing a heavy tray in the other. Grizzled and solemn, dark circles underline heavy-lidded eyes, only his voice remains full and commanding. He calls our waitress over, demands a plate of the twenty-four-hour breakfast special. Eyeing my leftovers he asks if I'm done with my bacon and cold toast, purring like a voracious old lion. *"But only, dear, if you aren't going to eat it."*

The other men challenge him on his high cholesterol and weight. His foul mood lifts as he rubs his ample belly. Food, he says, is his last pleasure. *"Gave up booze and pills, cigars and fine champagne, and nearly have given up sex ... oh, excuse me, dear."* He bends his head slightly to me, stops his rimless glasses from sliding off his nose into his plate, throws down a handful of toast, and says, *"Hell of a session this morning wasn't it boys?"* But he is not looking for an answer, and I notice Jim reach across the table, and squeeze his forearm.

Dr. Robert shakes his head, maybe knowing that all his education and knowledge, former prestige and precise scientific method of inquiry, will not help him answer the only questions that could save his life: Sobriety, how? Surrender, when? Process, why? Progress, Program, forgiveness, acceptance, faith, humility, and gratitude—how, when, where, why? He looks up at all of us, resigned but curious. Jim and Tom watch him thoughtfully, silently until one of them says, yeah, *"hell of a session,"* and nothing more.

Justin can't help but bring up Dexter and Ali. How their *"arrogance and self-righteous bullshit,"* called him to battle. Tom and Jim laugh, say together, *"Oh, we know you, Justin, must have been tempting!"* Dr. Robert gets the drift, slips out of melancholy, joins in, and says he's heard they were here.

"The Purleys of Dallas? They are Texas elite, up there with the Hunts, Bass brothers, and Bushes. Oil, gas, real estate, and sports teams now, of course."

Dr. Robert says he doesn't know Dexter but that he must be the son of the family patriarch, *"very proud, very old school."* Just a generation ago they were, *"roustabout-oil-driller poor, and now they're Princeton and Yale. Must be HELL for them. All their money can't comfort them here."*

We're all thinking similar hell thoughts; it's the same and different for us—no one is spared.

Justin speaks over our silence, tells the roommates that they must remember the night he took BJ to emergency. And, do they get that this is the kid of the broken-glass-and-spiders-in-his-hair delirium? And then those parents today, judging everyone else and pretending they don't know how serious the kid's problem is. Are they delusional? Or is it plain old denial? A rhetorical question, he interrupts any response and says, you know about denial, right, Mom? *"It ain't a river in Africa."* We all laugh at the joke often repeated at AA meetings, at Justin's inflections and eyebrow raising.

Yeah, it's not a river in Africa, Jim says. Rivers keep moving and clear stuff out. Denial is stagnant and keeps you in toxic waste. Tom applauds Jim's analogy.

"You have to keep looking for the humor—no doubt, no doubt."

❦ 51 ❦

Dr. Robert wants to play along, but he's jostled by the morning's session, equally drawn to and repelled by the memory. He interrupts our laughter with a verbal explosion.

"What the HELL does Martha mean by that goddamn AA quote, 'the bridge between sobriety and serenity is surrender.' Can you tell me that? What the hell does she mean?"

His voice rumbles out of him in exasperated thunder. He looks at us red faced, fists bunched up on either side of his plate, and then hangs his head over his partially eaten eggs, as if to divine truth from reading yolks and whites at close range.

I watch Tom and Jim nod to each other, reluctant to take this on. Their training, vocation, and discipline take over; they consider answers and attempt analysis. Martha's point, Jim says, is that to just stop the alcohol or end the drugs won't bring us a lasting, renewable, peace. To get there, will take something more, *"which, I can guess, also means harder to achieve..."*

Jim stops abruptly, and we wait. Idly, he says that there are other, deeper, levels of surrendering, his eyes distracted, staring into the middle of the crowded restaurant; he doesn't continue.

Dr. Robert slams his fist on the table, silverware raises and drops at the impact, and water sloshes from glasses.

"Surrender! Surrender! Surrender! What the hell does she mean by surrender? *And is serenity what we want? Is it happiness? Is it heavenly? And is heaven where I goddamn want to be? It sounds dead to me! Gonna' be dead soon enough."*

He doesn't like words without specific meanings, directives, or "without some damn proof" behind them. Surrender, to whom and for what? What is the payoff for all that surrender and serenity?

Dr. Robert growls incoherently, then turns back to his food. He takes large forkfuls of whatever is left on everyone's plate, mashes it together into boulders of congealing grease, and inhales the results. He grabs a coffee mug with his free hand, with no thought to ownership, and slugs down acidic brew as if swigging water at the end of a forced march across the desert. Follows it with a half glass of orange juice. His fist thuds the table again, and he looks up expecting an answer and ready for a fight. No one responds.

A tension of opposites exists at every stage of negotiation, whether personal or professional. And although each new development, deal point, or legal opinion, new relationship or old, creates a web of additional tensions, the basic one dominates: current reality versus a future we cannot wholly foresee. The past and the present appear to be understood and predictable; they may be flawed and may lead to less rather than more, but we're still secure in their recognizable familiarity. Safe. The opposite tension is the promise of the future, where the lure of success fuels the excitement of possibility and the drive for more and better of everything: money or market reach, status, sobriety, or happiness. The two tensions sit next to each other at every table, whether polished and lacquered or tacky with resin and spilled food. We look for the bridge to connect them; the way to leave the safety of the past for the promise of the future without the loss that is inherent in change. At this table, addiction is the past and sobriety the painful but promising, future. But, now something else has been proposed beyond, "just sober." It's something luminous and new. Peace and serenity are seductive thoughts and words that are also vague and difficult to grasp without a coherent action plan.

Dr. Robert is right: surrender is both bridge and thrown-down gauntlet. Fear of loss dominates plans for recovery. Bodies rebel after years of abuse, minds fold back over themselves, and rest is rendered useless. The only plan that makes sense is full frontal attack.

Tom says that for Martha the final goal isn't sobriety but *"another state of being entirely, which she calls serenity."* Dr. Robert half stands, ready to pounce and argue, but Jim grabs his arm, engages his wild eyes, and forces his attention with a command, *"let him talk."* He does not let go until the older man, deflates and backs down.

"It's a divine equilibrium for her. Sobriety alone can't bring you lasting happiness."

Tom says he's been wrestling with this and that he can *"feel, not prove,"* that Martha is right, and doesn't know whether to trust that instinct. After all, he adds, looking up at Jim, *"Feeling over logic, analysis, and proof is something we avoid at all costs."* He laughs, drops his head and seems to contemplate a future he can't imagine but which holds a promise he wants. When he speaks again, Tom's voice is clear and decisive, *"Serenity is the opposite of deadening. It's alive."*

Tom thinks about this a minute and then he looks at Dr. Robert directly.

"We were dead inside when we reached for the bottle or for pills and syringes. We reached from that dead place for the falsehood that something outside ourselves could make us alive, could wash away, drug away, the pain of dead insides, of dark holes, and of fear."

Addiction is demanded by one's very bones, by the course and pulse of blood and fluid. It's carried by veins and nerves connecting all internal systems to the brain, and body and back to one's aching, pounding heart, mind, and spirit. Of course it feels like self. It's etched in the lines of these men's faces, the shaking of their hands, the hollow yearning of their eyes. To an addict, booze and drugs are mother's milk, balance, and sustenance. It is the demon friend that has made them sick and kept them safe, if unconscious, for so long. Recovery is a high wire pulled on one end by the past of addiction, the temptation of forgetfulness, on the other by hope of sobriety and aliveness. Can sobriety, let alone the vagueness of serenity, anchor the opposite reality and lure the addict out of the familiar trap, and away from disease?

"Sober or dead." Dr. Robert interrupts our private thoughts. The quaking voice has returned, the grumble and storm are gone. *"Those are the real options. Sober or dead."* Sobriety, he says, has been elusive for so long that it has become both blessed and cursed.

"Let's face it boys, we're here because we have to be. Families, professions, and the law insist on it. Hell, the fear of death insists on it."

His eyes crazed again, Dr. Robert grasps the end of the table and hurls words at us in single syllables.

"I god ... damn killed ... someone. Me, me, the great doctor. I god ... damn killed some ... one."

He flattens his hands on the table to stop the shaking.

"And, God bless me, I still want a goddamn drink. I still want a shot of morphine. I vomit my guts out at night and, I'm afraid I have stomach cancer. I have lost everything, and face ... for god's sake, more jail time, and still I want a drink, a fix, a way out. How the hell can I surrender more? How the hell can I conceive of serenity?"

"Surrender to change ... Surrender to exploration ... to not knowing?"

Jim questions but doesn't know where the beginning of the thread is that can be pulled to reveal the intricate pattern. Surrender. It's a letting go. He says that he sees what Robert means, but, letting go of what? And, who surrenders in our society? Only losers? Victims? The defeated?

No one answers. Finally, Tom says that for all of us high achievers, or "overachievers," maybe surrender sounds like loss. It's a doctor's vocation and avocation to fight disease and only a patient's death makes him surrender. In this personal battle, the idea of surrender feels too much like death.

"It's the opposite of everything we have learned to value."

I hear my words, tender, low, dry. I sip some water and gather my thoughts. All four men turn to look at me, their faces unguarded. Only Justin's eyes question me. I smile and cover the hand he's placed on the table with mine. I don't know how it is for all of them, I say, but for me, as long as I have something to work for and toward, something to organize around or battle against, I feel capable and strong, worthwhile and accomplished. To surrender to *"powerless,"* to acknowledge I cannot do the one thing and most important in my life, *"save"* my son, well, *"that is much harder than full combat."* My voice, thin and reedy, requires more breath for timber and volume, but to stop and breathe would collapse the last of my resistance to tears. I take a small breath and say that surrender came for me when, in order to go forward, I had to let go of who I thought I was and who I wanted to be: *"Warrior mother, make-it-all-happen, take-no-prisoners, accomplish-to-survive."*

To surrender to people I don't know, at Anchor, in Al-Anon, to the Program itself, and to surrender to changes that may be *"necessary but are uncontrollable, unpredictable…"*

I stop, tears finally betray me, my hands tremble, and my voice catches. It is all I can do to shake my head no. I search for what is true, what describes this, the longest, steepest, most dangerous bridge I can imagine. I compose myself.

"When I go to cross the next bridge of surrender, if I seek serenity, what more do I give up? Do I surrender the life of my son? This is what I ask myself, when I can't sleep, when my mind races away from me, and when my head pounds. And, how could that be right, when it's against every instinct? Do I give up all that I have been in the world? All that I have the potential to be, to do, to go deeper within, and to find a peace, like Robert says, that is essentially vague and elusive?"

Heads nod as I finish but eyes are cast down or look out blankly into the parking lot or at the next table. These are exceptional men, no matter what their sins or slips from grace. But, today they know they cannot think and analyze their way over the bridge.

I don't have any answers, I go on, but I do know that there are flashes of light that have found me, brief as they may be. *"I know that grace comes in waves, and when it opens and the light pours out, it convinces me that I have to find that renewable, sustaining source of peace and staying centered."*

If it takes effort, commitment, striving, well, hell, I'm good at all that. What I fear is that it takes another surrender that I can't totally see or predict right now and that will take me on yet another journey over another bridge. I ask myself, what am I afraid of? Losing my son? Yes, that's the worst threat, but what else?

A deal doesn't appear as serious as the struggle for life or death going on every day at Anchor. It doesn't carry the weight or the despair, the physical pain, or the emotional rendering of the real battle between addiction and sobriety. But if you sit at enough of those deal tables, you realize why many feel as if their very lives are being negotiated out from under them. Their identified selves teeter on the tension between what was and what might be.

"To get to the future something of the past must always be lost, everyone in a deal knows that, but it's rarely articulated. So everyone argues about gaining or giving up 'points,' but never about surrender."

Deals test the limits of one type of courage. Here, in this small group of tentative resolve, surrender demands a type of courage that as yet has no name. Still, there is a universal similarity, a grasping after that which we know and which defines us—what seems safe and predictable.

Justin has grown very quiet. I cannot read his thoughts. I don't know if at nineteen-years-old, male and physically commanding, surrender can even be in his vocabulary. Dr. Robert, speaking with a face softened and willing, says that he understands *"what Bobbie is saying."*

"Maybe all great change takes surrender, and it's the change itself we fear most. And it is change alone that will keep us alive."

To get to the top of their chosen, often noble, profession, these men, like the lawyers I represent, like the pioneer women of my generation, paid close attention to the external markers noting the way, "turn left to get to the best medical school, the best residency program, and the most demanding specialty," "turn right to be chief resident." Outward rewards came by competition and earning fellowships and appointments, joining lucrative practices, and city hospital staffs, or university faculties. The inward rewards come without guideposts or applause. Any accomplishment now, if it comes at all, is drawn from the most foreign of notions: surrender, vulnerability, humility. Grace. I look at my son, knowing he and I will have to eventually face these things together, and say that I am left with more questions than answers. But, I am clear about this paradox.

"If the challenge wasn't there, the bridge wouldn't form."

In meditation, psychotherapy, and spiritual paths of all kinds, *"The bridge is always surrender."*

Surrender to what we don't know. Surrender to the truth, to "what's so." Surrender the falsehood of self-righteousness and surrender all our delusions and denial. I tell them about Nicole's advice: the future isn't about being less powerful.

"It's about surrendering the falseness of ego, about acceptance, and spiritual strength replacing egocentric control."

They nod; it's occurred to them, yes. They understand intellectually, but science and success are about predictability, and, at least the semblance of control.

"We only surrender when the patient dies," they repeat in unison.

* * *

Journal Entry, Anchor, 1990: What I will remember most about this day is the care with which we spoke, the poignant stretching on fine filaments of fresh understanding to try and comprehend that which is incomprehensible: how none of the past adequately answers the problems of the present. And I will remember that the fear of death and the fear of a new life sat at the table with us.

❧ 52 ❧

No one wants to leave. We small talk last thoughts and laugh some until the waitress, the stub of a number-five pencil tucked behind her ear, warm and chirpy despite the Sunday morning, eat-all-you-want, families-with-crying-babies chaos, approaches us.

"Don't want to hurry y'all, but if you need your check, I sure could use this table." The line at the hostess station stretches to the parking lot, and she draws our attention to it as she speaks.

I check my watch, noting I'll be crushed for time if I don't get going. Everyone finds dollar bills to split the check four ways evenly. We laugh together at the sum, so small compared to the mounds of food consumed, and add a generous tip. When we tell the waitress not to worry about the change, she bubbles over with gratitude. The plastic buttons that dot her peach and white ruffled apron, "Eat at Aunt Polly's, Down home Southern Cookin'" and "Take home a Georgia peach pie from deep in the heart of Georgia," bounce up and down and across her left breast in delight.

I am sorry to say good-bye to these men and wish we had hours more to talk. I give each a hug; try to say words of encouragement. I thank them for watching out for my son, who rolls his eyes at me. *"Are you kidding? It's me watching out for them,"* he says to their chorus of disagreement. Then Justin and I get into the car, and he leans out the window and waves to Jim who is driving to make sure they are behind us for the short drive to the airport.

"So, have you heard about the Al-Anon doll?" I can see the impish smile, know I'm generally the target of his next joke and think, am I going to fall for this?

I answer aloud, *"No, I haven't,"* distracted trying to find the freeway exit that reads car returns, *"Wait, there it is. Okay, yeah, the Al-Anon doll?"*

"Every time you wind it up, it walks into walls and says, 'I'm sorry, I'm sorry, I'm sorry.'" He is doubled over laughing in the passenger seat.

"Very funny!" I begin to protest, realize the ambient truth in it, and laugh in spite of myself.

We only have a few minutes now, and I am not sure when I will see him next. Who will he be then? What will have changed? I want to cling to his silly joke, look at him with his full smile, and listen to his laughter for a very long time.

The car carrying the doctors is behind me as I pull into the designated space at Hertz, look back to see they have pulled up on the other side of the chain-link fence. I'm going to miss those guys, I tell Justin. And, yes, I know, don't get delusional about them. You're right, but still, it's not often you get grown men, especially successful ones, willing to push themselves to the limit of their humility and understanding. *"To change and grow."*

"Change or DIE," Justin corrects me. *"Tom's the only real volunteer, myself included."*

"Right," I say back to him; no time left for more.

I turn off the ignition and get out to say good-bye. Justin is out first opening the trunk, pulls the bags onto the pavement, and then comes to my side of the car.

"Mom, I am really glad you came." He does not say take me home with you, but I know him so well that I think he wishes he could, so I say it. *"Wish it was time for you to come home."* He shrugs, says nothing more. It seems like such a short visit, like I just got here, I tell him. It sounds so inane, but it's all I can think to say. We hug each other a big, long time, and then I hold him at arm's length, get on my tip toes to make sure I have eye contact, and tell him again how proud I am of him, and how much I love him.

He brushes it off, an irritation in his voice. *"I don't know why you'd be proud of me, not like I am here by choice... not like I want to stay."*

He studies my face as he talks. I do not have time to give his question the thought it deserves but I say,

"There are all kinds of ways to rebel here, and screw up, like you did at the start, by just not participating, by arguing, resisting all help, staying in your story, *retreating, or being self-righteous, judgmental..."*

"Yeah," he interrupts with a sneer, *"I still do all of those at least once a day!"*

I ignore his comment, finish saying instead that wherever he started, wherever he is today, for the most part he's courageous and engaged.

"Look at how the doctors respect you. It's an acknowledgement of how much you give of yourself." It's more than most people can do, I tell him.

He squirms under my direct gaze and shrugs. I feel a well of sadness rise, knowing I cannot reflect the shine of his inner beauty for him to see.

There is no more time to explain or talk. The car carrying the doctors is waiting, engine running. The van that will take me to the terminal pulls up, Justin loads my bags, and I have to leave him with my insight and his self-assessment not seeing eye to eye.

He leans down and gives me a last peck on the cheek and then lopes to the waiting economy-size sedan stuffed with his roommates, and ducks his head to squeeze into the backseat. All four men turn for a last wave good-bye, Justin leaning from his waist out the car window, Dr. Robert turned completely around, his bobbing head smiling through the rear windshield.

I wave back trying to show confidence rather than the sadness tickling my throat. Then their car moves out of sight, and I step into the crowded bus for the ride to the Delta terminal, feeling suspended between competing worlds. The vulnerable tensions of departure and next adventure pull in opposite directions, and the suddenness of being alone again all weave into one tapestry.

❦ 53 ❦

I am dizzy riding in the Hertz van. There's no seat left, so I stand and hang onto the steel pole that separates the driver from the luggage rack. "So much, too much," tenderness and vulnerability, I diagnose internally my destabilized condition. The pushing apart and pulling together of dynamic forces, confrontations and profundities have left me quieted but also prickling with an energy peculiar and particular. "What's this about?" No masks, no social games, too much exposure? Maybe just being alive to it all.

"Being alive to the death of things known … to a known self … even poorly defined, to the destruction of a familiar self?"

I whisper the half-formed thought aloud and know it is perhaps crazy, self-destructive. But it follows logically that deconstruction may be necessary, vital even, to go further down this circuitous, convoluted, interior path. And where does the road lead—to emotional growth, to spiritual alignment, to recovery? Or is there a destination at all? Thoughts float unanchored by the comfort of strategy, agendas, or concrete solutions.

The van, packed with Sunday business travelers, briefcases and overnight bags dangling the logos of company loyalties. The faces are beginning to focus on the upcoming week's travels, as the van pulls up to the Delta passenger curb. I am happy to be distracted by the mundane paces of ticket check and seat assignment. I answer the ticket counter questions. Yes, checking two bags; yes, two carry-ons; yes, that's right, Los Angeles. I make small talk, *"No, L.A. is not as hot as Atlanta this time of year but we get those Santa Ana winds and they can be brutal. Fires spark when the winds come."*

"A shame," the Delta attendant says she saw something on TV about it, people losing so much because of the insanity of a few fire starters. Yes, terrible the losses, I agree.

I find my gate, look up at the departure board, and see that my flight is delayed fifteen minutes. I collapse into a gray-blue padded seat attached on both sides in neat rows, six deep, back to back, facing out in identical seating arrangements to my left and right. Fatigue finally pushing against further activity, I settle into the anonymity of an airport lounge, and allow the white noise and solitude to insulate me. I am utterly still, body and mind so used up that when I shut my eyes, I imagine hearing the "thud, bump" of my heart, the fluids course through my system. I breathe slowly, carefully into the quiet. Appreciate how rare this is, one moment, two, of "just so," the breath, no words.

The crackled voice of the PA system, intercedes, *"Flight 600 to LAX, Los Angeles International Airport. Sorry folks, plane's not here yet and will be delayed half an hour."* My mind comes out of stillness directly into one word, *"surrender."*

The creep of quiet dread starts slowly. I was confident an hour ago, less than that, I confirm, checking my watch. Confident that surrendering to truth, to the reality of addiction, to a higher power, to the mystery of life's unfolding, has started me on a path of greater truth and of clarity. About my son, yes, but, more importantly, about taking full responsibility for my life, too. And, in a new way: past, present, and future joining in one theme and one weaving to consider, to not run from.

I surrendered, after years of arrogance, of "I can fix it," of denial, into the promise of the Twelve Steps. I surrendered too, after years of reading about meditation, into a practice, into a discipline. But now I see that another layer of the onion must be peeled back, that I am only at a beginning, and that more must be tempted out of hiding, torn apart, understood, and, "yes, surrendered."

Lyndsey said it last night, and it is true of me. I am both eager and afraid of what is next. And, like her, I know I cannot stop here.

Quiet disappears in the rise of my agitated mind. *"It does not show on your son."* Where else will this challenge lead me? My mind fractures, does a U-turn to anxiety heading toward a reverie of tension. A tornado of worries whips me to a new crossroads: "Is it my son I must surrender to gain peace?" And how can that follow, in one breath, to lose and gain? "Surrender my son," is this what is required? And, to what do I surrender him? To a fate I can't completely define? "So I get, what? Serenity? No way. No way!" These are not new thoughts, but with the weekend's conclusion they burst through my raw mind and nerve-frazzled body, frantic and demanding escape.

"Maybe Dr. Robert is right, and losers lose, and then they surrender." But to whom and to what? Darkness? Unknown? To that which cannot be known? I have spent my life trying to understand, and solve, to succeed and gain, and now I must surrender? And, why, because "they" say so? What do they know of this kind of loss? Even Martha Morrison, no kids of her own ... what does she know ... how can she know about this loss, about this particular surrender?

I can surrender who I am. Give it all up, success, drive, ambition. Do I want to? No, I don't want to, but I can if I have to. "But my son?" Never. Do I give up "mother" to call myself serene? "I would rather die trying to save him, even if they say I can't, I would rather die than surrender his life!"

Thoughts falling over, bombarding each other, are loose and fractured in my mind and heart. Deep shimmers of nerves run electrical currents through my body. Inner calm shattering, I stand and pace, unhearing, unseeing, the clutter and noise surrounding me. The little I've eaten all day comes up from my stomach. Lands acidic in my throat. I try to force it down while I walk to the blue symbol for "women" identifying the place for toilets. Bitterness is in my mouth, up and out just as I arrive in the last empty stall, slam the door behind me, with no time to lock it. I crouch before the toilet a minute more. Allow the cold of the tile floor and the steel door to cool me down. I warn myself aloud, *"I do not throw up, and I do not cry!"* I command my stomach back into an uneasy quiver, catching my frayed breath, heart racing. I say silently to my shaking mind, "Calm, full breath in. Calm, full breath out." I force my agitation, the persistent rapid breath, into rhythm with silent words: "Concentrate, ten slow purposeful breaths in, ten slow purposeful breaths out."

I stand slowly, flush, and go to the water-spotted sink. Bending uncomfortably forward, I fill my mouth with enough cold water to wash the thick bile from my tongue. I cannot, I do not, look in the mirror. I straighten with a sigh, stretch my arms behind my back, loosen my bunched-up shoulders until I feel my limbs relax slightly, and make the effort to walk slowly. I pretend control and remind myself of an AA saying,

"Fake it 'til you make it."

I slow to more confident steps. Meditation mind in control of rebelling body, "lift and place left foot ... bend knee, soften and lift and place right, now left again ... now, more slowly, right." The twenty feet, bathroom back to long row of seats, takes several minutes. Tension eases, and the mind swerves out of panic into a low rumble, a distant reminder of its crack and thunder.

I cannot think of surrender, not of everything anyway, not yet. I am not ready. I understand the link—surrender to serenity. I know ego seeks control and that fear uses ego as a weapon. I have also learned that when fear travels the world under an assumed name, we get, *"I get,"* delusional and seek denial. What happens when I seek denial? I project into the world all the things I refuse to see within myself and all kinds of insanity follows.

What must I surrender to let truth in? Control. Ego. Fear. Projection. Surrender of the kind I seek leads to understanding and to compassion, which is the greatest power of all. But, like power and powerless, the bridge of surrender goes two ways. And, today, this moment, I cannot push through my fear.

"It will come," I tell myself aloud, *"stay conscious and it will come."*

I see that I have left all my belongings unguarded, purse, wallet, carry-on bag, and confidential papers. I do not have to check. Nothing is missing.

I sit and notice the shaking of my hands; I calm them and ease my mind with measured breaths. I remember what was asked of us in the last family session and take out my journal to give me a focal point, a clear action. When I write, the paper becomes the repository of feelings I otherwise find daunting. *"Fear of feeling."* I fear being overwhelmed by feeling. The messiness and vagueness of emotion unanchored makes my skin crawl; my mind wants precision and answers. But I have to come clean about how abysmally human and limited I am.

Less would be the wrong kind of surrender.

❧ 54 ❧

I ease into the writing and remind myself of what Martha said, *"Don't reach for familiar answers, explore sources and patterns, immerse yourself in the questions, and stay there until the truth reveals itself."*

What are the causes of disease and of the disease of which The Teacher speaks? What are the patterns of healing and its sources? Does disease feed disease and are they one? Are sources and patterns found, paradoxically, in the cause of the disease itself? And, if so it would follow that healing comes from plunging into the heart of the problem. The Teacher calls it *the wisdom of no escape.* In a world that seeks escape, the courage to deny it demands ruthless honesty.

Mind, body, spirit, past, present, generational influences and future results all stream through my thoughts. Cause and effect join, divide and join again. "Stay in the questions," I repeat for myself the familiar warning. Hard to do when I've trained myself on solutions, "and why have I trained myself this way?" Maybe because I'm afraid to know and not know at once.

And what of fear? Does fear give rise to illness? If I am afraid to look back and if I fear the unknown and of what will be found in the greater system, does my avoidance create more fear, pain, resistance, and disease? If I face my greatest fears, can I influence my son and daughter? Will opening and releasing the fears of the past bless the future or condemn it?

I remember with new understanding that The Teacher says *when you heal an injury, it is for the seven generations before you and the seven generations yet to come.*

It is a powerful thought: The patterns of the future influenced, perhaps changed forever, by the healing of the present and past. The sources that stretch back through the generations, healed in my parents, grandparents, in family I couldn't name, by my breaking the ties to suffering. By understanding cause and effect of the original sources, we are set free of patterns birthing patterns. "It is a powerful thought," capturing the future by healing the past.

I sit back and repeat what I've been taught: True Self is beyond illness and death, beyond even healing and human wholeness.

Let go of all identities and any limitation of spirit. Refuse the urge to attach to any extreme, seek the middle path, and surrender what is only limited human control anyway. Enter, instead, the realm of the deathless and become one with all things, where past, present, future weave without end.

Unified. Balanced. Mindful. Fully awake in the moment. No judgment. Limitless. I write it down; reread it. I resolve to think about it again later.

All I know and have become derives from striving and doing, from action and moving out of myself into the next challenge. And now I must surrender all of who I am and become unknown to myself to become my True Self? I write *Or is there a parallel path? A way to be in the world but not captured by it?*

I sit back. Stare into the faceless movement of people around me, into the noisy soundlessness of thought. I realize that, even now, I want to find an easier solution. To analyze, categorize, compartmentalize, create neat boxes and columns, and add them up. Come up with a strategy, a plan. Use words and action to take me out and away from emotion and questioning and away from the skin crawling, mouth drying, feeling of fire ants under my skin and eyelids. And then the aloneness threatens my meditation and instead of pushing it away, I welcome it and breathe into it knowing it must be explored to be fully known and understood.

I think of my husband again as I have all weekend. His handsome face glides across my thoughts. I reach for him in my mind but find him elusive, aloof. I find myself wanting and sad and unable to tell him all that my heart knows and yearns to know. I blame myself for not having magic words to bring him to me. Out of my longing I reach for my mobile phone and dial his number, his voicemail immediately responds. I hesitate then leave a message that my plane is delayed, but I'll be home tonight. Silence answers me back, and I have to push against it not to feel swallowed by the vacuum and ignored.

I don't know about his girlfriend yet, about deceptions and lies. That is all to come. Today, I am mystified only, and the hollowness of that mystification rings with self-recrimination but not warning.

"Flight 600, to Los Angeles, is now ready for boarding." The crackle of the PA system stops my internal rambling. I slide the journal into my

carry-on bag and shuffle slowly through my purse to find my ticket, and double-check to make sure my disheveled mind does not forget its earthly possessions.

I zone in, notice my thoughts shifting from personal to business and back to personal. In, then out, and in again so no one would know what had just transpired this morning, all day, or moments ago. The responsible party of have to, must, and keep moving is giving way to be, just be.

I talk to myself, *"Stay present, stay present, stay present."* No one sees me brush away moisture on my eyelashes. I cover anxiety with a smile. I cast away the grip of closure in the hiccup of my torn heart.

It's the way it is out there: stage center, stage left or right. Go forward. *"Suit up and show up."* You and I play the part required, even when we are not so sure what play we are in.

I smile at the flight attendant when she comments that first class is almost empty and how lucky I am to have it to myself. "She thinks I belong here." But I feel like a stowaway, after days in the belly of the beast, now delivered to the special treatment section, to isolation. I smile, thank her, find my seat, happy for the emptiness of the one adjacent to me.

I take out my merger file and remind myself that tomorrow is Monday. I look at my notes from the phone call to Howard, remember the urgency of getting to press contacts early, and take out a yellow ruled legal pad, and start the to-do and to-call lists. Balancing the file and legal pad, another slip of handwritten notes falls from the open sheaf and is retrieved by the attendant delivering water.

"Working already?" she asks. *"Always,"* I shrug and smile while reaching for the paper. I realize they are notes from my phone call with Justin before dinner Saturday night. We'd been talking about the education session with parents that morning and whether his doctor roommates agree with the concept of addiction as a disease.

Justin had put on a professional voice. I imagined him widening his chest, heard him speak in sonorous tones as he imitated their heated debates.

"They love to argue this shit. They stay up for hours quoting sources, giving opinion..."

"Well, why wouldn't they?" I asked Justin, *"after all, it's their field, medicine, science, and their problem at the same time... who would be better prepared to answer..."*

But I was hoping to prove something, too. That there is inestimable value if science had proof of disease, genes and DNA causing addiction. There would be a reason and understanding beyond psychology, family systems, lacking and failures, all the intangibles. I had said as much to him and finished with a strong statement on the importance of, *"medical, scientific, verifiable truth…"*

But Justin had interrupted, *"It doesn't matter! That's why I don't really listen to the, it's bullshit that's why—who cares if addiction follows a disease model, or if they are always looking for the alcohol gene for Christ's sake. It's bull! Choice is what matters and responsibility for the choices we make. Look, Mom, I don't want any more diseases. Hell, heard that all my life, learning disabilities, ADHD, hypoglycemia, whatever THAT is…"*

His voice was decisive but not angry, heated and focused. But, still I was nervous hearing this line of argument.

I stop him and say,

"Justin, what if some people are born with a much greater tendency let's call it … a greater natural tendency to addiction, wouldn't that help explain…?"

"It might explain something, but it could also, and DOES, just become another excuse, Mom. Another crybaby, poor-me, can't-help-myself, fucking excuse! Take Dr. Morrison, she listens, even speaks, the medical stuff, but then always tells us, 'choice, responsibility for your own choices, in the end it is all that will keep you sober. The wrong choice, hell, that'll kill you."

We were both silent a long time. Finally Justin said, *"I don't want to be 'diseased.' I want to admit when I've screwed up. I want to know I can change and make responsible choices for my own life."*

Rereading this now with the space of another day and all that has transpired, I am proud of him and scared for him at once. I admit I want an out, a context, if not an excuse then at least a concrete explanation, *"disease, can't be helped—not our fault."* But, like my son, I can't accept that either. Neither one of us can allow momentary relief that is without self-determination, without examination and full responsibility.

I read the notes over again, sit back, and see the faces, hear the voices of LA, Chicago, New York, and College Park. I recall words of anxiety, hope, hopelessness, faith, resilience, capitulation, authority, success, and failure spoken by lawyers, doctors, patients and parents. Objective and subjective. True Self, must be what truly determines us all. But it remains deep and elusive, and covered by definitions we accept without adequate inquiry.

I think of sources and patterns, of what we hide and find in the rooms of power and in the private sessions of powerless. I think too about our fragile quest for control, in our shared and loved and damned and vindicated humanity.

I wait until the plane takes off, the seat-belt sign releases us, to put the merger file in the pocket in front of my seat. I know I must attend to it thoroughly before I land but a need for closure, temporary as it may be, compels me. So I rip off a clean sheet of paper from the yellow pad, and I write to my son.

Dear Justin, I think I have an idea, at least, how hard this is for you, recovery, Anchor, away from home, and everything familiar. But you suit up and show up day after day in the face of incredible odds.

Thank you for telling the truth. Thank you for being willing to work with me. Thank you for being my son. I know I cannot change anyone but myself and that I too must choose to change and keep changing, until I am clearer and more together and whole. And only in that way can I walk this path with you, and does it become both of our journeys, alone yet together.

One thing more, you said you didn't believe in the disease model. That you believed in responsibility and in the power of choice. They tell me, as you do, that your sobriety is your responsibility. That sobriety and sanity and serenity are your choices. To me alcohol, addiction, is illness and pathway to an early death. Your courage, intelligence, humor, and your willingness to participate in life are a pathway to staying alive.

I ask that you keep considering the wisdom of recovery. I ask that as you make daily choices, as you say you can, that you turn away from death, and that you see your own beauty. I ask you please, Justin, choose life, choose life.

I want to say more, something big and profound and memorable. But, instead I think about labels and my own choices, smile to myself, and sign, *"I love you, your Mother."*

Epilogue:

On January 1, 2010, Justin marked thirteen years of sobriety. He doesn't celebrate, but we call each other and I congratulate him, and remind him what it has meant to me, to all of us, his courage, determination, his willingness to make a stand for his own life and in doing so for mine, his children's, and our community. He never fully gets it, not in the way I wish him to, not with all the admiration and love I extend, intend.

If I indulge my pride in him he cuts me off, *"One day at a time, Mom, one day at a time."* No promises, no false assurances, just the work that is there every day to do.

Justin was at Anchor for the better part of a year and stayed sober off and on for the next six years, trying everything from the Program to triathlon training and competitions to keep him straight. One day, married and with two sons who needed a father, he gave up all pretense, got ruthlessly honest, and stopped drinking.

The percentage of people who are recognized as addicted, or admit that of themselves and are able to get sober and stay sober before their thirtieth birthdays, is less than five percent. No matter what Justin says, it is an act of tremendous courage to face ones demons, to deal with illnesses, as they say in AA, of the mind, body and spirit, without excuses. I can't help but be proud of him. No apologies.

Several weeks after that first Family Weekend in Atlanta my sister Nicole and I were headed home from a client dinner in Los Angeles, discussing, for the hundredth time, whether the Katten Muchin-Wyman merger would close. It was a conversation that had dominated my thoughts and actions that year. Each day was a roller coaster of breakdowns that threatened to crater the deal, followed by promising negotiations that revived it. *"Schizophrenic,"* I was saying to Nicole, the deal, everyone's nerves and emotions, up and positive one minute, crazed, done-with the next. I was frustrated by my inability to predict an outcome. So much hung on personal trust, the relationships and competitiveness of powerful men. I could influence, but not determine.

We were heading west on Santa Monica Boulevard and as I turned to say something more, we slowed for a light in front of La Dulce Vita, a famous old hangout of the entertainment industry. Incredulous, I laughed, drew Nicole's attention to the men walking out the front door. The soft yellow light of the sconces on either side of the restaurant's awning framed Allan Muchin, Howard Weitzman and Michael Zavis, Allan lighting the cigars he had most likely just provided for the others. The dinner, I learned later, was an impromptu semi-celebration after a long day of negotiations that had gone well. We watched as they laughed together, waiting for Howard's car to be delivered by the valet. Their common spirit was lighthearted, jovial. I shook my head in wonder of it all: the timing, the surprise, my part in it, the never boring twists and turns.

"This deal is done!" I said to Nicole, and although we weren't through all the hurdles, indeed, that night sealed the merger.

The first few years of the merger were tumultuous. Howard and Michael, with similar styles and energies, never were completely comfortable with each other, always testing the other's ability to be a team player and leader. Michael insisted on a level of accountability that Howard felt was restrictive and small. Within three years Howard left the firm to become President of Universal Studios, during the reign of Edgar Bronfman and Seagram's. Today, returned to private law practice with his own firm of Kinsella, Weitzman, Kump, (et al.) in Santa Monica, California, he is again one of Hollywood's most influential counselors and power brokers.

Allan Muchin continues to be a guiding light of the firm named after him, with offices across the U.S and in London, but is more often found running charities and civic boards in Chicago.

Michael Zavis retired and became a scratch golfer, continuing to make waves wherever he goes, specifically on Southern U.S golf courses.

The Los Angeles office of Katten Muchin is one of the most successful law practices of any out-of-state firm. Craig and Alan still practice there and the company, now run by a talented group of next generation leaders, heads the list of prominent Century City business practices, specializing in work for the entertainment industry's major studios, and new media outlets.

Tommy Fallon retired to Florida, his old policeman injuries deciding his future and the need for warm weather year round.

Lee Van Leuween pretends to have gone fishing, moved out of L.A into retirement. But a group of his clients won't have it, so he is often coaxed back into executive search for specific high-end assignments that require unusual judgment and analysis.

I wish I knew more about the Anchor kids and families. A few years after Justin left Anchor the teen program was discontinued for reasons never well articulated. Justin and I kept up with BJ, his parents and Don for sometime after that, enough to know that BJ's path was as difficult as Justin's, but we have no resolution to report. Geographic moves on everyone's part and life in general interrupted, caused us to become far-flung.

Don, we know, has gone on to head re-hab programs and finish all his post-doctoral studies. Even after my many years in the Program, and in community projects and among caregivers of all kinds, he stands out as a model of what is best in this work and in human beings.

Because Justin was at Anchor for awhile, I participated in many Family Weekend Workshops and other activities in Atlanta and around the U.S. that concentrated on the principles and practices of AA and Al-Anon. The families all changed and rarely did I see the same faces on any of my subsequent visits.

Sometimes word would drift back, this child doing well, that other one having "gone out" again, back on the streets, in jail, drugged up. Dead.

In a certain way I am never sure how much I want to know about the people we met in those intense and difficult days. The odds of sobriety are long, and longer still if serenity, peace, and transformation of the family system are what we strive for. But not impossible.

Miracles happen every hour of every day in the work of the Program, and in spiritual paths of all kinds. Reading my journal entries and reliving my relationships with children, parents and staff in the process of writing this book, has warmed and deepened me in ways I cannot adequately express. I am left with a great deal of faith that those who participated continue to be informed by the Anchor and AA experiences; that, in whatever manner, they have found some grounding force to better their days, even if the full impact of the Program and sobriety eludes them.

As for me, I am selfish. This story may appear to you to be about certain things: a mother and son, a mother and both her children, a woman trying to find her way in the world as she is pulled by an inner voice. All those are true in their own way, but each is limited. I thank Justin and Lyndsey often for having been the catalysts for my own inner work. Without them, I would have chosen to avoid confronting the past and present, and I would have continued to duck and deny the hardest questions, never knowing I was cheating myself of the lessons and answers that form my life and that have become my path. I never had the luxury of abandoning either the outer or inner path and so had to come to my own peace with both. It took a long time. And so I would say this is a book about continuing along a path of transforming oneself and ones experience of the world, using whatever life brings as grist for the mill. I think my children see that as circular and that my work catalyzes them as they inspire me. This is a Program of progress, not perfection. As Lyndsey said, *"That doesn't exist."*

Acknowledgments: To All My Teachers

In the period this memoir takes place, I began to question every tenet of belief that made up my personal world and generally accepted thought. The questions that moved me then and now have to do with the sources and patterns of science, spirituality, psychology, and philosophy. With that in mind, I took myself down many circuitous paths of inquiry, fortunate to find brilliant teachers all along the way. While there are not sufficient words or space to acknowledge the many contributors to my education in its numerous and varied forms—formal, informal, spiritual and emotional—I'd like to try. I owe so much to the many thinkers, scholars, and teachers who opened my heart and mind and underpin my personal philosophy.

My deep gratitude to Bill W. and Dr. Bob, the founders of AA; Thich Nhat Hahn, Chogyam Trungpa Rinpoche, and Ram Dass; the American Buddhists, especially Jack Kornfield, Joseph Goldstein, Michele McDonald, Susan Salzberg, and Pema Chodron; The Daoist family of Drs. and teachers, Master Ni, Mao Shing Ni and especially Daoshing Ni. To the teachers of India, especially Vivekenanda, Ramakrishna, Sri Aurobindo, Sweet Mother, Krishnamurti, and Mother Meera. In Western spiritual traditions, Elaine Pagels, Abraham Herschel, Hans Kung, Teilhard de Chardin, Thomas Merton, Brother David Steindl-Rast, and so many more.

Acknowledgements, as well, to a group of thinkers that to this day light my life and deep understanding: Paul Watzlawick, Peter Senge, Gregory Bateson, David Bohm, Carl Jung, Robert Johnson, Linda Schierse Leonard, Marion Woodman, Marie-Louise Von Franz, Fritjof Capra, Gary Zukav, Joan Borysenko, and to the Mar Vista Family Center, especially the Factors, June Payne, Lucia Diaz; and the Lakota tribe, especially Bear, Sean and the White Whirlwind.

A special thanks to my personal teachers, without whom *Seven Days* would not have been written or published: most importantly, my brave and inspirational children, Lyndsey and Justin McMorrow, and my husband, Ralph

J. Savarese, the wolf counselor, whose strength and elegant mind gave me the courage to finally write; this book is dedicated to them. Thanks also to the inimitable Ray Stark, who believed in me before I believed in myself; Katrina Dewey, my great, good, gifted friend and the original editor who never let me off the hook and never let me hang there alone; Jay Worenklein who refused my concerns and encouraged this publication; my wonderful sisters, Nicole Spicer and Traci Porreco who read drafts chapter by chapter, insisting I be honest about our shared childhood and take pride in my life. Their love and support have been invaluable. To John Schureman, whose brilliance and unwavering support informed all my thinking on all levels and continues to today. To my son-in-law, Steve Finkel, who never swayed in his belief in me or my work, and who lent humor, imagination, precision and executive skill to getting this book edited, published and in the meantime helped usher in the completion of my personal dreams.

Lastly, a special thank you and blessing to Connor and Dillon McMorrow. When I started my business I kept a picture of Justin and Lyndsey on my desk for inspiration, especially on days when quitting felt desirable. Today I am blessed with ten grandsons and two granddaughters, but when I began writing, Connor and Dillon, Justin's beautiful boys, were my only grandchildren. More than anything else it was their pure and accepting love, their little boy bravery and clear-eyed wonder, and, yes, their pictures on my desk, that encouraged me during the many challenging hours of truth-telling. It is my hope that this book, and my direct experience, might light a small candle to guide them through their heritage and give them strength to face whatever comes their way.

About the Author

Bobbie McMorrow, co-founder of McMorrow Savarese, is one of the leading mergers and acquisition professionals in the country and an expert in leveraging the power of change. She has been profiled in *The American Lawyer* and on *Lawdragon* and her writing has appeared in the *Daily Journal*, California's largest legal news provider. A former teacher, activist, and civic leader, Bobbie has always been passionate about transforming both communities and individual lives. In the 1980s the Los Angeles School District recognized Bobbie as a Teacher of the Year and throughout the following decade she served on the board of the Mar Vista Family Center and as Youth Council Advisor.

Inspired by her own challenging experiences of family systems and addiction, McMorrow has spent the last thirty years studying with some of the greatest minds in the fields of psychology, spirituality, quantum physics, divinity and biochemistry. These studies, integrated with decades of board room success, inform her work today as she leads individuals and organizations on journeys of self-awareness, uncovering truths and possibilities that enable profound transformation and opportunity in the midst of crisis and change.

A mother and a grandmother, Bobbie lives in Santa Ynez, California, with husband Ralph Savarese, their dog Misty, and a white buffalo.

www.BobbieMcMorrow.com

8263306R0

Made in the USA
Lexington, KY
19 January 2011